Fourth Edition

Be Prepared
for the

Computer
Science
Exam in Java

Maria Litvin
Phillips Academy, Andover, Massachusetts

Gary Litvin
Skylight Publishing, Andover, Massachusetts

Skylight Publishing
Andover, Massachusetts

Library of Congress Control Number: 2009904716

ISBN 978-0-9824775-0-2

Skylight Publishing
9 Bartlet Street, Suite 70
Andover, MA 01810

web: www.skylit.com
e-mail: sales@skylit.com
         support@skylit.com

1 2 3 4 5 6 7 8 9 10   14 13 12 11 10 09

Printed in the United States of America

Brief Contents

Contents

Preface

The AP exam in computer science tests your understanding of basic concepts in computer science as well as your fluency in Java programming. The exam covers roughly the material of a one-semester introductory college course in computer science (CS-1).

In the past, the College Board offered two computer science exams, called "A" and "AB." Recently the College Board has made a decision to drop the more advanced AB exam and, starting in 2010, will offer only one exam (still called "A").

Exam questions are developed by The College Board's AP CS Test Development Committee, and exams are put together by Educational Testing Service (ETS). The College Board offers exams in more than 30 subjects. In 2008, 1,559,665 students took 2,694,569 exams in the US and Canada. The most up-to-date information on the AP exams offered and participation statistics can be found on The College Board's *AP Central* web site, http://apcentral.collegeboard.com.

In the spring of 2004, the computer science exams used Java for the first time. At the same time, the AP CS program's emphasis shifted from implementation of algorithms and coding proficiency to object-oriented software design and development. The 2009 exam, however, shows some renewed interest in algorithms.

Developing exams is a very big effort for The College Board; training teachers in a new programming language is another big undertaking. So it is safe to say that Java is here to stay for a few more years, as long as it remains a popular programming language in colleges and in the industry.

> **Answers to exam questions written in a programming language other than Java will not receive credit.**

A working knowledge of Java is necessary but not sufficient for a good grade on the exam. First and foremost, you must understand the basic concepts of computer science, object-oriented programming (OOP), and some common algorithms. As for Java: you don't have to know the whole language, just the subset described in The College Board's *Advanced Placement Course Description for Computer Science* (www.collegeboard.com/student/testing/ap/sub_compscia.html). You must also be familiar with The College Board's material developed specifically for the AP CS exam: the GridWorld case study.

This is a lot of material to cover, and it is certainly not the goal of this book to teach you everything you need to know from scratch. For that, you need a complete textbook with exercises and programming projects. Most students who take the exam are enrolled in an AP computer science course at their school. A determined student can prepare for the exam on his or her own; it may take anywhere between two and twelve months, and a good textbook will be even more important.

The goals of this book are:

- to describe the exam format and requirements

- to describe the AP Java subset

- to provide an effective review of what you should know with emphasis on the more difficult topics and on common omissions and mistakes

- to help you identify and fill the gaps in your knowledge

- to offer sample exam questions with answers, hints, and solutions for you to practice with and analyze your mistakes

The AP exam in computer science is a paper-and-pencil affair. While you need a computer with a Java compiler to learn how to program and how to implement common algorithms in Java, this book does not require the use of a computer. In fact, it is a good idea not to use one when you work on practice questions, so that you can get used to the exam's format and environment. One-hundred-percent correct Java syntax is not the emphasis here. Small mistakes (a missed semicolon or a brace) that a compiler would normally help you catch will probably not affect your exam score. You'll need a computer only to access collegeboard.com, *AP Central*, and our web site for the latest updates and past exam free-response solutions.

Chapter 1 of this book explains the format, required materials, and the Java subset for the exam and provides information about exam grading and exam-taking hints. Chapter 2 and Chapter 3 cover the elements of Java required for the exam. Chapter 4 deals with OOP topics. Chapter 5 deals with common algorithms for searching and sorting. Chapter 6 reviews the GridWorld case study. The review chapters contain sample multiple-choice questions with detailed explanations of all the right and wrong answers. Chapter 7 is actually on the web at this book's companion web site, `www.skylit.com/beprepared/`. It offers annotated solutions to free-response questions from past exams. At the end of the book are four complete practice exams followed by answers and solutions.

Good luck!

Our colleague and friend Dave Wittry passed away in a tragic accident while training for a triathlon, on February 5, 2008. He was 41. Dave contributed practice exam questions for the 2nd and 3rd editions of this book. Dave taught at Troy High School, a magnet school for science, math, and technology in Fullerton, California, and contributed to Troy's immense success in Computer Science. In 2005 Dave moved to Taiwan and taught AP Computer Science and mathematics at the Taipei American School. He was a reader for the AP Computer Science Exams for several years. Dave was always ready to help friends, students, and colleagues, and he developed valuable resources for computer science teachers. We miss Dave!

We are grateful to David Levine of St. Bonaventure University who recommended many important improvements, helped us catch technical and stylistic mistakes, and pointed out questions that needed clarification in the first edition of *Be Prepared*, which came out in 1999.

Roger Frank and Judy Hromcik contributed practice questions to the second and third editions; some of the questions in this book are based on their ideas. Roger also went very thoroughly over the draft of the earlier editions and recommended many corrections and improvements.

We thank teachers and students who alerted us to several mistakes in the earlier editions of this book.

Our special thanks to Margaret Litvin for making this book more readable with her thorough and thoughtful editing.

Finally, we thank the Boy Scouts of America for allowing us to allude to their motto in the book's title.

About the Authors

Maria Litvin has taught computer science and mathematics at Phillips Academy in Andover, Massachusetts, since 1987. She is an AP Computer Science exam reader and Question Leader and, as a consultant for The College Board, provides AP training for high school computer science teachers. Maria is a recipient of the 1999 Siemens Award for Advanced Placement for Mathematics, Science, and Technology for New England and of the 2003 RadioShack National Teacher Award. Prior to joining Phillips Academy, Maria taught computer science at Boston University. Maria is the author of the earlier, C++ version of *Be Prepared* and co-author of *C++ for You++: An Introduction to Programming and Computer Science*, which became one of the leading high school textbooks for AP Computer Science courses. More recently, Maria and Gary Litvin co-wrote *Java Methods A & AB: Object-Oriented Programming and Data Structures* (Skylight Publishing, 2006) that were used for AP CS courses in hundreds of schools. Their latest book is *Mathematics for the Digital Age and Programming in Python* (Skylight Publishing, 2008).

Gary Litvin is a co-author of *C++ for You++*, the *Java Methods* series, and *Mathematics for the Digital Age and Programming in Python*. Gary has worked in many areas of software development including artificial intelligence, pattern recognition, computer graphics, and neural networks. As founder of Skylight Software, Inc., he developed SKYLIGHTS/GX, one of the first visual programming tools for C and C++ programmers. Gary led in the development of several state-of-the-art software products including interactive touch screen development tools, OCR and handwritten character recognition systems, and credit card fraud detection software.

How to Use This Book

Multiple-choice questions in the review chapters are marked by their number in a box:

Their solutions are delimited by ☞ and ☜.

The companion web site

        www.skylit.com/beprepared/

is an integral part of the book. It contains annotated solutions to free-response questions from past exams, the latest case study information, and relevant links. The GridWorld case study was used for the first time in 2008 and will probably stay for a few years. Check this book's web site for the current information, and be sure you have the latest edition of *Be Prepared*.

> **Our practice exams may be more difficult than the actual exams, so don't panic if they take more time. We have included three parts in many of our free-response questions, while actual exam questions may have only two parts.**

Chapter 1. Exam Format, Grading, and Tips

1.1. Exam Format and Materials

Figure 1-1 shows the format of the AP Computer Science exam. The exam takes 3 hours of test time (plus breaks and time for instructions). It is divided into two sections. Section I consists of 40 multiple-choice questions with a total allotted time of 1 hour and 15 minutes (1.5 to 2 minutes per question on average). Section II consists of four free-response questions with a total allotted time of 1 hour and 45 minutes (20-30 minutes per question). The free-response questions usually consist of two or three parts each. No computers, calculators, other devices, books, or materials are allowed.

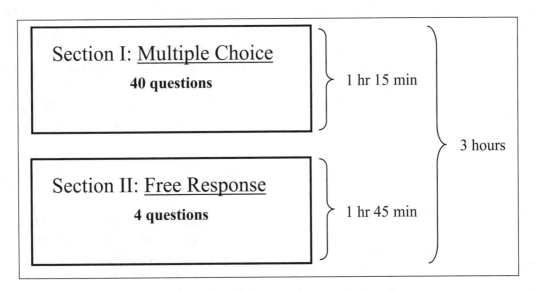

Figure 1-1. AP Computer Science exam format

Exam materials given to you at the exam will include a booklet containing the needed case study code and *Quick Reference* — a list of the library classes and their methods included in the AP subset. These materials are provided for reference — it is expected that you will already be very familiar and comfortable with the case study and the required library classes before the exam. www.skylit.com/beprepared/ has current links to these materials.

The multiple-choice section is a mixture of questions related to general computer science terms, program design decisions, specific elements of Java syntax, properties of classes, logical analysis of fragments of Java code, OOP concepts, and five-six questions related to the case study.

The free-response questions usually aim to cover a wide range of material: one- and two-dimensional arrays, strings, classes and interfaces, Java library classes (within the AP subset), and so on. In past exams, students have not been asked to write complete programs. Usually, they were asked to write a constructor or a method that performs a specified task under a given header for the method. The second part of the question often refers to the class or method implemented in the first part, but each part is graded separately, and your implementation of Part (a) does not have to be correct in order for you to get full credit for Part (b). Part (c) may ask questions about your implementation or ask you to write an additional method that uses Parts (a) and/or (b). In that case you are to assume that the methods in the previous parts work as intended, regardless of what you wrote for them.

Free-response questions may also include a "design" question, in which you are asked to design a small class, then write it or some fragments of it or just use it in other parts of the question. Your design will be graded based on the appropriateness of the features of your class, appropriate names for methods and variables, and other criteria.

One free-response question is based on the case study. It may ask you to extend a case study class and to write a new method or rewrite an existing method.

1.2. The Java Subset

The Development Committee has defined a restricted subset of Java to be tested on the exams. The purpose of the subset is to focus the AP CS program more on general concepts than on the specifics of Java and to limit the scope, especially of material related to the peculiarities of Java. The subset is described in The College Board's *Advanced Placement Course Description for Computer Science*; we have a link to it from this book's web site `www.skylit.com/beprepared/`.

What is in the subset? Actually, quite a bit:

- `boolean`, `int`, and `double` primitive data types. `(int)` and `(double)` casts. **Other primitive data types, including** `char`, **are not in the subset and should be avoided on the exam.**

- Assignment (=), arithmetic (+, -, *, /, %), increment/decrement (++, --), compound assignment (+=, -=, *=, /=, %=), relational (<, >, <=, >=, ==, !=), and logical (&&, ||, !) operators. **Use only the postfix form of ++ and -- (x++ or x--), and do not use them in expressions**.

- + and += operators for concatenating strings. `String`'s `compareTo`, `equals`, `length`, `substring`, and `indexOf(String s)` methods. `\n`, `\\`, and `\"` escape sequences in literal strings.

- `System.out.print` and `System.out.println`.

- One- and two-dimensional arrays, `array.length`, arrays of objects, initialized arrays such as `int[] x = {1,2,3};`

- `if-else`, `for`, including the "for each" form, `for(type x : values)...`, `while`, `return`. **But do-while and switch are not included.**

- Classes. Constructors, the `new` operator, `public` and `private` methods, `static` methods, `static` variables and `static final` variables (constants), overloaded methods, `null`. **All instance variables are private**. Default initialization rules are <u>not</u> in the subset and won't come up on the exam.

- Inheritance, interfaces and abstract classes, `extends`, `implements`. Calling a superclass's constructor from a subclass (as in `super(...)`). Calling a superclass's method from a subclass (as in `super.someMethod(...)`). Passing `this` object to a method (as in `otherObject.someMethod(this)`).

- `NullPointerException`, `ArrayIndexOutOfBoundsException`, `ArithmeticException`, `IllegalArgumentException`, `ClassCastException`.

- Library classes, methods, and constants:
String:	`length()`, `substring(...)`, `indexOf(String s)`
Integer:	`Integer(int x)`, `intValue()`;
	`Integer.MIN_VALUE` and `Integer.MAX_VALUE`.
Double:	`Double(double x)`, `doubleValue()`
Math:	`abs(int x)`, `abs(double x)`,
	`pow(double base, double exp)`, `sqrt(double x)`,
	`random()`

  Also understand `toString` methods for all objects, the `equals` and `compareTo` methods for `String`, `Integer`, and `Double`, and the `Comparable<T>` interface.

- The `List<E>` interface and the `ArrayList<E>` class (see Section 2.6).

> **If you feel you must stray from the subset in your free-response solution, you might have misunderstood the problem and be making it harder than it is.**

Things that are <u>not</u> in the AP subset and should be avoided include the following:

- Java syntax abominations, such as the `?_:_` operator and the "comma" operator
- `++` and `--` in expressions (as in `a[i++]`)
- Primitive data types other than `boolean`, `int`, and `double` (`char` is <u>not</u> in the subset)
- All bit-wise logical operators

> **Also not in the subset and will not be tested:**

- The `switch` statement, the `do-while` loop, `continue` in loops
- The prefix form of `++` and `--` operators (`++k`, `--k`)
- Library classes (such as `StringBuffer`, `Arrays`, `DecimalFormat`, etc.), unless specifically listed in the subset
- checked exceptions and `try-catch-finally` statements
- `System.in` and `Scanner`; any input and output other than `System.out.print` and `System.out.println`
- `enum` data types

1.3.   Grading

The exams are graded on a scale from 1 to 5. Grades of 5 and 4 are called "extremely well qualified" and "well qualified," respectively, and usually will be honored by colleges that give credit or placement for AP exams in computer science. A grade of 3, "qualified," may be denied credit or placement at some colleges. Grades of 2, "possibly qualified," and 1, "no recommendation," will not get you college credit or placement.

2009 was the last year when the College Board offered two AP Computer Science exams, A and, more advanced, AB. Table 1-1 presents published statistics and grade distributions on the 2004 A and AB exams. In 2004, 13,834 candidates took the A exam and 5,807 candidates took the AB exam.

	Computer Science A		Computer Science AB	
	Number	%	Number	%
Students	13,834	100.0	5,807	100.0
Grade:				
5	2,572	18.6	1,574	27.1
4	3,270	23.6	1,058	18.2
3	2,102	15.2	1,020	17.6
2	1,309	9.5	702	12.1
1	4,581	33.1	1,453	25.0
3 or Higher	7,944	57.4	3,652	62.9

Table 1-1. 2004 grade distributions for A and AB exams

The multiple-choice and free-response sections weigh equally in the final grade.

The College Board uses a weighted combination of the multiple-choice (MC) and free-response (FR) scores to determine the final total score:

```
totalScore =
    MC_coeff * (countCorrect - 0.25*countWrong) +
    FR_coeff * FR_score;
```

For multiple-choice questions, one point is given for each correct answer and 1/4 point is subtracted for each wrong answer. There is no subtraction for an answer left blank. Free-response questions are graded by a group of high school teachers and college professors. Scores are based on a *rubric* established by the Chief Reader, Exam Leader, and Question Leaders. Each free-response question is graded out of 9 points, with partial credit given according to the rubric.

The final score is obtained by adding the MC and FR weighted scores. The MC and FR coefficients are chosen in such a way that they give equal weights to the multiple-choice and free-response sections of the exam. For example, if the exam has 40 multiple-choice questions and 4 free-response questions, weights of 1.25 for multiple-choice and 1.3889 for free-response will give each section a maximum total of 50, for a maximum possible total score of 100.

Four cut-off points determine the grade. Table 1-2 shows the maximum composite scores and cut-off points used for the 1999 and 2004 exams. In 2004, 79% or more correct answers on the A exam and 68% or more correct answers on the AB exam would get you a 5. The cut-off points are determined by the Chief Reader and may vary slightly from year to year based on the score distributions and close examination of a sample of individual exams.

	A			AB	
	Max composite score 80 $(1.00 * MC + 1.1111 * FR)$			Max composite score 100 $(1.25 * MC + 1.3889 * FR)$	
AP Grade	1999	2004	AP Grade	1999	2004
5	60 - 80	63 - 80	5	70 - 100	68 -100
4	45 - 59	49 - 62	4	60 - 69	56 - 67
3	33 - 44	39 - 48	3	41 - 59	44 - 55
2	25 - 32	32 - 38	2	31 - 40	35 - 43
1	0 - 24	0 - 31	1	0 - 30	0 - 34

Table 1-2. Score-to-grade conversion

Statistical analysis of published results from the 2004 exam shows that over 98% of students who got at least 27 out of 40 on the multiple-choice section received a 4 or a 5 for the whole exam. This may or may not be true for our practice exams. You will know only after the exam!

1.4. College Credit

Most colleges will take your AP courses and exam grades into account in admissions decisions if you take your exams early enough. But acceptance of AP exam results for credit and/or placement varies widely among colleges. In general, the AP Computer Science course corresponds to a CS-1 course (Introductory Computer Science or Computer Programming I), a one-semester course for computer science majors. Some colleges may base their decision on your grade, and some may not give any credit at all.

The AP program in computer science is a rigorous and demanding program that is comparable to or exceeds the level of the respective first-semester computer science courses at most colleges.

If you plan to major in computer science and your college of choice does not recognize a good grade on the AP exam for credit and/or placement, you should examine the reasons carefully. Decide for yourself whether these reasons are valid or just stem from the bias of that college or its computer science department.

1.5. Exam Taking Tips

Some things are obvious:

- If you took the time to read a multiple-choice question and all the answer choices but decided to skip it, take an extra ten seconds and guess. Most likely you have eliminated one or two wrong answers even without noticing.

- If a common paragraph refers to a group of questions and you took the time to read it, try each question in the group.

- Do read the question before jumping to the code included in the question.

There are a few important things to know about answering free-response questions.

> **Remember that all free-response questions have equal weight. Don't assume that the first question is the easiest and the last is the hardest.**

> **In a nutshell: be neat, straightforward, and professional; keep your exam reader in mind; don't show off.**

More specifically:

1. Stay within the AP Java subset.

2. Remember that the elegance of your code <u>does not</u> count. More often than not, a brute-force approach is the best. You may waste a lot of time writing tricky, non-standard code and trick yourself in the process or mislead your exam reader who, after all, is only human. No one will test your code on a computer.

3. Superior efficiency of your code does not count, unless the desired performance of the solution is specifically stated in the question.

4. Remember that Parts (b) and (c) of a question are graded independently from the previous parts, and may actually be easier: Part (a) may ask you to write a method, while Part (b) or Part (c) may simply ask you to use it.

    It is common for method(s) specified in Part (a) to be called in subsequent parts. Do so, even if your Part (a) is incorrect or left blank. <u>Do not</u> re-implement code from earlier parts in later parts — you will waste valuable time and may lose points for doing so.

5. Bits of "good thinking" count. You may not know the whole solution, but if you have read and understood the question, go ahead and write fragments of code that may earn you partial credit points. But don't spend too much time improvising incorrect code.

6. Don't waste your time erasing large portions of work. Instead, cross out your work with one neat line, but only after you have something better to replace it with. Do not cross out a solution if you have no time to redo it, even if you think it is wrong. You <u>won't</u> be penalized for incorrect code and may get partial credit for it. Exam readers are instructed not to read any code that you have crossed out. But if you wrote two solutions, be sure to cross one out: otherwise only the first one on the page will be graded.

7. Read the comment above the method header quickly — it usually restates the task in a more formal way and sometimes gives hints. Assume that all preconditions are satisfied — don't add unnecessary checks to your code.

8. One common mistake is to forget a `return` statement in a non-`void` method. Make sure the returned value matches the specified type.

9. Do not ignore any hints in the question description. If an algorithm is suggested for a method (as in "you may use the following algorithm"), don't fight it, just do it! If the description says "you may use a helper method," be sure to write and use one: chances are it is much more difficult to come up with a solution without a helper method.

10. Remember that the exam readers grade a vast number of exams in quick succession during a marathon grading session every June. Write as neatly as possible. Space out your code (don't save paper).

11. Always indent your code properly. This helps you and your exam reader. If you miss a brace but your code is properly indented, the reader (as opposed to a Java compiler) may accept it as correct. Similarly, if you put each statement on a separate line, a forgotten semicolon may not be held against you.

12. Follow the Java naming style: the names of all methods, variables, and parameters start with a lowercase letter. Use meaningful, but not too verbose, names for variables. `count` may be better than `a`; `sum` may be better than `temp`; `row`, `col` may be better than `i`, `j`. But `k` is better than `loopControlVariable`. If the question contains examples of code with names, use the same names when appropriate.

13. Don't bother with comments; they do not count and you will lose valuable time. Occasionally you can put a very brief comment that indicates your intentions for the fragment of code that follows. For example:

```
// Find the first empty seat:
...
...
```

14. Don't worry about `imports` — assume that all the necessary library classes are imported.

15. Code strictly according to the specifications and preconditions. Avoid extraneous "bells and whistles" — you will lose points. Never add `System.out.print/println` in solutions unless specifically asked to do so.

16. Use recursion when appropriate: if specifically requested or especially tempting.

17. Don't try to catch the exam authors on ambiguities: there will be no one to hear your case, and you'll waste your time. Instead, try to grasp quickly what was meant and write your answer.

18. Don't quit until the time is up. Use all the time you have and keep trying. The test will be over before you know it.

Chapter 2. Java Features, Part 1

2.1. Variables; Arithmetic, Relational, and Logical Operators

Primitive data types included in the subset are `boolean`, `int`, and `double`. In Java, an `int` always takes four bytes, regardless of a particular computer or Java compiler, and its range is from -2^{31} to $2^{31} - 1$ ($-2,147,483,648$ and $2,147,483,647$, respectively). These values are defined in Java as symbolic constants `Integer.MIN_VALUE` and `Integer.MAX_VALUE`; use these symbolic constants if you need to refer to the limits of the `int` range. A `double` takes 8 bytes and has a huge range, but its precision is about 15 significant digits.

▌ **Remember to declare local variables.**

It is safer to declare all variables at the top of the method body. If you declare a variable inside a nested block, make sure it is used only in that block. If you declare a variable in a `for` loop, it will be undefined outside that loop.

For example:

```
public int find(int[] a, int target)
{
  if (a.length > 0)
  {
    int iMin = 0;

    for (int i = 1; i < a.length; i++)
      if (a[i] < a[iMin])
        iMin = i;

    int count = 0;

    for (i = 0; i < a.length; i++)
      if (a[i] == a[iMin])
        count++;
  }
  return count;
}
```

Error: i is undefined

Error: count is undefined here

A safer version:

```
public int countMins(int[] a)
{
  int iMin = 0;
  int count = 0;

  if (a.length > 0)
  {
    iMin = 0;
    for (int i = 1; i < a.length; i++)
      if (a[i] < a[iMin])
        iMin = i;

    count = 0;

    for (int i = 0; i < a.length; i++)
      if (a[i] == a[iMin])
        count++;
  }
  return count;
}
```

> *Do not declare* count *here:*
> **int** count = 0;
> *would be a mistake*

You won't be penalized for declarations inside the code, but if you declare important variables above the code, it makes it easier to read and may help you avoid mistakes.

Which of the following statements is true?

(A)   In Java, data types in declarations of symbolic constants are needed only for documentation purposes.

(B)   When a Java interpreter is running, variables of the `double` data type are represented in memory as strings of decimal digits with a decimal point and an optional sign.

(C)   A variable's data type determines where it is stored in computer memory when the program is running.

(D)   A variable's data type determines whether that variable may be passed as a parameter to a particular method.

(E)   A variable of the `int` type cannot serve as an operand for the / operator.

☞ This question gives us a chance to review what we know about data types.

A is false: symbolic constants are not so different from variables. The difference is that a constant declaration includes the keyword `final`. Class constants are often declared as `static final` variables. For example:

```
public static final double LBS_IN_KG = 2.20462262;
public static final int maxNumSeats = 120;
```

B is false, too. While real numbers may be written in programs in decimal notation, a Java compiler converts them into a special floating-point format that takes eight bytes and is convenient for computations.

C is false. The data type by itself does not determine where the variable is stored. Its location in memory is determined by where the variable is used and its allocation: whether it is a local variable in a method or an instance variable of a class.

E is false, too. In Java, you can write `a/b`, where both `a` and `b` are of type `int`. The result is truncated to an integer.

D is true. Sometimes an parameter of a different type may be promoted to the type expected by the method (for example, an `int` can be promoted into `double` when you call, say, `Math.sqrt(x)` for an `int x`). But this is not always the case (for example, a `double` won't work in place of a `String`). The answer is D. ☜

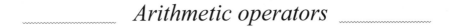

Arithmetic operators

> **The most important thing to remember about Java's arithmetic operators is that the data type of the result, even each intermediate result, is the same as the data type of the operands. In particular, the result of division of one integer by another integer is truncated to an integer.**

For example:

```
int n = 3;
double result;

result = (n + 1) * n / 2;        // result is 6.0
result = (n / 2) * (n + 1);      // result is 4.0
result = (1 / 2) * n * (n + 1);  // result is 0.0
```

To avoid truncation you have to watch the data types and sometimes use the *cast operator*. For example:

```
int a, b;
double ratio;
...
ratio = (double)a / b;       // Or a / (double) b;
// But not ratio = (double)(a/b) -- this is a cast applied too late!
```

If at least one of the operands is a `double`, there is no need to cast the other one — it is promoted to a `double` automatically. For example:

```
double x;
int factor = 3;
x = 2.0 / factor;  // Correct result: x = .6666...
```

2

Which of the following expressions does not evaluate to 0.4?

(A)   `(int)4.5 / (double)10;`
(B)   `(double)(4 / 10);`
(C)   `4.0 / 10;`
(D)   `4 / 10.0;`
(E)   `(double)4 / (double)10;`

☞ In B the cast to `double` is applied too late — after the ratio is truncated to 0 — so it evaluates to 0. The answer is B. ☜

In the real world we have to worry about the range of values for different data types. For example, a method that calculates the factorial of *n* as an `int` may overflow the result, even for relatively small *n*.

> **For the AP exam, you have to be aware of what overflow is, and you need to be aware of the `Integer.MIN_VALUE` and `Integer.MAX_VALUE` constants, but you don't have to know their specific values.**

Modulo division

> **The % (modulo division) operator usually applies to two integers: it calculates the remainder when the first operand is divided by the second.**

For example:

```
int r;
r = 17 % 3;   // r is set to 2
r = 8 % 2;    // r is set to 0
r = 4 % 5;    // r is set to 4
```

Compound assignments, ++ and --

Compound assignment operators are +=, -=, *= , /=, and %=. x += y is the same as x = x + y. Other operations follow the same pattern.

There are two forms of the ++ and -- operators in Java. The prefix form increments (or decrements) the variable before its value is used in the rest of the expression; the postfix form increments (or decrements) it afterwards.

> **The AP Development Committee discourages the use of ++ and -- in expressions. Use ++ and -- only in separate statements.**

For example:

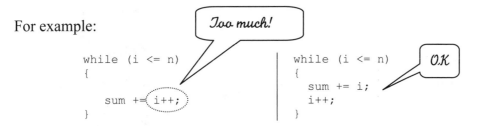

You won't lose points over ++ or -- in expressions if you use them correctly, but they won't earn you any credit, either.

> **It is bad style <u>not</u> to use increment or compound assignment operators where appropriate.**

For example:

```
for (int i = 0; i < n; i = i + 1)          for (int i = 0; i < n; i++)
{                                          {
   count = count + 1;                          count++;
   sum = sum + a[i];                           sum += a[i];
}                                          }
```

Works, but looks bad   *O.K*

Again, this incurs no penalty but looks ugly.

Arithmetic expressions are too easy to be tested alone. You may encounter them in questions that combine them with logic, iterations, recursion, and so on.

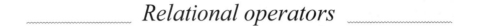

Relational operators

In the subset, the relational operators ==, !=, <, >, <=, >= will apply to `ints` and `doubles`. Remember that "is equal to" is represented by == (not to be confused with =, the assignment operator). Write it clearly. `a != b` is equivalent to `!(a == b)`, but `!=` is stylistically better.

> **The == and != operators can be also applied to any objects, but their meanings are different from what you might expect: they compare the <u>addresses</u> of two objects. The result of == is true if and only if the two variables refer to exactly the same object. You rarely care about that: most likely you want to compare the <u>contents</u> of two objects, for instance two strings. Then you need to use the `equals` or `compareTo` method.**

For example:

```
if (str.equals("Stop")) ...
```

> **On the other hand, == or != must be used when you need to compare an object to `null`.**

`null` is a Java reserved word that stands for a reference with a value of zero. It is used to indicate that a variable currently does not refer to any valid object. For example:

```
if (str != null && str.equals("Stop")) ...
// str != null avoids NullPointerException --
// can't call a null's method
```

You can also write

```
if ("Stop".equals(str)) ...
```

This works because `"Stop"` is not `null`; it works even if `str` is `null`.

_____ *Logical operators* _____

The logical operators `&&`, `||`, and `!` normally apply to Boolean values and expressions. For example:

```
boolean found = false;          boolean found = false;
...                             ...
while (i >= 0 && !found)         while (i >= 0 && found == false)
{                                {
   ...                              ...
}                                }
```

Works, but is more verbose

Do not write

```
while (... && !found == true)
```

— this works, but is redundant.

3

Assuming that x, y, and z are integer variables, which of the following three logical expressions are equivalent to each other, that is, have the same values for all possible values of x, y, and z?

 I.   `(x == y && x != z) || (x != y && x == z)`

 II. `(x == y || x == z) && (x != y || x != z)`

 III. `(x == y) != (x == z)`

(A)   I and II only
(B)   II and III only
(C)   I and III only
(D)   I, II, and III
(E)   None of the three

 Expression III is the key to the answer: all three expressions state the fact that exactly one out of the two equalities, x == y or x == z, is true. Expression I states that either the first and not the second or the second and not the first is true. Expression II states that one of the two is true and one of the two is false. Expression III simply states that they have different values. All three boil down to the same thing. The answer is D.

De Morgan's Laws

The exam may include questions on De Morgan's Laws:

!(a && b) is the same as !a || !b
!(a || b) is the same as !a && !b

4

The expression !((x <= y) && (y > 5)) is equivalent to which of the following?

(A)   (x <= y) && (y > 5)
(B)   (x <= y) || (y > 5)
(C)   (x >= y) || (y < 5)
(D)   (x > y) || (y <= 5)
(E)   (x > y) && (y <= 5)

The given expression is pretty long, so if you try to plug in specific numbers you may lose a lot of time. Use De Morgan's Laws instead:

$$!((x <= y) \quad \&\& \quad (y > 5))$$

$$!(x <= y) \quad || \quad !(y > 5)$$

$$(x > y) \quad || \quad (y <= 5)$$

> When ! is distributed, && changes into || and vice-versa

The answer is D.

Short-circuit evaluation

An important thing to remember about the Java logical operators, && and ||, is *short-circuit evaluation*. If the value of the first operand is sufficient to determine the result, then the second operand is <u>not</u> evaluated.

Consider the following code segment:

```
int x = 0, y = 3;
String op = "/";

if (op.equals("/") && (x != 0) && (y/x > 2))
{
  System.out.println("OK");
}
else
{
  System.out.println("Failed");
}
```

Which of the following statements about this code is true?

(A)   There will be a compile error because `String` and `int` variables are intermixed in the same condition.
(B)   There will be a run-time divide-by-zero error.
(C)   The code will compile and execute without error; the output will be `OK`.
(D)   The code will compile and execute without error; the output will be `Failed`.
(E)   The code will compile and execute without error; there will be no output.

☞   A and E are just filler answers. Since `x` is equal to 0, the condition cannot be true, so C should be rejected, too. The question remains whether it crashes or executes. In Java, once `x != 0` fails, the rest of the condition, `y/x > 2`, won't be evaluated, and `y/x` won't be computed. The answer is D. ☜

The relational expressions in the above question are parenthesized. This is not necessary because relational operators always take precedence over logical operators. If you are used to lots of parentheses, use them, but you can skip them as well. For example, the Boolean expression from Question 5 can be written with fewer parentheses:

```
if (op.equals("/") && x != 0 && y/x > 2)
```

`&&` also takes precedence over `||`, but it's clearer to use parentheses when `&&` and `||` appear in the same expression. For example:

```
if ((0 < a && a < top) || (0 < b && b < top)) ...
```

Bit-wise logical operators

> The bit-wise logical operators, &, |, ^, and ~, are <u>not</u> in the AP Java subset and are <u>not</u> tested on the AP exam. You don't have to worry about them.

Programmers use these operators to perform logical operations on individual bits, usually in `int` values. Unfortunately, Java also allows you to apply these operators to `boolean` values, and, when used that way, these operators do not comply with short-circuit evaluation. This may lead to a nasty bug if you inadvertently write & instead of && or | instead of ||. For example,

```
if (x != 0 & y/x > 2)
```

Error: & instead of &&

results in a division by 0 exception when `x = 0`.

2.2. Conditional Statements and Loops

> You can use simplified indentation for `if-else-if` statements.

For example:

```
if (score >= 70)
  grade = 5;
else if (score >= 60)
  grade = 4;
...
else
  grade = 1;
```

But don't forget braces and proper indentation for nested `if`s. For example:

```
if (exam.equals("AB"))
{
  if (score >= 60)
    grade = 5;
  else if ...
    ...
}
else if (exam.equals("BC"))
{
  if (score >= 70)
    grade = 5;
  else if ...
    ...
}
```

6

Consider the following code segment, where `m` is a variable of the type `int`:

```
if (m > 0)
{
  if (1000 / m) % 2 == 0)
    System.out.println("even");
  else
    System.out.println("odd");
}
else
  System.out.println("not positive");
```

Which of the following code segments are equivalent to the one above (that is, produce the same output as the one above regardless of the value of m)?

I.
```
if (m <= 0)
   System.out.println("not positive");
else if ((1000 / m) % 2 == 0)
   System.out.println("even");
else
   System.out.println("odd");
```

II.
```
if (m > 0 && (1000 / m) % 2 == 0)
   System.out.println("even");
else if (m <= 0)
   System.out.println("not positive");
else
   System.out.println("odd");
```

III.
```
if ((1000 / m) % 2 == 0)
{
  if (m <= 0)
    System.out.println("not positive");
  else
    System.out.println("even");
}
else
{
  if (m <= 0)
    System.out.println("not positive");
  else
    System.out.println("odd");
}
```

(A) I only
(B) II only
(C) I and II
(D) II and III
(E) I, II, and III

Segment I can actually be reformatted as:

```
if (m <= 0)
  System.out.println("not positive");
else
{
  if ((1000 / m) % 2 == 0)
    System.out.println("even");
  else
    System.out.println("odd");
}
```

So it's the same as the given segment with the condition negated and `if` and `else` swapped. Segment II restructures the sequence, but gives the same result. To see this we can try different combinations of true/false for `m <= 0` and `(1000 / m) % 2 == 0`. Segment III would work, too, but it has a catch: it doesn't work when `m` is equal to 0. The answer is C.

for and `while` *loops*

The `for` loop,

```
for (initialize; condition; change)
{
  ...   // Do something
}
```

is equivalent to the `while` loop:

```
initialize;
while (condition)
{
  ...   // Do something
  change;
}
```

change can mean any change in the values of the variables that control the loop, such as incrementing or decrementing an index or a counter.

`for` loops are shorter and more idiomatic in some instances. They shouldn't be discriminated against. For example:

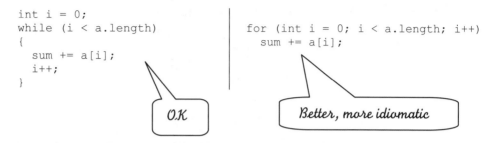

```
int i = 0;
while (i < a.length)
{
  sum += a[i];
  i++;
}
```

O.K

```
for (int i = 0; i < a.length; i++)
  sum += a[i];
```

Better, more idiomatic

> **In a `for` or `while` loop, the condition is evaluated at the beginning of the loop and the program does not go inside the loop if the condition is false. Thus, the body of the loop may be skipped entirely if the condition is false at the very beginning.**

7

Consider the following methods:

```
public int fun1(int n)
{
  int product = 1;
  int k;
  for (k = 2; k <= n; k++)
  {
    product *= k;
  }
  return product;
}
```

```
public int fun2(int n)
{
  int product = 1;
  int k = 2;
  while (k <= n)
  {
    product *= k;
    k++;
  }
  return product;
}
```

For which integer values of n do `fun1(n)` and `fun2(n)` return the same result?

(A)   Only $n > 1$
(B)   Only $n < 1$
(C)   Only $n == 1$
(D)   Only $n >= 1$
(E)   Any integer n

  The best approach here is purely formal: since the initialization, condition, and increment in the `for` loop in `fun1` are the same as the ones used with the `while` loop in `fun2`, the two methods are equivalent. The answer is E.

8

Consider the following code segment:

```
while (x > y)
{
  x--;
  y++;
}
System.out.print(x - y);
```

Assume that x and y are int variables and their values satisfy the conditions $0 \le x \le 2$ and $0 \le y \le 2$. Which of the following describes the set of all possible outputs?

(A) 0
(B) –1, 1
(C) –1, –2
(D) 0, –1, –2
(E) 0, –1, 1, –2, 2

☞ If $x \le y$, then the while loop is never entered and the possible outputs are 0, –1, and –2 (for the pairs (0,0), (0,1), (0,2), (1,1), (1,2), (2,2)). If $x > y$, then the loop is entered and after the loop we must have $x \le y$, so $x - y$ cannot be positive. The answer is D. ↵

───────────── *OBOBs* ─────────────

When coding loops, beware of the so-called "off-by-one bugs" ("OBOBs"). These are mistakes of running through the iterations one time too many or one time too few.

9

Suppose the `isPrime` method is defined:

```
// returns true if p is a prime number, false otherwise
// precondition: p >= 2
public static boolean isPrime(int p) { < code not shown > }
```

Given

```
int n = 101;
int sum = 0;
```

Which of the following code segments correctly computes the sum of all prime numbers from 2 to 101?

(A)
```
while (n != 2)
{
   n--;
   if (isPrime(n)) sum += n;
}
```

(B)
```
while (n >= 2)
{
   n--;
   if (isPrime(n)) sum += n;
}
```

(C)
```
while (n != 2)
{
   if (isPrime(n)) sum += n;
   n--;
}
```

(D)
```
while (n >= 2)
{
   if (isPrime(n)) sum += n;
   n--;
}
```

(E)
```
while (n >= 2 && isPrime(n))
{
   sum += n;
   n--;
}
```

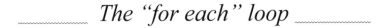   It is bad style to start the body of a loop with a decrement, so choices A and B are most likely wrong. Indeed, both A and B miss 101 (which happens to be a prime) because n is decremented too early. In addition, B eventually calls `isPrime(1)`, violating `isPrime`'s precondition. C misses 2 — an OBOB on the other end. E might look plausible for a moment, but it actually quits as soon at it encounters the first non-prime number. The answer is D.

The "for each" loop

The "for each" loop was first introduced in Java 5.0. This loop has the form

```
for (SomeType x : a)  // read: "for each x in a"
{
   ...   // do something
}
```

where a is an array or an `ArrayList` (or another `List` or "collection") that holds values of *SomeType*.

For example:

```
int[] scores = {87, 95, 76};
for (int score : scores)
  System.out.print(score + " ");
```

works the same way as

```
int[] scores = {87, 95, 76};
for (int i = 0; i < scores.length; i++)
{
  int score = scores[i];
  System.out.print(score + " ");
}
```

Both will display

```
87 95 76
```

Another example:

```
List<String> plants = new ArrayList<String>();
plants.add("Bougainvillea");
plants.add("Hibiscus");
plants.add("Poinciana");

for (String name : plants)
   System.out.print(name + " ");
```

will display

```
Bougainvillea Hibiscus Poinciana
```

Note that the "for each" loop traverses the array or list only in the forward direction and does not give you access to the indices of the values stored in the array or list. For example, a "for each" loop won't be very useful if you need to find the <u>position</u> of the first occurrence of a target value in a list.

If you need access to indices, use a for or while loop.

break *and* return *in loops*

In Java it is okay to use break and return inside loops. return immediately quits the method from any place inside or outside a loop. This may be a convenient shortcut, especially when you have to write nested loops and you are pressed for time. For example:

```
// returns true if all values in list are different, false otherwise
public boolean allDifferent(int[] list)
{
  for (int i = 0; i < list.length; i++)
    for (int j = i + 1; j < list.length; j++)
      if (list[i] == list[j])
        return false;
  return true;
}
```

You can also use break, but it may be dangerous and is not in the AP subset. Remember that in a nested loop, break takes you out of the inner loop but not out of the outer loop. Avoid redundant, verbose, and incorrect code like this:

```
// returns true if all values in list are different, false otherwise
public boolean allDifferent(int[] list)
{
  boolean foundDuplicates;

  for (int i = 0; i < list.length; i++)
  {
    for (int j = i + 1; j < list.length; j++)
    {
      if (list[i] == list[j])
      {
        foundDuplicates = true;
        break;
      }
      else
      {
        foundDuplicates = false;
      }
    }
  }
  if (foundDuplicates == true)
    return false;
  else
    return true;
}
```

Out of the inner for *but still in the outer* for.

If you insist on using Boolean flags, you need to be extra careful:

```
// returns true if all values in list are different, false otherwise
public boolean allDifferent(int[] list)
{
  boolean foundDuplicates = false;

  for (int i = 0; i < list.length; i++)
  {
    for (int j = i + 1; j < list.length; j++)
    {
      if (list[i] == list[j])
      {
        foundDuplicates = true;
        break;
      }
    }
  }
  return !foundDuplicates;
}
```

The continue statement is not in the AP subset and should be avoided.

2.3. Strings

In Java, a string is an object of the type `String`, and, as with other types of objects, a `String` variable holds a reference to (the address of) the string. Strings are immutable: no string methods can change the string. An assignment statement

```
str1 = str2;
```

copies the reference from `str2` into `str1`, so they both refer to the same memory location.

A *literal string* is a string of characters within double quotes. A literal string may include "escape sequences" \n (newline), \" (a double quote), and \\ (one backslash). For example,

```
System.out.print("Hello\n");
```

has the same effect as

```
System.out.println("Hello");
```

The `String` class supports the + and += operators for concatenating strings.

> **`String` is the only class in Java that supports special syntax for using operators on its objects.**

The operator

```
s1 += s2;
```

appends `s2` to `s1`. In reality it creates a new string by concatenating `s1` and `s2` and then sets `s1` to refer to it. It is equivalent to

```
s1 = s1 + s2;
```

10

What is the output of the following code segment?

```
String str1 = "Happy ";
String str2 = str1;
str2 += "New Year! ";
str2.substring(6);
System.out.println(str1 + str2);
```

(A) Happy New Year!
(B) Happy Happy New Year!
(C) Happy New Year! New Year!
(D) Happy New Year! Happy New Year!
(E) Happy New Year! Happy

☞ After `str2 = str1`, `str1` and `str2` point to the same memory location that contains "`Happy `". But after `str2 += "New Year! "`, these variables point to different things: `str1` remains "`Happy `" (strings are immutable) while `str2` becomes "`Happy New Year! `". `str2.substring(6)` does not change `str2` — it calls its `substring` but does not use its returned value (a common beginner's mistake: again, strings are immutable). The answer is B.

_____ *String methods* _____

The `String` methods included in the subset are:

```
int length()
boolean equals(String other)
int compareTo(String other)
String substring(int from)
String substring(int from, int to)
int indexOf(String s)
```

> **Always use the `equals` method to compare a string to another string. The == and != operators, applied to two strings, compare their <u>addresses</u>, not their values.**

`str1.equals(str2)` returns `true` if and only if `str1` and `str2` have the same values (that is, consist of the same characters).

`str1.compareTo(str2)` returns a positive number if `str1` is greater than `str2` (lexicographically), zero if they are equal, and a negative number if `str1` is less than `str2`.

`str.substring(from)` returns a substring of `str` starting at the `from` position to the end, and `str.substring(from, to)` returns `str`'s substring starting at the `from` position and up to but <u>not including</u> the `to` position (so the length of the returned substring is `to - from`). Positions are counted from 0. For example, `"Happy".substring(1,4)` would return `"app"`.

`str.indexOf(s)` returns the starting position of the first occurrence of `s` in `str`, or `-1` if not found.

Consider the following method:

```java
public String process(String msg, String delim)
{
  int pos = msg.indexOf(delim);
  while (pos >= 0)
  {
    msg = msg.substring(0, pos) + " "
                    + msg.substring(pos + delim.length());
    pos = msg.indexOf(delim);
  }
  return msg;
}
```

What is the output of the following code segment?

```java
String rhyme = "Twinkle\ntwinkle\nlittle star";
String rhyme2 = process(rhyme, "\n")
System.out.println(rhyme + "\n" + rhyme2);
```

(A)   ```
       little star
       Twinkle twinkle little star
       ```

(B)    ```
       little star
       Twinkle
       twinkle
       little star
       ```

(C)   ```
       Twinkle
       twinkle
       little star
       Twinkle winkle ittle tar
       ```

(D)    ```
       Twinkle
       twinkle
       little star
       Twinkle twinkle
       little star
       ```

(E)   ```
       Twinkle
       twinkle
       little star
       Twinkle twinkle little star
       ```

☞  `process` receives and works with a <u>copy</u> of a reference to the original string (see Section 3.3). The method can reassign the copy, as it does here, but the original reference still refers to the same string. This consideration, combined with immutability of strings, assures us that `rhyme` remains unchanged after the call `process(rhyme)`.

The `rhyme` string includes two newline characters, and, when printed, it produces

```
Twinkle
twinkle
little star
```

So the only possible answers are C, D or E. Note that we can come to this conclusion before we even look at the `process` method! This method repeatedly finds the first occurrence of `delim` in `msg`, cuts it out, and replaces it with a space. No other characters are replaced or lost. The resulting message prints on one line. The answer is E. ↵
```

2.4. `Integer` and `Double` Classes

In Java, variables of primitive data types (`int`, `double`, etc.) are not objects. In some situations it is convenient to represent numbers as objects. For example, you might want to store numeric values in an `ArrayList` (see Section 2.6), but the elements of an `ArrayList` must be objects. The `java.lang` package provides several "wrapper" classes that represent primitive data types as objects. Two of these classes, `Integer` and `Double`, are in the AP subset.

The `Integer` class has a constructor that takes an `int` value and creates an `Integer` object representing that value. The `intValue` method of an `Integer` object returns the value represented by that object as an `int`. For example:

```
Integer obj = new Integer(123);
...
int num = obj.intValue();  // num gets the value of 123
```

Likewise, `Double`'s constructor creates a `Double` object that represents a given `double` value. The method `doubleValue` returns the `double` represented by a `Double` object:

```
Double obj = new Double(123.45);
...
double x = obj.doubleValue();  // x gets the value of 123.45
```

The `Integer` class also provides two symbolic constants that describe the range for `int` values:

```
public static final int MIN_VALUE = -2147483648;
public static final int MAX_VALUE = 2147483647;
```

> Use the `equals` method of the `Integer` or of the `Double` class if you want to compare two `Integer` or two `Double` variables, respectively.

For example:

```
Integer a = new Integer(...);
Integer b = new Integer(...);
...
if (a.equals(b))
  ...
```

If you apply a relational operator == or != to two Integer or two Double variables, you will compare their <u>addresses</u>, not values. This is rarely, if ever, what you want to do.

The Integer and Double classes implement the Comparable<Integer> and Comparable<Double> interfaces respectively (see Section 4.6), so each of these classes has a compareTo method. As usual, obj1.compareTo(obj2) returns a positive integer if obj1 is greater than obj2 (that is, obj1's numeric value is greater than obj2's numeric value), a negative integer if obj1 is less than obj2, and zero if their numeric values are equal.

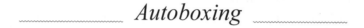

Autoboxing

Starting with Java 5.0, the compiler in certain situations automatically converts values of primitive data types, (int, double, etc.) into the corresponding wrapper types (Integer, Double, etc.). This feature is called *autoboxing* (or *autowrapping*). For example, in

```
ArrayList<Integer> numbers = new ArrayList<Integer>();
numbers.add(5);
```

the second line is compiled as

```
numbers.add(new Integer(5));
```

Likewise, where appropriate, the compiler performs *autounboxing*. For example,

```
int num = numbers.get(0);
```

in effect compiles as

```
int num = numbers.get(0).intValue();
```

Autoboxing and autounboxing are <u>not</u> in the AP subset, but you won't be penalized for relying on them.

2.5. Arrays

There are two ways to declare and create a one-dimensional array:

```
SomeType[] a = new SomeType[ size ];
SomeType[] b = {value0, value1, ..., valueN-1};
```

For example:

```
double[] samples = new double[100];
int[] numbers = {1, 2, 3};
String[] cities = {"Atlanta", "Boston", "Cincinnati", "Dallas"};
```

The first declaration declares an array of `double`s of size 100. Its elements get default values (zeroes), but this fact is not in the AP subset. The second declaration creates an array of `int`s of size 3 with its elements initialized to the values 1, 2, and 3. The third declaration declares and initializes an array of four given strings.

We can refer to `a`'s elements as `a[i]`, where `a` is the name of the array and `i` is an index (subscript), which can be an integer constant, variable, or expression.

> **Indices start from 0.**

`a.length` refers to the size of the array. (In an array, `length` is not a method, but rather works as an instance variable, hence <u>no parentheses</u>.) `a[a.length - 1]` refers to the last element.

Once an array is created, its size cannot be changed. The only way to expand an array is to create a bigger array and copy the contents of the original array into the new one. The old array is discarded (or, more precisely, recycled by a process called "garbage collection"). For example:

```
int[] a = new int[100];
...
int[] temp = new int[a.length * 2];
for (int i = 0; i < a.length; i++)
  temp[i] = a[i];
a = temp;   // reassign a to the new array; the old array is discarded
```

> **If `a` and `b` are arrays, `a = b` does not copy elements from `b` into `a`: it just reassigns the reference `a` to `b`, so that both `a` and `b` refer to the same array.**

The following method reverses the order of elements in an array of strings:

```
public void reverse(String[] words)
{
  int i = 0, j = words.length - 1;
  String temp;

  while (i < j)
  {
    temp = words[i]; words[i] = words[j]; words[j] = temp;
    i++;
    j--;
  }
}
```

The Java Virtual Machine (the run-time interpreter) checks that an array index is within the valid range, from 0 to `array.length - 1`. If an index value is invalid, the interpreter "throws" an `ArrayIndexOutOfBoundsException` — reports a run-time error, the line number for the offending program statement, and a trace of the method calls that led to it.

An exception is a run-time error, not a compile-time error.

The compiler cannot catch errors that will be caused by certain circumstances that occur during program execution, such as a variable used as an array index whose value has gone out of the appropriate range.

12

Suppose the method `int sign(int x)` returns 1 if x is positive, -1 if x is negative, and 0 if x is 0. Given

```
int[] nums = {-2, -1, 0, 1, 2};
```

what are the values of the elements of `nums` after the following code is executed?

```
int k;
for (k = 0; k < nums.length; k++)
{
  nums[k] -= sign(nums[k]);
  nums[k] += sign(nums[k]);
}
```

(A) -2, -1, 0, 1, 2
(B) -1, 0, 0, 0, 1
(C)   0, 0, 0, 0, 0
(D) -2, 0, 0, 2, 3
(E) -2, 0, 0, 0, 2

Remember that the first statement within the loop changes `nums[k]`, which may change the sign of `nums[k]`, too. Jot down a little table:

Before		After -=		After +=
a[k]	sign of a[k]	a[k]	sign of a[k]	a[k]
-2	-1	-1	-1	-2
-1	-1	0	0	0
0	0	0	0	0
1	1	0	0	0
2	1	1	1	2

The answer is E.

| 13 |

Consider the following method:

```
// returns true if there are no two elements among
// counts[0], ... counts[n-1], whose values are the same
// or are consecutive integers; otherwise, returns false
// precondition: counts contains n values, n > 1
public boolean isSparse(int[] counts, int n)
{
  int j, k, diff;

  < code >
}
```

Which of the following code segments can be used to replace < *code* > so that the method isSparse works as specified?

I.
```
for (j = 0; j < n; j++)
{
  for (k = j + 1; k < n; k++)
  {
    diff = counts[j] - counts[k];
    if (diff >= -1 && diff <= 1)
      return false;
  }
}
return true;
```

II.
```
for (j = 1; j < n; j++)
{
  for (k = 0; k < j; k++)
  {
    diff = counts[j] - counts[k];
    if (diff >= -1 && diff <= 1)
      return false;
  }
}
return true;
```

III.
```
for (j = 0; j < n; j++)
{
  for (k = 1; k < n; k++)
  {
    diff = counts[j] - counts[k];
    if (Math.abs(diff) <= 1)
      return false;
  }
}
return true;
```

(A) I only
(B) II only
(C) I and II only
(D) I and III only
(E) I, II, and III

Note that in this question not all `counts.length` elements of `counts` are used, just the first *n*. Their subscripts range from 0 to *n*-1. The precondition states that *n* > 1, so there is no need to worry about an empty array or an array of just one element. Looking at the inner loop in each segment you can quickly see that they work the same way. So the difference is how the loops are set up; more precisely, the limits in which the indices vary. In Segment I the outer loop starts with the first item in the list; the inner loop compares it with each of the subsequent items. In Segment II the outer loop starts with the second item in the list; the inner loop compares it with each of the preceding items. Both of these are correct and quite standard in similar algorithms. This eliminates A, B, and D. Segment III at first seems harmless, too, but it has a catch: the inner loop doesn't set a limit for `k` that depends on `j`, so when `j` is greater than 0, `k` may eventually take the same value as `j` (such as `j` = 1, `k` = 1). The method will erroneously detect the same value in `counts` when it is actually comparing an item to itself. The answer is C.

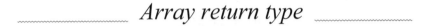

Array return type

Occasionally you may need to return an array from a method. Suppose you want to restructure the `reverse` method above so that it <u>returns</u> a new array containing the values from a given array in reverse order. The original array remains unchanged. The method can be coded as follows:

```
public String[] reverse(String[] words)
{
  String[] result = new String[words.length];

  for (int i = 0; i < words.length; i++)
    result[i] = words[words.length - 1 - i];

  return result;
}
```

Two-dimensional arrays

The AP subset includes rectangular two-dimensional arrays. These are similar to one-dimensional arrays but use two indices, one for the row and one for the column. For example:

```
double[][] matrix = new double[3][5]; // 3 rows by 5 cols
int r, c;
...
matrix[r][c] = 1.23;
```

> **If m is a two-dimensional array, m.length represents the number of rows and m[0].length (that is, the length of the first row) represents the number of columns.**

Only rectangular 2-D arrays are considered in the AP subset; therefore, the lengths of all the rows are the same, and m[0].length represents the length of any row.

The following method calculates and returns the sums of the values in each column of a 2-D array:

```
// returns a 1-D array containing sums of all the values
// in each column of table
public double[] totalsByColumn(double[][] table)
{
  int nRows = table.length;
  int nCols = table[0].length;
  double[] totals = new double[nCols];

  for (int c = 0; c < nCols; c++)
  {
    totals[c] = 0.0;
    for (int r = 0; r < nRows; r++)
      totals[c] += table[r][c];
  }
  return totals;
}
```

14

Consider the following code segment:

```
String[][] m = new String[6][3];

for (int k = 0; k < m.length; k++)
{
  m[k][m[0].length - 1] = "*";
}
```

Which of the following best describes the result when this code segment is executed?

(A) All elements in the first row of m are set to "*"
(B) All elements in the last row of m are set to "*"
(C) All elements in the last column of m are set to "*"
(D) The code has no effect
(E) `ArrayIndexOutOfBoundsException` is reported

☞ The first index is the row, and the `for` loop is set up for all rows. The answer is C. ↵

> **Note that in Java, a two-dimensional array is viewed as an array of one-dimensional arrays, its rows. So a straight "for each" loop won't work for traversing a 2-D array.**

To make it work, you need nested loops. For example:

```
int[][] a = {{1, 2, 3}, {4, 5, 6}};

for (int[] row : a)
{
  for (int x : row)
    System.out.print(x + " ");
  System.out.println();
}
```

2.6. The `List` Interface and the `ArrayList` Class

`java.util.List<E>` is a Java library interface that defines a list of objects of some type *E*.

> **Starting with Java 5.0, a `List<E>` holds objects of the specified type *E* (for example, `Strings` or `Integers`).**

Java developers say that in Java 5.0, `List` and other *collections* have become *generic*. The term implies that the same code works with collections of elements of different data types. As far as we are concerned, collections have become type-specific: a collection holds elements of a specified type. Before the 5.0 release, Java collection classes and interfaces only worked with elements of the `Object` type.

The Java library provides two classes that implement `List<E>`: `java.util.ArrayList<E>` and `java.util.LinkedList<E>`. An `ArrayList` stores the items in an array; a `LinkedList` uses a linked list structure.

> **The `java.util.LinkedList<E>` class is <u>not</u> included in the AP subset.**

Note the syntax for declaring `ArrayLists` introduced in Java 5.0. The class name is `ArrayList` followed by angle brackets that hold the data type of the objects stored in the list. For example:

```
ArrayList<Student> list = new ArrayList<Student>();
```

Since `ArrayList<E>` implements the `List<E>` interface, you can also write:

```
List<Student> list = new ArrayList<Student>();
```

> **You cannot instantiate an interface, so it is a mistake to write something like this:**
>
> **`List<String> list = new `<u>`List`</u>`<String>();`**

> **An `ArrayList` cannot hold values of a primitive data type. For instance, `ArrayList<int>` or `ArrayList<double>` are not allowed.**

However, an `int` or `double` value can be added to an `ArrayList<Integer>` or `ArrayList<Double>` respectively, due to autoboxing. For example:

```
List<Double> prices = new ArrayList<Double>();
prices.add(29.95);
```

`ArrayList` provides methods for getting and setting the value of a particular element, adding a value at the end of the list, removing a value, and inserting a value at a given position. As in standard arrays, indices start from 0.

An `ArrayList` is automatically resized when it runs out of space. `ArrayList`'s "no-args" constructor (that is, the constructor that takes no parameters) allocates an array of some default initial capacity and size 0 (no values stored in it). As values are added, their number may exceed the current capacity. Then the capacity is doubled, a new array is allocated, the old values are copied into the new array, and the old array is discarded. All this happens behind the scenes — you don't have to worry about any of it.

The AP subset includes the following methods of `List<E>` and `ArrayList<E>`:

`int size()`	Returns the number of values currently stored in the list
`boolean add(E x)`	Adds x at the end of the list; returns `true`
`E get(int index)`	Returns the value stored at `index`
`E set(int index, E x)`	Sets the value of the element at `index` to x; returns the old value
`E remove(int index)`	Removes the value at `index` and shifts the subsequent values toward the beginning of the list; returns the old value stored at `index`
`void add(int index, E x)`	Inserts x at `index`, shifting the current value stored at `index` and all the subsequent values toward the end of the list

The `add` and `remove` methods adjust the size of the `ArrayList` appropriately. The methods that take an `index` parameter check that the index is in the valid range, from 0 to `size() - 1` and "throw" `IndexOutOfBoundsException` if the index is not in that range.

Since the compiler knows what type of objects are stored in an `ArrayList`, it automatically casts values retrieved from the list into their type. For example:

```
List<Fish> list = new ArrayList<Fish>();
...
Fish f = list.get(i);
```

What is the output of the following code segment?

```
ArrayList<String> list = new ArrayList<String>();
list.add("A");
list.add("B");
list.add("C");
list.add("D");
list.add("E");

for (int k = 1; k <= 3; k++)
{
  list.remove(1);
}

for (int k = 1; k <= 3; k++)
{
  list.add(1, "*");
}

for (String word : list)
{
  System.out.print(word + " ");
}
```

(A)   A C D E * * *
(B)   * * * B C D E
(C)   A * * * E
(D)   A E * * *
(E)   IndexOutOfBoundsException

This question is not as tricky as it might seem. First we create an empty list and add five values to it: `"A"`, `"B"`, `"C"`, `"D"`, `"E"`. Then we remove the value at index 1 three times. This is the second element and each time we remove it, the subsequent values shift to the left by one position. `"A"` and `"E"` remain. Then we insert three asterisks. Note that we always insert at index 1. After the first insertion we get `"A"`, `"*"`, `"E"`. After the second we get `"A"`, `"*"`, `"*"`, `"E"`. The third insertion produces `"A"`, `"*"`, `"*"`, `"*"`, `"E"`. The third loop (a "for each" loop) traverses the whole list and prints out the values. The answer is C.

Chapter 3. Java Features, Part 2

3.1. Classes

A Java program consists of classes. The term *class* refers to a class of objects.

You should know the following concepts and terms:

class	*private* and *public* fields and methods
object	*encapsulation* and *information hiding*
instance of a class	*static* methods and fields
constructor	*public static final* fields (constants)
new operator	*accessor*
garbage collection	*modifier*
instance variables (*fields*)	*client* of a class

An object that belongs to a particular class is also called an *instance* of that class, and the process of creating an object is called *instantiation*.

A class definition includes *constructors*, *methods*, and data fields. The constructors describe how objects of the class can be created; the methods describe what an object of this class can do; the data fields (a.k.a. *instance variables* or simply *fields*) describe the object's attributes — the current state of an object.

────────── *Constructors* ──────────

Constructors describe ways to create an object of a class and initialize the object's instance variables.

> **All constructors have the same name as the class. Constructors do not have any return data type, not even void.**

A constructor may take parameters that help define a new object. A constructor that takes no parameters is called a "no-args" constructor.

> **The term *parameter* is often interchangeable with the term *argument* (as in function argument in math), especially when it refers to the actual values passed to a constructor or method.**

Hence such usage as "no-args" constructor, `IllegalArgumentException`, or `main(String[] args)`. The *Course Description* seems to favor "parameter" but occasionally uses "argument," and so do we.

A new object is created using the `new` operator. For example, suppose you have defined a class `School`:

```
public class School
{
  // constructor
  public School(String name, int numStudents) { < code not shown > }
  ...
}
```

Then you can create a `School` object elsewhere in the code:

```
School sgt = new School("School for Gifted and Talented", 1200);
```

If a class has instance variables `name` and `numStudents` —

```
public class School
{
  ...
  private String name;
  private int numStudents;
}
```

— the constructor can set them to values of the arguments passed to it:

```
public School(String nm, int num)
{
  name = nm;
  numStudents = num;
}
```

In Java, objects that are no longer accessible in the program (that is no longer referred to by any variable) are automatically destroyed and the memory they occupy is recycled. This mechanism is called *garbage collection*.

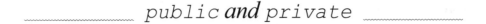 *public and private*

Data fields and methods may be *public* or *private*.

Public fields and methods are accessible anywhere in the code. Private fields and methods are accessible only within constructors and methods of the same class.

The concept of "privacy" applies <u>to the class as a whole</u> and not to individual objects. Different objects of the same class have full access to each other's fields and methods.

In the AP subset, constructors are always public.

It is a common practice in OOP (and a requirement on the AP exam) to make <u>all instance variables private</u>.

Private fields and methods hide the implementation details of a class from other classes, its clients. This concept is known as *encapsulation*. A *client* class uses your class through constructors and public methods. In general, it is a good idea to supply as little information to client classes as possible. This concept is known as *information hiding*. For example, if a method is used only internally within that class, it should be made <u>private</u>.

Accessors and modifiers

Since all instance variables are private, they are not directly accessible in client classes. It is common to provide special public methods, called *accessors*, that return the values of instance variables. For example:

```
public class School
{
  ...
  public String getName()
  {
    return name;
  }
  ...
}
```

Accessors' names often start with a "get." Accessors can have any name, but starting with "get" makes their purpose easier to remember. Accessors do not change the state of the object.

A public method that sets a new value of an instance variable is called a *modifier*. Modifiers' names often start with a "set." For example:

```java
public class School
{
  ...
  public void setName(String nm)
  {
    name = nm;
  }
  ...
}
```

The "accessor" and "modifier" designations are somewhat informal — a class may have a method that sets an instance variable to a new value and at the same time returns, say, the old value.

Consider the following class:

```java
public class Clock
{
  private int hours;
  private int mins;

  public Clock(int h, int m)
  {
    hours = h;
    mins = m;
  }

  // moves this clock one minute forward
  public void move()
  {
    < missing code >
  }

  public void set(int h, int m)
  {
    hours = h;
    mins = m;
    normalize();
  }

  private void normalize()
  {
    while (mins >= 60)
    {
      mins -= 60;
      hours++;
    }
    hours = hours % 12;
  }
}
```

Which of the following could replace < *missing code* > in the `move` method?

I.   `this = new Clock(hours, mins + 1);`

II.   `mins++;`
      `normalize();`

III. `set(hours, mins + 1);`

(A) I only
(B) II only
(C) I and II only
(D) II and III only
(E) I, II, and III

☞ Option I is wrong: it attempts to replace `this` with a new object instead of changing this one, which results in a syntax error. The other two options are acceptable: it is okay to access private instance variables and call private and public methods inside the same class. The answer is D.

(Note that it would be better to add a call to `normalize` in `Clock`'s constructor, too, just to make sure the clock is set correctly, even if `mins` ≥ 60. Alternatively, the constructor could throw an `IllegalArgumentException` if its arguments didn't make sense.) ↵

3.2. Static Variables and Methods

Sometimes an attribute belongs to a class as a whole, not to individual objects (instances) of that class. Such an attribute is represented by a variable called *class* or *static variable*, which is declared with the keyword `static`.

Static variables are used to keep track of a property or quantity shared by all objects of the class. For example,

```
public class School
{
  private static int numSchools;
  private static int[] totalNationalEnrollmentByGrade;
  ...
}
```

A static variable can be also used to define a public symbolic constant. In that case, the keyword `final` is used in their declaration. For example:

```
public class School
{
  public static final int HIGHEST_GRADE = 12;
  ...
}
```

A class may also have static methods — methods that do not involve any particular instances of a class. For example,

```
public class School
{
  public static final int HIGHEST_GRADE = 12;
  private static int numSchools;
  private static int[] totalNationalEnrollmentByGrade;
  ...
  public static void initializeStatistics()
  {
    numSchools = 0;
    totalNationalEnrollmentByGrade = new int[highestGrade + 1];
  }
  ...
}
```

> **Static methods cannot access or modify any instance variables and cannot refer to `this` (a reference to a particular object), because `this` is undefined when a static method is running.**

Static variables can be initialized in a class constructor and they can be accessed and modified in instance methods. For example:

```
public class School
{
  // Static variables:
  public static final int HIGHEST_GRADE = 12;
  private static int numSchools;
  private static int[] totalNationalEnrollmentByGrade;

  // Static methods:
  public int getNationalEnrollment(int grade)
  {
    return totalNationalEnrollmentByGrade[grade];
  }

  ...

  // Instance variables:
  private int[] enrollmentByGrade;
  ...

  // Constructor:
  public School(int[] numStudents)
  {
    numSchools++;

    enrollmentByGrade = new int[HIGHEST_GRADE + 1];

    for (int grade = 0; grade <= HIGHEST_GRADE; grade++)
    {
      enrollmentByGrade[grade] = numStudents[grade];
      totalNationalEnrollmentByGrade[grade] += numStudents[grade];
    }
    ...
  }

  // Instance methods:
  public void enrollOneStudent(int grade)
  {
    enrollmentByGrade[grade]++;
    totalNationalEnrollmentByGrade[grade]++;
  }

  ...
}
```

17

Consider a class with the following fields:

```
public class TestPow2
{
  private static int[] powersOfTwo = {1, 2, 4, 8, 16};
  private int num;
  ...
}
```

Which of the following methods inside the `TestPow2` class will compile with no errors?

I.
```
public int pow2()
{
  return powersOfTwo[num];
}
```

II.
```
public static int pow2(int x)
{
  return powersOfTwo[x];
}
```

III.
```
public static int pow2()
{
  return powersOfTwo[num];
}
```

(A)   I only
(B)   II only
(C)   I and II only
(D)   II and III only
(E)   I, II, and III

☞   The code in Option I would compile, because here an instance (non-static) method `pow2` can work with both the instance variable `num` and the static variable `powersOfTwo`. The code in Option II would compile, too, because here a static method `pow2` works only with its own parameter and the static variable `powersOfTwo`. The code in Option III would cause a syntax error, because a static method `pow2` attempts to access the instance variable `num`. The answer is C. ☜

Java library class `Math` has static methods `abs`, `sqrt`, `pow`, `random`. For your convenience, it also includes the `public static final` "variables" `Math.PI`, which represents π, the ratio of a circle's circumference to its diameter, and `Math.E`, which represents e, the base of the natural logarithm.

Outside the class, public static methods are called and public static constants are accessed using the dot notation, with the class's name as the prefix. For example:

```
double volume = 4.0 / 3.0 * Math.PI * Math.pow(r, 3);
```

3.3. Method Calls

In Java, all methods belong to classes. It is universal Java style that all method names start with a lowercase letter.

An *instance* method is called for a particular object; then the object's name and a dot are used as a prefix in a call, as in `obj.someMethod(...)`. If a method is called from another method of <u>the same</u> object, the prefix is not needed and you write simply `someMethod(...)`. Class (`static`) methods belong to the class as a whole and are called using the class's name with a dot as a prefix. For example: `Math.sqrt(...)`.

A method takes a specific number of parameters of specific data types. (Starting with Java 5.0, a method can be defined with a variable number of parameters, as in `System.out.printf`; however, this feature is not in the AP subset.) Some methods take no parameters. A method call may include a whole expression as an argument; then the expression is evaluated first and the result is passed to the method. An expression may include calls to other methods. For example:

```
double x, y;
...
x = Math.sqrt(Math.abs(2*y - 1));
```

A method usually returns a value of the specified data type, but a `void` method does not return any value. The return type is specified in the method signature. The return <u>value</u> is specified in the `return` statement.

> **It is considered a "major error" (–1 point) to read the new values for a method's parameters from `System.in` from inside the method.**
>
> **It is a minor error (–1/2 point) to print the return value to `System.out` from inside the method (when it is not requested) and an additional error if a required `return` statement is missing in a non-`void` method.**

For example:

```
// returns the sum of all integers from 1 to n
// precondition: n >= 1
public int addNumbers(int n)
{
  int k;
  int sum = 0;



  n = System.in.read();


  for (k = 1; k <= n; k++)
  {
    sum += k;
  }

  System.out.println(sum);

  return sum;
}
```

Mistake: n *is passed to this method from* main *or from another calling method* 👎

Mistake: Not intended and not described in the method specifications 👎

18

Recall that Math's static method min returns the value of the smaller of two integers. If a, b, c, and m are integer variables, which of the following best describes the behavior of a program with the following statement?

```
m = Math.min(Math.min(a, c), Math.min(b, c));
```

(A)   The statement has a syntax error and will not compile.
(B)   The program will run but go into an infinite loop.
(C)   a will get the smaller value of a and c; b will get the smaller value of b and c; m will get the smallest value of a, b, and c.
(D)   m will be assigned the smallest of the values a, b, and c.
(E)   None of the above

👉 Any expression of the appropriate data type, including a method call that returns a value of the appropriate data type, may be used in a larger expression or as an argument to a method. The code above is basically equivalent to:

```
int temp1 = Math.min(a, c);
int temp2 = Math.min(b, c);
m = Math.min(temp1, temp2);
```

So m gets the smallest of the three values. The answer is D. 👈

Parameters of primitive data types

In Java, all parameters of primitive data types are passed to methods "by value."

When a parameter is passed by value, the method works with a copy of the variable passed to it, so it has no way of changing the value of the original.

19

Consider the following method:

```
public void fun(int a, int b)
{
  a += b;
  b += a;
}
```

What is the output from the following code?

```
int x = 3, y = 5;
fun(x, y);
System.out.println(x + " " + y);
```

(A) 3 5
(B) 3 8
(C) 3 13
(D) 8 8
(E) 8 13

  x and y are ints, so they are passed to fun by value. fun works with copies of x and y, named a and b. What is happening inside fun is irrelevant here because x and y do not change after the method call. The answer is A.

Objects passed to methods

All objects are passed to methods as references. A method receives a <u>copy</u> of a reference to (the address of) the object.

When a variable gets an "object" as a value, what it actually holds is a reference to (the address of) that object. Likewise, when an object is passed to a method, the method receives a copy of the object's address, and therefore it potentially <u>can</u> change the original object. Usually all instance variables of an object are private, so to change the object, the method would have to call one of the object's *modifier* methods.

But note that the `String`, `Integer`, and `Double` classes represent *immutable* objects, that is, objects without modifier methods. Even though these objects are passed to methods as references, no method can change them. For example, there is no way in Java to write a method

```
// converts s to upper case
public void toUpperCase(String s)
{
   ...
}
```

because the method has no way to change the string passed to it. For immutable objects, the method has to create and return a new object with the desired properties:

```
// returns s converted to upper case
public String toUpperCase(String s)
{
   ...
}
```

Aliasing

A more complicated concept is *aliasing*. It is good to understand in general, but it is unlikely to come up on the exam. The following explanation is for a more inquisitive reader.

Suppose a class `Point` represents a point on the plane. Consider a method:

```
// point2 receives coordinates of point1 rotated 90 degrees
// counterclockwise around the origin
public void rotate90 (Point point1, Point point2)
{
  point2.setY(point1.getX());
  point2.setX(-point1.getY());
}
```

In this example, `rotate90` takes two `Point` objects as parameters. Like all objects, these are passed to the method as references. Note that a `Point` object here is not immutable because it has the `setX` and `setY` methods. The code looks pretty harmless: it sets `point2` coordinates to the new values obtained from `point1` coordinates. However, suppose you call `rotate90(point, point)` hoping to change the coordinates of `point` appropriately. The compiler will not prevent you from doing that, but the result will not be what you expected. Inside the method, `point1` and `point2` actually both refer to `point`. The first statement will set `point`'s y equal to x, and the original value of y will be lost. If `point` coordinates are, say, x = 3, y = 5, instead of getting x = –5, y = 3, as intended, you will get x = –3, y = 3. This type of error is called an aliasing error.

In Java, aliasing may happen only when parameters are objects and they are mutable (or when parameters are arrays and the method moves values from one array to another). In the above example, it would be safer to make `rotate90` return a new value, as in

```
public Point rotate90 (Point point)
{
   return new Point(point.getX(), -point.getY());
}
```

return

A method that is not `void` must return a value of the designated type using the `return` statement. `return` works with any expression, not just variables. For example:

```
return (-b + Math.sqrt(b*b - 4*a*c)) / (2*a);
```

An often overlooked fact is that a `boolean` method can return the value of a Boolean expression. For example, you can write simply

```
return x >= a && x <= b;
```

as opposed to the redundant and verbose

```
if (x >= a && x <= b)
   return true;
else
   return false;
```

A `void` method can use a `return` (within `if` or `else`) to quit early, but there is no need for a `return` at the end of the method.

Returning objects

A method's return type can be a class, and a method can return an object of that class. Often a new object is created in the method and then returned from it. For example:

```
public String getFullName(String firstName, String lastName)
{
  return firstName + " " + lastName;
}
```

A method whose return type is a class can also return a `null` (a reference with a zero value that indicates that it does not refer to any valid object). For example:

```
public String getAddress(String name)
{
  for (int i = 0; i < listOfNames.length; i++)
  {
    if (listOfNames[i].equals(name))
      return listOfAddresses[i];
  }
  return null; // not found
}
```

If a method returns an `ArrayList`, write the full `ArrayList` type, including its elements' type in angle brackets, as the method's return type. For example:

```
public ArrayList<Integer> getCourseNumbers()
{
  ArrayList<Integer> courseNumbers = new ArrayList<Integer>();
  ...
  return courseNumbers;
}
```

Overloaded methods

Methods of the same class with the same name but different numbers or types of parameters are called *overloaded* methods. (The order of different types of parameters is important, too.)

> **The compiler treats overloaded methods as different methods. It figures out which one to call depending on the number and types of the parameters.**

The `String` class, for example, has two forms of the `substring` method:

```
String substring(int from)
String substring(int from, int to)
```

If you call `"Happy".substring(2)`, then the first overloaded method will be called, but if you call `"Happy".substring(1, 3)` then the second overloaded method will be called. Another example of overloading is `Math.abs(x)`, which has different versions of the static method `abs`, including `abs(int)` and `abs(double)`. `System.out.print(x)` has overloaded versions for all primitive data types as well as for `String` and `Object`.

The `ArrayList` class has two overloaded `add` methods: `add(x)`, which adds `x` at the end of the list, and `add(index, x)`, which inserts `x` at a given index.

Overloading methods is basically a stylistic device. You could instead give different names to different forms of a method, but it would be hard to remember them. Overloaded methods do not have to have the same return type, but often they do, because they perform similar tasks. The return type alone cannot distinguish between overloaded methods.

> **All constructors of a class have the same name, so they are overloaded by definition and must differ from each other in the number and/or types of their parameters.**

20

Consider the following class declaration:

```
public class Date
{
  public Date()
  { < code not shown > }

  public Date(String monthName, int day, int year)
  { < code not shown > }

  public void setDate(int month, int day, int year)
  { < code not shown > }

    < fields and other methods not shown >
}
```

Consider modifying the `Date` class to make it possible to initialize variables of the type `Date` with month (given as a month name or number), day, and year information when they are declared, as well as to set their values later using the method `setDate`. For example, the following code should define and initialize three `Date` variables:

```
Date d1 = new Date();
d1.setDate("May", 11, 2006);
Date d2 = new Date("June", 30, 2010);
Date d3 = new Date(6, 30, 2010);
```

Which of the following best describes the additional features that should be present?

(A)   An overloaded version of `setDate` with three `int` parameters
(B)   An overloaded version of `setDate` with one `String` and two `int` parameters
(C)   A constructor with three `int` parameters
(D)   Both an overloaded version of `setDate` with three `int` parameters and a
      constructor with three `int` parameters
(E)   Both an overloaded version of `setDate` with one `String` and two `int`
      parameters and a constructor with three `int` parameters

☞   This is a wordy but simple question. Just match the declarations against the
provided class features:

```
Date d1 = new Date();            ─────────────  ✓ Date()

Date d2 = new Date("June", 30, 2010);  ────  ✓ Date(String, int, int)

Date d3 = new Date(6, 30, 2010);   ─────────    Date(int, int, int)

d1.setDate("May", 11, 2004);     ─────────────    void setDate(String, int, int)

            not used               ─────────  ✓ void setDate(int, int, int)
```

As we can see, what's missing is a constructor with three `int` parameters and a
version of `setDate` with one `String` and two `int` parameters. The answer is E.

Questions 21-23 refer to the following partial class definition:

```
public class TicketSales
{
  public  TicketSales(String movieName) { < code not shown > }

  // sets box office receipts for a given week
  // precondition: 1 <= week <= 52
  public void setWeekSales(int week, double dollars)
  { < code not shown > }

  // finds and returns the week with best sales
  private int findBestWeek() { < code not shown > }

  < Other methods not shown >

  private String name;
  private double[] sales;
       // sales[0], ..., sales[51] hold sales totals for 52 weeks
}
```

21

The method `findBestWeek` is declared `private` because

(A) `findBestWeek` is not intended to be used by clients of the class.
(B) `findBestWeek` is intended to be used only by clients of the class.
(C) Methods that work with private instance variables of the `array` type cannot be public.
(D) Methods that have a loop in their code cannot be public.
(E) Methods that return a value cannot be public.

☞ In this question only the first two choices deserve any consideration — the other three are fillers. You might get confused for a moment about what a "client" means, but common sense helps: a client is anyone who is not yourself, so if a client needs to use something of yours, you have to make it public. Private things are for yourself, not for clients. The answer is A. ↵

22

The constructor for the `TicketSales` class initializes the `sales` array to hold 52 values. Which of the following statements will do that?

(A) `double sales[52];`
(B) `double sales = new double[52];`
(C) `double[] sales = new double[52];`
(D) `sales = new double[52];`
(E) `sales.setSize(52);`

☞ This is a syntax question. Choice A has invalid syntax. E is absurd: an array does not have a `setSize` method (or any other methods). B assigns an array to a `double` variable — a syntax error. Both C and D appear syntactically plausible and in fact either one will compile with no errors. But C, instead of initializing an instance variable `sales`, will declare and initialize a <u>local</u> variable with the same name. This is a very common nasty bug in Java programs. The answer is D. ↵

23

Given the declaration

```
TicketSales movie = new TicketSales("Monsters, Inc.");
```

which of the following statements sets the third week sales for that movie to 245,000?

(A) `movie = TicketSales(3, 245000.00);`
(B) `setWeekSales(movie, 3, 245000.00);`
(C) `movie.setWeekSales(3, 245000.00);`
(D) `movie(setWeekSales, 3, 245000.00);`
(E) `setWeekSales(3, 245000.00);`

☞ This is another syntax question. The variable `movie` of the type `TicketSales` is defined outside the class, in a client of the class. The key word in this question is "sets." It indicates that a method, a modifier, is called, and the way to call a method from a client class is with dot notation. (Besides, A assumes that there is a constructor with two parameters; B and D look like calls to non-existing methods; E forgets to mention `movie` altogether.) The answer is C.

3.4.   Random Numbers

Random numbers simulate chance in computer programs. For example, if you want to simulate a roll of a die, you need to obtain a random number from 1 to 6 (with any one of these values appearing with the same probability). "Random" numbers are not truly random — their sequence is generated using a certain formula — but they are good enough for many applications.

One way to get random numbers in a Java program is to call the static method `random` of the `Math` class. It returns a random `double` from 0 (inclusive) to 1 (exclusive). To get a random integer from 1 to *n* use:

```
int r =  (int)(n * Math.random()) + 1;
```

24

Which of the following is a list of all possible outputs of the following code segment?

```
String memo = "MEMO";
System.out.print("[" +
      memo.substring((int)(3 * Math.random()),
                                    (int)(3 * Math.random()) + 2) +
            "]");
```

(A)   [ME], [EM]
(B)   [ME], [EM], [MO]
(C)   [EM], [MO], [O], []
(D)   [], [M], [ME], [EM], [MO]
(E)   [], [M], [E], [ME], [EM], [MO], [MEM], [EMO], [MEMO]

The two calls to `Math.random()` look the same, but they return different values — two successive values in the random number sequence. The "from" parameter of `memo.substring` can be 0, 1, or 2, and the "to" parameter can be 2, 3, or 4. Any combination of these from/to values results in a valid substring (including `substring(2,2)`, which returns an empty string). The answer is E.

Another way to get random numbers relies on the `java.util.Random` class, but it is not in the AP subset.

3.5. Input and Output

The AP subset does not include any classes or methods for data input. In particular, the `Scanner` class is not in the AP subset. If a question involves user input it may be stated as follows:

```
double x = < call to a method that reads a floating-point number >
```

or

```
int x = IO.readInt();   // Reads user input
```

Output is limited to `System.out.print` and `System.out.println` calls.

You do not have to worry about formatting numbers. Java converts an `int` or a `double` value passed to `System.out.print` or `System.out.println` into a string using default formatting. Starting with Java 5.0, `System.out.printf`, a new method with a variable number of parameters, can be used for more precisely formatted output of one or several numbers and strings. `printf` is not in the AP subset.

You can pass any object to `System.out.print`, `System.out.println`, or `System.out.printf`. These methods handle an object by calling its `toString` method. `Integer` and `Double` classes have reasonable `toString` methods defined. If you are designing a class, it is a good idea to supply a reasonable `toString` method for it. For example:

```
public class Fraction
{
  ...
  public string toString()
  {
    return num + "/" + denom;
  }
}
```

Otherwise, your class inherits a generic `toString` method from `Object`, which returns the object's class name followed by the object's address.

> **The `System.out.print` and `System.out.println` methods take only <u>one</u> parameter.**

If you need to print several things, use the + operator for concatenating strings (or the `printf` method). You can also concatenate a string and an `int` or a `double`: the latter will be converted into a string. For example:

```
System.out.println(3 + " hours " + 15 + " minutes.");
```

The displayed result will be

```
3 hours 15 minutes.
```

You can also concatenate a string and an object: the object's `toString` method will be called to convert it into a string. For example:

```
int n = 3, d = 4;
Fraction f = new Fraction(n, d);
System.out.println(f + " = " + (double)n / (double)d);
```

The displayed result will be

```
3/4 = 0.75
```

Just be careful not to apply a + operator to two numbers or two objects other than strings: in the former case the numbers will be added rather than concatenated; the latter will cause a syntax error.

3.6. Exceptions

An exception is a <u>run-time</u> event that signals an abnormal condition in the program. Some run-time errors, such as invalid user input or an attempt to read past the end of a file, are considered fixable. The `try-catch-finally` syntax allows the programmer to catch and process the exception and have the program recover. This type of exception is called a *checked exception*.

> **Checked exceptions and the `try-catch` statements are not in the AP subset.**

Other errors, such as an array index out of bounds or an attempt to call a method of a non-existing object (null reference) are considered fatal: the program displays an error message with information about where the error occurred, then quits. This type of exception is called an *unchecked exception*.

In Java, an exception is an object. The Java library implements many types of exceptions, and if necessary you can derive your own exception class from one of the library classes. For an AP CS exam, you are expected to understand what `ArithmeticException`, `IndexOutOfBoundsException`, `ArrayIndexOutOfBoundsException`, `NullPointerException`, `IllegalArgumentException`, and `ClassCastException` mean.

We say that a program "throws" an exception. An `ArithmeticException` is thrown in case of an arithmetic error, such as integer division by zero. (You would expect `Math.sqrt(x)` to throw an `ArithmeticException` for a negative x, but it doesn't. Java exception handling is inconsistent at times.)

`ArrayIndexOutOfBoundsException` is self-explanatory: it is thrown when an array index is negative or is greater than `array.length - 1`. `ArrayList` methods throw a similar `IndexOutOfBoundsException`.

`NullPointerException` is thrown when you forget to initialize an object-type instance variable or an element of an array and then try to call its method. For example:

```
public class MyClass
{
  private String name;   // name is set to null
    ...
    int n = name.length();   // if name has not been initialized
                             // by MyClass's constructor, this statement
                             // will throw a NullPointerException
  ...
}
```

Another example:

```
public class Dice
{
  private Random gen;   // gen is set to null
    ...
    int n = gen.nextInt(6);  // gen has to be initialized here or
                             // by Dice's constructor --
                             //    gen = new Random();
                             // if not, this will throw a
                             // NullPointerException
```

A third example:

```
        Integer[] a = new Integer[10];
        int x = a[0].intValue();      // a[0] is null --
                                      // throws a NullPointerException
```

A `ClassCastException` is thrown when you are trying to cast an object into a class type to which it does not belong. For example:

```
        ArrayList<Object> list = new ArrayList<Object>();
        list.add("123.456");
        Double x = (Double)list.get(0);  // ClassCastException: trying to cast
                                         //    a string "123.456" into a Double
```

Throwing your own exceptions

Occasionally you need to "throw" your own exception. For example, you are implementing the `remove` method for a queue data structure. What is your method to do when the queue is empty? Throw a `NoSuchElementException`.

`throw` is a Java reserved word. The syntax for using it is

```
throw < exception >;
```

For example:

```
if (items.size() == 0)
   throw new NoSuchElementException();
```

Throw an `IllegalStateException` if an object is not ready for a particular method call. For example:

```
public void stop()
{
  if (!isMoving())
    throw new IllegalStateException();  // displays a message
                                        //   and quits
  speed = 0;
  ...
}
```

Your code does not need to explicitly throw an `ArithmeticException`, `NullPointerException`, `ClassCastException`, or `ArrayIndexOutOfBoundsException` — Java does it automatically when the triggering condition occurs.

25

Consider the following class:

```
public class TestSample
{
  private ArrayList<Integer> samples;

  public TestSample(int n)
  {
    for (int k = 0; k < n; k++)
    {
      samples.add(k);
    }
  }

  public double getBestRatio()
  {
    double maxRatio = samples.get(1).intValue() /
                            samples.get(0).intValue();

    for (int k = 1; k < samples.size() - 1; k++)
    {
      double ratio = samples.get(k+1).intValue() /
                            samples.get(k).intValue();
      if (ratio > maxRatio)
      {
        maxRatio = ratio;
      }
    }
    return maxRatio;
  }
}
```

What is the result of the following code segment?

```
        TestSample t = new TestSample(1);
        System.out.println(t.getBestRatio());
```

(A)   NullPointerException
(B)   ArithmeticException
(C)   IndexOutOfBoundsException
(D)   ClassCastException
(E)   Infinity

Luckily we don't have to look at the `getBestRatio` method. The programmer has forgotten to initialize `samples` and calls its `add` method in the constructor. The answer is A.

Now suppose we added

```
samples = new ArrayList<Integer>();
```

at the top of the constructor. What would happen then? `getBestRatio` would call `samples.get(1)`, but we would have added only one value to `samples`. The answer would be C, `IndexOutOfBoundsException`.

Now suppose we changed

```
TestSample t = new TestSample(1);
```

to

```
TestSample t = new TestSample(2);
```

What would happen then? The answer would be B, `ArithmeticException`, because we would have an integer division by 0.

Actually, the programmer probably meant to write

```
double maxRatio = (double)samples.get(1).intValue() /
                          samples.get(0).intValue();
```

What would happen if we added this cast to a `double`? We would still expect an `ArithmeticException` for floating-point division by 0, but Java actually prints "Infinity." The answer would be E (but you do not have to know that).

Note that the numbers and objects *are* cast correctly into `Integer`s automatically where necessary due to autounboxing, so `ClassCastException` does not occur.

Chapter 4. Program Design and OOP Concepts

4.1. Computer Systems

You are probably aware by now that a typical computer system's *hardware* has at least one *processor*, (a.k.a. CPU), some *RAM* (*random-access memory*), secondary storage devices (such as magnetic disks, CD-ROM drives, floppy disk drives, etc.) and *peripherals* (modems, printers, sound cards and speakers, mice or other pointing devices, etc.).

Chances are you also have worked with an *operating system*, a piece of *software* that controls the computer system and interacts with a user. Linux, Windows XP, and OS X, are examples of operating systems. A *compiler* is also a piece of software. It checks syntax in programs written in a high-level programming language and translates them into machine code. In Java, a compiler translates the *source code* (program text) into machine-independent *bytecodes* — instructions for the *Java Virtual Machine*. The virtual machine acts as a run-time *interpreter* that reads bytecodes and executes the appropriate instructions on a particular computer. A *debugger* is a program that helps you run and test your program in a controlled way and find errors ("bugs") in it. The editor, compiler, interpreter, debugger, and other *software development tools* may be combined in one package called an *IDE* (Integrated Development Environment), which has a *GUI* (Graphical User Interface).

Issues of system reliability and security and the legal and ethical issues related to computer use are not precisely defined in the AP exam guidelines. Questions about these topics would have to be rather general.

4.2. Program Design and Development Methodology

Computer science courses try to emphasize *problem solving*, as opposed to just programming in a particular language or using specific hardware platforms. The exam topics related to general software design and development methodology emphasize *procedural* and *data abstraction*, *functional decomposition*, and the *reusability* of code. These topics are discussed in the context of *object-oriented* software design and development. Here is a very brief glossary of the relevant terms:

Specifications — a detailed description of what a piece of software should accomplish and how it should behave and interact with the user. Specifications may be given for a whole system, one module, or even one class or method.

Object-oriented programming (OOP) — a programming methodology based on designing the program as a world of interacting objects arranged in hierarchies of classes and using encapsulation and polymorphism.

Top-down design — a design methodology in which you first define the general structure of the program, laying out high-level classes and their interaction, and then refine the design of each class, identifying subtasks and smaller classes or methods. Then you refine the design of subtasks, individual methods, and so on.

Top-down development — similar to top-down design: you first lay out your code at a high level, defining general classes and methods. These methods may call lower-level methods, which are not yet implemented. You can compile and sometimes even test high-level pieces of your code by substituting "stubs" — empty or greatly simplified placeholders — for low-level methods that are still not coded.

Data structure — a way of organizing data combined with methods of accessing and manipulating the data. For example, a two-dimensional array with methods or operators for retrieving and changing the values of its elements is a data structure that may be useful for representing tables.

Encapsulation and information hiding — the practice of making all instance variables and helper methods that are used only inside the class private. The clients of a class can use such a class only through its public constructors and methods.

Procedural abstraction — a description of a procedure that is not tied to a specific hardware platform, particular data types, or other details. A high-level programming language, such as Java, already assures a degree of procedural abstraction by isolating a programmer from the particular hardware platform. An algorithm is even more abstract. It can be described using pseudocode, flowcharts, or other tools independent of any particular programming language.

Reusable code — debugged and tested libraries, classes, or fragments of code that are somewhat general in nature and ready to be reused in other projects. Reusing code shortens software development projects, no matter what methodology is being employed.

Team development — OO languages, such as Java, allow you to split a project into separate pieces and assign their development to different team members. Encapsulation and information hiding facilitate team development by limiting the amount of interaction needed between developers.

User interface — the behavior of a program as it interacts with a user: screens, menus, commands, messages, graphics, sounds, and so on.

These are very general concepts, and it is not easy to come up with multiple-choice or free-response questions that test in-depth understanding of these concepts. In past exams, design and implementation questions have been limited to specific data structures and algorithms, which sometimes used these terms in their descriptions. An exam may include a free-response "design" question that asks you to design a small class, then use some of its features (see Section 4.7).

4.3. Inheritance

Inheritance allows a programmer to state that one class *extends* another class, inheriting its features. In Java terminology, a *subclass* extends a *superclass*. `extends` is a Java reserved word. For example:

```
                  𝒮𝓊𝒷𝒸𝓁𝒶𝓈𝓈              𝒮𝓊𝓅𝑒𝓇𝒸𝓁𝒶𝓈𝓈
                    /                  /
                   /                  /
public class HighSchool extends School
{
   ...
}
```

Inheritance implements the IS-A relationship between objects: an object of a subclass type IS-A (is also an object of the) superclass. A high school is a kind of school. A `HighSchool` object IS-A (kind of) `School` object. Technically this means that in your program you can use an object of a subclass whenever an object of its superclass is expected. For example:

```
School sch = new HighSchool(...);
```

If a constructor or a method in a client class expects a `School` type of parameter to be passed to it, you can call it with a `HighSchool` type of argument. Objects of a subclass inherit the data type of the superclass.

In Java, a class can directly extend only one superclass — there is no *multiple inheritance* for classes. But more than one subclass can be derived from the same superclass:

```
public class HighSchool extends School ...
public class ElementarySchool extends School ...
public class DrivingSchool extends School ...
```

The IS-A relationship of inheritance is not to be confused with the HAS-A relationship between objects. That *X* "has a" *Y* simply means that *Y* is a data field (an instance variable) in *X*. For example, you might say that a `HighSchool` HAS-A `MarchingBand`, but not a `HighSchool` IS-A `MarchingBand`.

Subclass methods

A subclass inherits all the public methods of its superclass, and you can call them in the subclass without any "dot prefix." For example, if `School` has a method

```
public String getName() { ... }
```

then `HighSchool`'s method `registerForAP` can call it directly:

```
public class HighSchool extends School
{
  ...
  public void registerForAP()
  {
    String registrationForm = getName() + ...;
    ...
  }
  ...
}
```

`HighSchool`'s clients can call `getName`, too, for any `HighSchool` object:

```
HighSchool hs = new HighSchool(...);
String name = hs.getName();
```

A subclass can add its own methods. It can also *override* (redefine) a method of the superclass by providing its own version with exactly the same *signature* (the same name, return type, and number and types of parameters). For example, `School` may have a `toString` method, and `HighSchool`'s `toString` may override it.

Occasionally it may be necessary to make an explicit call to a superclass's public (or protected) method from a subclass. This is accomplished using the `super.` prefix. For example:

```
public class HighSchool extends School
{
  ...
  public String toString()
  {
    return super.toString() + collegeAcceptance() + ...;
  }
  ...
}
```

The superclass's <u>private</u> methods are not callable in the subclass.

Subclass constructors

> **Constructors are not inherited: a subclass has to provide its own.**

A subclass's constructors can explicitly call the superclass's constructors using the keyword `super`. For example:

```
public class School
{
  private String name;
  private int numStudents;

  public School(String nm, int num)
  {
    name = nm;
    numStudents = num;
  }
  ...
}

public class ElementarySchool extends School
{
  private int highestGrade;

  public ElementarySchool(String nm, int num, int grade)
  {
    super(nm, num); // calls School's constructor
    highestGrade = grade;
  }
  ...
}
```

If `super` is used, it must be the <u>first</u> statement in the subclass's constructor.

Subclass variables

A subclass inherits all the class (static) variables and instance variables of its superclass. However, the instance variables are usually private (always private in the AP subset).

> **The superclass's private variables are <u>not</u> directly accessible in its subclass. So you might as well forget that they are inherited — instead, use public accessors and modifiers to get and set values of the superclass's instance variables.**

Superclass public constants (`public static final` variables) are directly accessible everywhere.

A subclass can add its own static or instance variables. For example, the class
ElementarySchool above, a subclass of School, adds an instance variable

```
private int highestGrade;
```

Consider the following partial definitions:

```
public class MailingList
{
  private ArrayList<String> people;

  public MailingList() { people = new ArrayList<String>(); }
  public void add(String name) { people.add(name); }
  public ArrayList<String> getPeople() { return people; }

}

public class Subscribers extends MailingList
{
  public Subscribers() { super(); }

  // returns the number of names in people
  private int size()
  {
    return < expression >;
  }

  < Other methods not shown >
}
```

Which of the following should replace < *expression* > in the size method of the
Subscribers class so that the method works as specified?

(A) super.size();
(B) people.size();
(C) super.people.size();
(D) getPeople().size();
(E) None of the above

The `MailingList` class HAS-A(n) `ArrayList<String> people` as an instance variable, but `MailingList` Is-Not-A(n) `ArrayList`: it does not extend `ArrayList`. The programmer has not provided a `size` method for the `MailingList` class (a design mistake), so choice A is wrong. B or C might look plausible at first, but `people` is private in `MailingList`, so it is not directly accessible in `Subscribers`. But `MailingList` has a public method `getPeople`, and this method is inherited and accessible in the `Subscribers` class. `getPeople` returns an `ArrayList<String>`, which has a method `size` that returns the size of the list. The answer is D.

Also note that

```
return getPeople().size();
```

is equivalent to

```
ArrayList<String> temp = getPeople();
return temp.size();
```

4.4. Class Hierarchies

If you have a class, you can derive one or several subclasses from it. Each of these classes can in turn serve as a superclass for other subclasses. You can build a whole tree-like hierarchy of classes, in which each class has one superclass. For example:

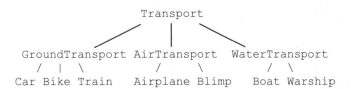

```
                      Transport
                    /     |     \
   GroundTransport  AirTransport  WaterTransport
      /  |  \          /    \        /  \
   Car Bike Train  Airplane Blimp  Boat Warship
```

In fact, in Java all classes belong to one big hierarchy; it starts at a class called `Object`. If you do not specify that your class extends any particular class, then it extends `Object` by default. Therefore, every object IS-A(n) `Object`. The `Object` class provides a few common methods, including `equals` and `toString`, but these methods are not very useful and usually get redefined in classes lower in the hierarchy.

Class hierarchies exist to allow reuse of code from higher classes in the lower classes without duplication and to promote a more logical design. A class lower in the hierarchy inherits the data types of all classes above it.

For example, if we have classes

```
public class Animal { ... }
public class Dog extends Animal { ... }
public class Spaniel extends Dog { ... }
```

all of the following declarations are legal:

```
Spaniel s = new Spaniel(...);
Dog d = new Spaniel(...);
Animal a = new Spaniel(...);
```

But if you also define

```
public class Horse extends Animal { ... }
```

then

```
Horse x = new Spaniel(...);
```

is an error, of course: `Spaniel` does not extend `Horse`.

Abstract classes

Classes closer to the top of the hierarchy are more abstract — the properties and methods of their objects are more general. As you proceed down the hierarchy, the classes become more specific and the properties of their objects are more concretely spelled out. Java syntax allows you to define a class that is officially designated `abstract`. For example:

```
public abstract class Solid { ... }
```

An abstract class can have constructors and methods; however, some of its methods may be declared `abstract` and left without code. For example:

```
public abstract class Solid
{
  ...
  public abstract double getVolume();
  ...
}
```

This indicates that every `Solid` object has a method that returns its volume; but the actual code may depend on the specific type of solid. For example, the `Sphere` and `Cube` subclasses of `Solid` will define `getVolume` differently.

A class in which all the methods are defined is called *concrete*. Naturally, abstract classes appear near the top of the hierarchy and concrete classes sit below. You cannot instantiate an abstract class, but you can declare variables or arrays of its type. For example:

```
Solid s1 = new Sphere(radius);
Solid s2 = new Cube(side);
Solid[] solids = { new Sphere(100), new Cube(100) };
```

Questions 27-28 refer to the following partial class definitions:

```
public abstract class Account
{
  public Account() { ... }
}

public class BankAccount extends Account
{
  private double balance;

  public BankAccount(double amount)
  {
    super();
    balance = amount;
  }
}

public class CheckingAccount extends BankAccount
{
  private String customerName;

  public CheckingAccount(String name, double amount)
  {
    < Missing statements >
  }
  ...
}
```

27

Which of the following is an acceptable replacement for < *Missing statements* > in `CheckingAccount`'s constructor?

     I.   `balance = amount;`
          `customerName = name;`

    II.   `super(amount);`
          `customerName = name;`

   III.   `super(name, amount);`

(A)   I only
(B)   II only
(C)   I and II
(D)   II and III
(E)   I, II and III

`balance` is private in `BankAccount`, so it is not accessible in `CheckingAccount`. Option I cannot be right. `BankAccount` does not have a constructor with two arguments, so III cannot be right either. Option II is the way to go. The answer is B.

28

Which of the following declarations are valid?

     I.   `Account acct = new BankAccount(10.00);`

    II.   `CheckingAccount acct = new BankAccount(10.00);`

   III.   `BankAccount acct = new CheckingAccount("Amy", 10.00);`

(A)   I and II
(B)   II and III only
(C)   I and III
(D)   I, II, and III
(E)   None of the three

It may appear that Option I is wrong because an abstract class `Account` cannot be instantiated. But in fact we are not instantiating `Account` — we are instantiating `BankAccount` and assigning the newly created `BankAccount` object to an `Account` variable. Since a `BankAccount` IS-A(n) `Account`, we are okay. We only have to make sure that `BankAccount` has a constructor that takes one `double` parameter (which it does). Options II and III are clearly problematic as a pair: either a `BankAccount` IS-A `CheckingAccount` or a `CheckingAccount` IS-A `BankAccount`, but not both. Here `CheckingAccount` extends `BankAccount`, so Option III is okay (again, provided `CheckingAccount` has a constructor that takes a `String` and `double` parameters). The answer is C.

4.5. Polymorphism

Polymorphism is a mechanism that ensures that the correct method is called for an object disguised as a more generic type. In the above example, if we call

```
double volume = solids[0].getVolume();
```

the compiler does not know whether `solids[0]` is a `Sphere` or a `Cube`. The decision of which `getVolume` method to call is postponed until run-time. In Java implementation, each object holds a pointer to a table of entry points to its methods; thus the object itself "knows" what type of object it is. This technique is called *dynamic method binding* — which method to call is decided at run time, not compile time.

> **Polymorphism is implemented in the language; all you have to do is understand it and use it correctly.**

One common situation when polymorphism comes into play occurs when different types of objects are mixed together in an array or list, as shown in the above example. This code

```
for (Solid solid : solids)
  totalVolume += solid.getVolume();
```

works no matter what `Solids` are stored in the `solids` array because the appropriate `getVolume` method is called for each element of the array. This is true even if several different `Solids` are in the `solids` array.

Another situation for polymorphism occurs when a method takes a more generic type of parameter and a client class passes a more specific type of argument to the method. For example, one of the overloaded versions of `System.out`'s `print` method takes an `Object` type as a parameter. This method may be implemented as follows:

```
public void print(Object x)
{
  if (x != null)
    print(x.toString());
  else
    print("<null>");
}
```

This method works for any type of object x with a reasonable `toString` method defined (including `Integer`, `Double`, etc.). Polymorphism assures that the correct `toString` is called for each type of x.

Given

```
public class Person
{
  private String name;

  Person(String nm) { name = nm; }
  public String getName() { return name; }
  public String toString { return getName(); }
}

public class OldLady extends Person
{
  private int age;

  public OldLady(String nm, int yrs) { super(name); age = yrs; }
  public String getName() { return "Mrs. " + super.getName(); }
  public int getAge() { return age; }
}
```

what is the output of the following statements?

```
Person p = new OldLady("Robinson", 92);
System.out.println(p + ", " + ((OldLady)p).getAge());
```

(A) `Mrs. Robinson, 92`
(B) `Robinson, 92`
(C) `Robinson`
(D) `ClassCastException`
(E) No output due to infinite recursion

⇗ In this question we have to restore a somewhat convoluted sequence of events:

1. The variable p is disguised as a Person type, but it is actually an OldLady.

2. p + ", " calls p's toString method. OldLady inherits toString from Person, so Person's toString is called.

3. toString in turn calls getName. Which one? This is the trickiest point. Both Person and OldLady have a getName method, but, due to polymorphism, OldLady's getName will be called (notwithstanding the fact that we call it from Person's toString method).

4. OldLady's getName takes "Mrs. " and appends to it the result of super.getName(). The latter explicitly calls Person's getName, which simply returns the name.

5. Finally we cast p back to the OldLady type — we need this to call its getAge method. A Person does not have getAge, and the compiler does not keep track of what type we assigned to p. getAge's result is appended to the output string.

Choice B tries to make you forget about polymorphism or suggests that polymorphism does not apply here. It does. Choice C is an awkward attempt to confuse you about p's data type. Deep inside, p is not just a Person but an OldLady, so it does have a getAge method once we cast it to OldLady. If p were only a Person, the cast to OldLady would cause a ClassCastException, as suggested in D. E hints that getName infinitely calls itself. This does not happen here: OldLady's getName explicitly calls Person's getName as indicated by the super. prefix. We would have infinite recursion only if we forgot super. The answer is A. ⇗

4.6. Interfaces

In Java, an interface is even more "abstract" than an abstract class. An interface has no constructors or instance variables and no code at all — just headings for methods. All its methods are public and abstract. For example:

```
public interface Fillable
{
  void fill(int x);
  int getCurrentAmount();
  int getMaximumCapacity();
}
```

(No need to repeat "public abstract" for each method in an interface — it is understood.)

A class "implements" an interface by supplying code for all the interface methods. `implements` is a reserved word. For example:

```
public class Car implements Fillable
{
  ...
  public void fill(int gallons) { fuelAmount += gallons; }
  public int getCurrentAmount() { return fuelAmount; }
  public int getMaximumCapacity() { return fuelTankCapacity; }
}

public class VendingMachine implements Fillable
{
  ...
  public void fill(int qty) { currentStock += qty; }
  public int getCurrentAmount() { return currentStock; }
  public int getMaximumCapacity() { return 20; }
}
```

> **For a concrete class to implement an interface, it must define <u>all</u> the methods required by the interface. It must also explicitly state that it implements the interface. A class that claims it implements an interface but does not define some of the interface methods must be declared `abstract`.**

A class can extend only one class, but it can implement several interfaces. For example:

```
public class Car extends Vehicle implements Fillable, Sellable { ... }
```

Each interface adds a secondary data type to the objects of the class that implements it. If a class *C* implements interface *I*, objects of *C* can be disguised as type *I* objects and polymorphism applies (the same way as for subclasses). For example, we can have a method:

```
// fills all objects in the array a to capacity
public void fillUp(Fillable[] a)
{
  for (Fillable f : a)
    f.fill (f.getMaximumCapacity() - f.getCurrentAmount());
}
```

The formula works polymorphically for any types of different `Fillable` objects that might be stored in the array `a`.

> **If class *C* implements interface *I*, all subclasses of *C* automatically implement *I*.**

Interfaces help us write more general methods, facilitating code reuse.

The `Comparable<T>` *interface*

The library (built-in) interface `java.lang.Comparable<T>` is widely used for designating objects that can be compared in some way. We need to compare objects in order to arrange them in order (sorting), perform a binary search, or implement certain data structures. Objects of a class that implements `Comparable` are said to have a *natural ordering* defined.

Starting with Java 5.0, the `Comparable<T>` interface is a "generic" interface, that is, it works with objects of a specific type. The `Comparable<T>` interface specifies only one method:

```
int compareTo(T other);
```

The method returns a positive integer if this object is "greater than" the other, zero if they are "equal," and a negative integer if this object is "less than" the other. (Sort of like `this` minus `other`.) It is up to the programmer to define what "smaller" and "greater" might mean when comparing objects of his class and whether the value returned by `compareTo` has any meaning besides telling which object is larger or smaller.

`compareTo` takes one parameter of the type `T` — and it is usually assumed that the parameter belongs to the same class that implements `Comparable<T>`. For example:

```
public class Flight implements Comparable<Flight>
{
  ...
  public int compareTo(Flight other)
  {
    return getDepartureTime() - other.getDepartureTime();
  }
}
```

`String`, `Integer`, and `Double` all implement `Comparable`, but naturally they do so in different ways. Strings are compared lexicographically. The comparison is case-sensitive, and all uppercase letters precede all lowercase letters. `Integer` and `Double` objects are compared as usual, based on their numeric values.

The `Comparable<T>` interface does not specify an `equals` method, and a class that implements `Comparable<T>` does not need an `equals` method to compile. But it is better to override the `equals` method inherited from `Object` and make it consistent with `compareTo`, to avoid possible errors later. For example:

```
public boolean equals(Object x)
{
  return x instanceof Flight && compareTo((Flight)x) == 0;
}
```

The Boolean operator `instanceof` is not in the AP subset.

Note that the argument to your `equals` method should have the type `Object`, so that your `equals` indeed overrides `Object`'s `equals`.

Consider the following class:

```
public class Fraction implements Comparable<Fraction>
{
  private int num, denom;

  public int getNum() { return num; }
  public int getDenom() { return denom; }
  public double doubleValue() { return (double)num / denom; }

  < Other constructors and methods not shown >
}
```

Which of the following would appropriately implement a `compareTo` method, required by the `Comparable<Fraction>` interface?

I.
```
public int compareTo(Object other)
{
  Fraction f = (Fraction)other;
  return getNum() * f.getDenom() -
         getDenom() * f.getNum();
}
```

II.
```
public int compareTo(Fraction other)
{
  double x = doubleValue();
  double y = other.doubleValue();
  if (x < y)
    return -1;
  else if (x > y)
    return 1;
  else
    return 0;
}
```

III.
```
public int compareTo(Fraction other)
{
  return (int)(doubleValue() - other.doubleValue());
}
```

(A) I only
(B) II only
(C) I and II
(D) II and III
(E) I, II, and III

☞ Option I would be problematic on an actual exam. First, it assumes that students know how to subtract fractions, which can't be taken for granted. Second, it is ambiguous with regard to possible arithmetic overflow: can we assume that the numerators and denominators of the fractions are small enough so that their products do not overflow the `int` range? Luckily we can eliminate this answer because the `compareTo` method is defined incorrectly: the parameter must be a `Fraction`, not an `Object`. If we put `Object` there, the compiler will display a cryptic error message "Fraction must be declared abstract" (because `compareTo(Fraction)` is not defined). Option II works, even though it provides a rather truncated result of the comparison: `compareTo` can return only 0, 1, or -1. Recall that only the sign of a comparison result really matters. Option III fulfills the formal requirements, but fractions that differ "by a small fraction" will be deemed equal. This is not in the spirit of `compareTo` for arithmetic objects. If a question like this happened to slip past exam editors, we'd say the answer was B. ↵

31

What is the output from the following code segment?

```
Comparable<Integer> x = new Integer(123);     // Line 1
System.out.println(x.compareTo("123"));       // Line 2
```

(A) 0
(B) A positive integer
(C) A syntax error on Line 1
(D) A syntax error on Line 2
(E) A `ClassCastException`

☞ There are three separate issues here. First, on Line 1, we are assigning an `Integer` object to a variable of the `Comparable<Integer>` type. Is this okay? Yes, because the `Integer` class implements `Comparable<Integer>`. Second, on Line 2 we are passing a string to x's `compareTo` method. Is this okay? No, because starting with Java 5.0, `compareTo`'s parameter has the type of the compared objects, in this case `Integer`. So the compiler won't let pass a call to `compareTo` with a `String` argument. The answer is D. ↵

4.7. "Design" Question

The free-response section of the exam may include a "design" question. This type of question asks you to design <u>but not implement</u> a simple class that represents a given situation or model. This is the "design" part of the question. Other parts may ask you to implement a method or constructor in your class or to write some code of a client class that uses some constructors or methods from the class you designed.

> **Note that you are not asked to implement your class in the design part, only to design it. It would be a huge waste of time to write code for your class if you are not asked to do so.**

Designing a class means specifying its constructors and their parameters, public (and possibly private) methods, and fields (public static constants and private instance variables).

> **In the context of the AP exams, all instance variables should be declared <u>private</u>.**

In writing the design part, pay special attention to the following:

- Use reasonable and consistent style with proper indentation and generous spacing between statements.

- Do not include comments or preconditions — they are not required.

- Choose meaningful names for your class, its methods and their parameters, and fields and local variables. Follow the same naming style as shown in the other parts of the exam: a class name starts with an uppercase letter; the names of all methods, their parameters, and instance variables start with a lowercase letter. Make sure that all constructors have the same name as the class.

- Make all instance variables private and group them together at the top of the class.

- Put all constructors and public methods first. Make all methods public, unless there is a specific hint in the question that some of them are "helper" methods used only inside this class — then make them private.

- In addition to specified constructors, it may be a good idea to provide a no-args constructor that takes no arguments.

- Specify appropriate return types for all methods. Recall that constructors do not have a return type, not even `void`.

- Provide public "accessor" methods as specified in the question. An accessor returns the value of the respective data field. Accessor names may start with "get." For example:

```
public double getBalance() { ... }
```

- Provide "modifier" methods as specified in the question. Modifiers set the values of one or several data fields. Modifier names may start with "set" or "make." For example:

```
public void makeDeposit(double amount) { ... }
```

- Group all accessors together in a group and all modifiers in another group to make your class definition more readable.

Again, do not write any code in the design part of the question unless you are asked to do so.

Part (b) may ask you to write a fragment of code from a client class that uses your class designed in Part (a). In answering such a question, pay special attention to the following:

- Use constructors and call public methods of your Part (a) class with appropriate numbers and types of arguments, consistent with what you wrote in Part (a). Use this opportunity to double-check your definitions in Part (a).

- Never refer directly to private instance variables of your Part (a) class in the client class; rather, call accessors and modifiers.

- It is allowed (and often desirable) to reuse in the client class the same names for variables as you used for similar formal parameters in methods in Part (a). For example, if in Part (a) you wrote

```
public void makeDeposit(double amount) { ... }
```

then in Part (b) you may write

```
double amount = ...;
...
account.makeDeposit(amount);
```

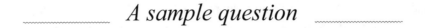

A sample question

The World Population Institute keeps track of demographic trends in different countries or "population zones." Each population zone is described by its name, population growth rate, and a table of population counts by age. The age ranges from 0 (under one year old) to some maximum age.

When a new population zone is created in the program, it receives a name and a list of population counts by age. It may also receive a growth rate parameter. If not supplied, the growth rate is set to 1.0 (no growth).

Operations on a population zone include the following:

- retrieve zone's name

- retrieve zone's growth rate

- set a new growth rate

- retrieve the total population

- retrieve the total population below a given age

- adjust the distribution to simulate aging of the population by one year (filling the "zero" slot with a new value calculated from a formula that includes the growth rate factor).

This simplified model does not take into account deaths at different ages. It simply assumes that people who go beyond the maximum age in the counts-by-age array immediately die.

A population zone will be represented in a program by a class called `PopulationZone`. A separate class, `Demographics`, will store a list of population zones, such as all countries in the world.

(a)   Write a class definition for `PopulationZone`, putting only "`...`" in the bodies of its constructors and methods. In writing this definition you must:

- choose appropriate names for methods, data fields, and parameters;

- use overloaded methods where appropriate;

- provide the functionality specified above;

- make data representation consistent with the above specifications;

- make design decisions that are consistent with information-hiding principles.

Comments are not required but may be used if desired.

DO NOT write the implementations of the constructors or methods of the `PopulationZone` class.

(b)   Consider the class `Demographics` partially specified below.

```
public class Demographics
{
  private ArrayList<PopulationZone> countries;

  public double teenRatio(PopulationZone z)
  {
    < Code not shown >
  }

  public String findMostTeens()
  {
    < Code not shown >
  }
}
```

Write a method `teenRatio` that computes and returns the ratio of all teenagers (ages 13 through 19) to the total population in a given population zone. In writing `teenRatio`, you may use any of the methods of the `PopulationZone` class that you specified in Part (a). Assume that these methods work as specified, regardless of what you wrote in Part (a).

Complete the method `teenRatio` below.

```
// returns the ratio of all teenagers (ages 13 through 19)
// to the total population in z
public double teenRatio(PopulationZone z)
```

(c)   Write the method `findMostTeens` of the `Demographics` class. This method returns the name of the country from the `countries` list with the highest ratio of teenagers to the total population. (In the unlikely event that two or several population zones have exactly the same highest teen ratio, the method returns any one of them.) In writing this method you can use the class from Part (a) and the method from Part (b) and assume that they work as specified regardless of what you wrote in those parts.

Complete the method `findMostTeens` below.

```
// returns the name of the country from the list countries
// with the highest ratio of teenagers to the total population;
// if several countries have the same highest ratio, returns
// any one of their names
public String findMostTeens()
```

(a)

```
public class PopulationZone
{
  private String name;
  private double growthRate;
  private int[] countsByAge;

  public PopulationZone() { ... }

  public PopulationZone(String nm, int[] countsByAge) { ... }

  public PopulationZone(String nm, int[] counts,
                                   double rate) { ... }
  public String getName() { ... }
  public double getGrowthRate() { ... }
  public int getPopulation() { ... }
  public int getPopulation(int ageLimit) { ... }
  public void setGrowthRate(double rate) { ... }
  public void ageByOneYear() { ... }
}
```

(b)

```
public double teenRatio(PopulationZone z)
{
  return (double)(z.getPopulation(20) - z.getPopulation(13))
                                  / z.getPopulation();
}
```

(c)

```
public String findMostTeens()
{
  int kMax = 0;

  for (int k = 1; k < countries.size(); k++)
  {
    if (teenRatio(countries.get(k)) >
                          teenRatio(countries.get(kMax)))
      kMax = k;
  }
  return (countries.get(kMax)).getName();
}
```

Chapter 5. Algorithms

5.1. Iterations

Most programming languages provide iteration control structures, such as the `while` and `for` loops in Java. Simple loops are good for iterating (repeating the same operation) over a range of numbers or over the elements of a one-dimensional array or a list.

A `for` loop is a convenient and idiomatic way to *traverse* a one-dimensional array:

```
for (int k = 0; k < a.length; k++)
{
  System.out.println(a[k]);        // ... or do whatever you need to do
                                   //        with each element
}
```

or

```
for (T x : a)
{
  System.out.println(x);
}
```

where *T* is the data type of the elements of a.

For working with two-dimensional arrays you usually need *nested* loops. The following code, for example, traverses a two-dimensional array m:

```
int nRows = m.length, nCols = m[0].length;

for (int r = 0; r < nRows; r++)
{
  for (int c = 0; c < nCols; c++)
  {
    System.out.println(m[r][c]);   // ... or do whatever...
  }
}
```

Note that braces are optional if the body of the loop has only one statement:

```
for (int i = 1; i < n; i++)
  for (int j = 0; j < i; j++)
    if (a[i] == a[j])
      count++;
```

In "triangular" nested loops, the outer loop may run, say, for *i* from 1 to *n*-1 and the inner loop may run for *j* from 0 to *i*-1. In the above example the inner loop runs *i* times for *i* = 1, ..., *n*-1, so the total number of comparisons is

$$1 + 2 + ... + (n-1) = \frac{n(n-1)}{2}$$

The "for each" loop makes it easy to traverse a `List`:

```
List<String> list = new ArrayList<String>();
...
for (String s : list)
{
   ...
}
```

Max and min

A common example of using loops is to find a maximum or a minimum value (or its position) in an array:

```
// returns maxValue such that maxValue >= a[k] for any 0 <= k <= n-1 and
// maxValue = a[k] for some k
// precondition: array a holds values a[0], ..., a[n-1]; n >= 1
public double max(double[] a, int n)
{
  double maxValue = a[0];

  for (int k = 1; k < n; k++)
  {
    if (a[k] > maxValue)
      maxValue = a[k];
  }
  return maxValue;
}
```

32

Consider the following method:

```
public int mysteryMax(int[] a)
{
  int m = 0;

  for (int i = 0; i < a.length; i++)
  {
    int sum = 0;

    for (int k = i; k < a.length; k++)
    {
      sum += a[k];
      if (sum > m)
        m = sum;
    }
  }

  return m;
}
```

If a contains $-1, -3, 2, -3, 2, 1$, what value will be returned by `mysteryMax(a)`?

(A)   -2
(B)   -1
(C)   1
(D)   2
(E)   3

☞ The method returns the largest sum of several consecutive elements in a (or 0 if all the values are negative). The answer is E. ☜

33

Consider the following method:

```
// returns the largest sum of any two elements
// precondition: n >= 2; a[0] ... a[n-1] are filled with values
public double maxSum(double[] a, int n)
{
  < code >
}
```

Which of the following code segments can replace *< code >* so that the method works as specified?

I.
```
double max = a[0] + a[1];

for (int i = 1; i < n; i++)
  for (int j = 0; j < i; j++)
    if (a[i] + a[j] > max)
      max = a[i] + a[j];
return max;
```

II.
```
double max1 = a[0], max2 = a[0];

for (int i = 1; i < n; i++)
  if (a[i] > max1)
    max1 = a[i];

for (int i = 1; i < n; i++)
  if (a[i] != max1 && a[i] > max2)
    max2 = a[i];

return max1 + max2;
```

III.
```
double max1 = a[0], max2 = a[1];

if (a[1] > a[0])
{
  max1 = a[1];
  max2 = a[0];
}

for (int i = 2; i < n; i++)
{
  if (a[i] > max1)
  {
    max2 = max1;
    max1 = a[i];
  }
  else if (a[i] > max2)
    max2 = a[i];
}

return max1 + max2;
```

(A) I only
(B) II only
(C) I and II
(D) I and III
(E) I, II, and III

☞   This is a lot of code for one question, so we need to focus on the key points. Segment I is inefficient but most straightforward: using triangular nested loops we generate sums for all the different pairs of elements and choose the largest of them. Segment II is based on a different idea: finding the largest value and then the second largest value in two separate traversals of the array. But it has two problems. First, if the largest value happens to be `a[0]`, then the second `for` loop will never update `max2`. Second, it will fail if the largest value appears in the array more than once. The method description states that the method is looking for the largest sum of two different elements, but these could have the same value.

To work, this approach would need a couple of minor fixes:

```
int iMax1 = 0, iMax2 = 0;

for (int i = 1; i < n; i++)
  if (a[i] > a[iMax1])
    iMax1 = i;

if (iMax1 == 0)
  iMax2 = 1;

for (int i = 1; i < n; i++)
  if (i != iMax1 && a[i] > a[iMax2])
    iMax2 = i;

return a[iMax1] + a[iMax2];
```

In Segment III we find both the largest and the second largest elements in one sweep. Note how the largest element becomes the second largest when we find another one with a greater value. It works fine. The answer is D. ☜

Insert in order

Many applications, including Insertion Sort, require you to insert a value into a sorted array while preserving the order:

```
// shifts values a[k], ..., a[n-1] appropriately into
// a[k+1], ..., a[n] and inserts newValue into a[k] so that the
// ascending order is preserved
// precondition:  a[0] <= a[1] <= ... <= a[n-1]; n < a.length
void insertInOrder(int[] a, int n, int newValue)
{
  // Shift values to the right by one until you find the
  //     place to insert:

  int k = n;               // Start at the end
  while (k > 0 && a[k-1] > newValue)
  {
    a[k] = a[k-1];
    k--;
  }
  a[k] = newValue;
}
```

In the above code, we shift the values in the array to the right by one to create a vacant slot and then insert the new value into the vacancy thus created. Note that the shifting has to proceed from the end, so that each shifted value is placed into a vacant slot and does not overwrite any data (Figure 5-1).

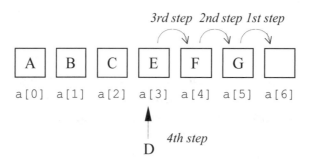

Figure 5-1. Inserting a new value in the middle of a sorted array

34

Consider an array a that contains n integer values sorted in ascending order (n < a.length). Which of the following code segments correctly inserts newValue into a, preserving the ascending order?

I.
```
for (int k = n; k > 0; k--)
{
  if (a[k-1] <= newValue)
  {
    a[k] = newValue;
    k = 0;
  }
  else
    a[k] = a[k-1];
}
```

II.
```
int k = n;
while (k > 0 && a[k-1] > newValue)
{
  a[k] = a[k-1];
  k--;
}
a[k] = newValue;
```

III.
```
int k = 0;

while (k < n && a[k] < newValue)
  k++;

for (int j = n-1; j >= k; j--)
{
  a[j+1] = a[j];
}
a[k] = newValue;
```

(A) I only
(B) II only
(C) III only
(D) I and II
(E) II and III

When you have to decide whether such code is correct, check the boundary conditions first: does it work if you have to insert the value at the very beginning or at the very end of the array? Segment I, for example, looks good at first — similar to the insertInOrder method described above. But if newValue is smaller than all the values in the array, nothing is inserted. Segment II is equivalent to the insertInOrder code above. Segment III uses a more step-wise approach: first find the place to insert, then shift the values above that place, then insert. In Segment III, it is sufficient to check that this code works for newValue being the smallest and the largest — that means there are no tricks. The answer is E.

Loop invariants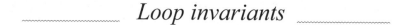

You might find useful the concept of a *loop invariant*. A loop invariant is an assertion about the loop that is relevant to the purpose of the loop and that holds true before and after each iteration through the loop. This assertion is usually expressed as a relation between the variables involved in the loop. Loop invariants are used to reason about programs formally and to prove their correctness without tracing all the iterations through a loop. If you can establish that an assertion is true before the first iteration, and also prove that for any iteration if the assertion is true before that iteration it will remain true after that iteration, then your assertion is a loop invariant. If you are familiar with mathematical induction, you can see how it works here. If not, you can still reason about loop invariants without too much trouble.

35

Consider the following code segment:

```
int count = 0;
int n = 41;
int k = 2;

while (k <= n)
{
  if (isPrime(k))
    count++;
  k++;
}
```

Which of the following statements are loop invariants for the above code?

    I. k is a prime.
   II.   41 is a prime.
  III.   `count` is equal to the number of primes from 2 to $k-1$.

(A)   I only
(B)   II only
(C)   III only
(D)   I and II
(E)   None of the three

☞   Statement I is not an invariant because it varies: k may or may not be a prime as we iterate through the loop. More precisely, k is a prime before the first iteration ($k = 2$) and before the second iteration ($k = 3$), but not after the second iteration ($k = 4$). This eliminates A and D. Statement II is not an invariant for a different reason. Certainly 41 is a prime — so are 37, 43, 47, and an infinite number of other integers. Also, Washington, DC, is the capital of the United States. These facts, while true, do not help us reason about the purpose or correctness of the above code. But Statement III is a typical invariant: it links the values of the variables count and k and reflects the purpose of the loop, namely counting all the primes from 2 to n. The answer is C.   ☟

5.2. Sequential Search and Binary Search

A typical application of a simple loop is *Sequential Search*:

```
// returns pos such that 0 <= pos < n and a[pos] == target,
// or -1 if target is not among a[0], ..., a[n-1]
// precondition: array a holds values a[0], ..., a[n-1]
public int sequentialSearch(int[] a, int n, int target)
{
  for (int k = 0; k < n; k++)
  {
    if (a[k] == target)
      return k;
  }
  return -1;
}
```

Sequential Search works for any array: the values in the array may be in random order. If an array is sorted (that is, if its elements are arranged in ascending or descending order), then Binary Search is a much more efficient method.

Binary Search is a "divide and conquer" method for quickly finding a target value in a sorted array. Suppose the array is sorted in ascending order. We take an element in the middle (or approximately in the middle) of the array and compare it to the target. If they are equal, we're done. If the target is greater, we continue the search in the right half of the array; if it's smaller, we continue in the left half.

102 CHAPTER 5 ~ ALGORITHMS

For example:

```
// returns the position of the element equal to target or -1 if target
// is not in the array
// precondition: array a contains n values sorted in ascending order
public int binarySearch(int[] a, int n, int target)
{
  int left = 0;
  int right = n - 1;
  int middle;

  while (left <= right)
  {
    middle = (left + right) / 2;
    if (target == a[middle])
      return middle;
    else if (target < a[middle])
      right = middle - 1;     // Continue search in the left half
    else
      left = middle + 1;      // Continue search in the right half
  }
  return -1;
}
```

Binary Search in an array of $2^k - 1$ elements requires at most k iterations. In other words, Binary Search in an array of n elements requires $\log_2 n$ iterations. Thus in an array of 1,000,000 elements it would need at most 20 iterations. By comparison, Sequential Search in an array of n elements takes, on average, $n/2$ iterations, and in the worst case it may take n iterations.

36

Suppose that two programs, one using Binary Search and the other using Sequential Search, take (on average) the same amount of time to find a random target value in a sorted array of 30 elements. Roughly how much faster than the Sequential Search program will the Binary Search program run on an array of 1000 elements?

(A) 2 times faster
(B) 10 times faster
(C) 16 times faster
(D) 33 times faster
(E) 50 times faster

☞ Binary Search takes 5 iterations for 30 elements $(32 = 2^5)$ and 10 iterations for 1000 elements $(1024 = 2^{10})$. So Binary Search will run roughly two times longer on a 1000-element array than on a 30-element array. Sequential search will run roughly 33 times longer $(1000 \approx 30 \cdot 33)$. On 1000 elements, Binary Search will be $33/2 = 16.5$ faster. The answer is C. ↵

37

An e-mail address is a string made up of alphanumeric characters, one or several "dots," and one "@." The short substring after the last dot is called the domain name suffix. For example, in `jane.lee@math.bestacad.org`, "org" is the suffix. Which of the following methods can be used to find the beginning position of the suffix?

    I.   A modified Sequential Search in which we scan through the whole array keeping track of the last occurrence of a given character

    II.   A modified Sequential Search which proceeds backwards, starting at the end of the array

    III.   A modified Binary Search in which each alphanumeric character is treated as '0' and a dot and @ are treated as '1'

(A)   I only
(B)   II only
(C)   III only
(D)   I and II
(E)   II and III

The task is basically to find the last dot in a string. Method I is not the most efficient, but it works:

```
for (int k = 0; k < email.length(); k++)
  if (email.charAt(k) == '.')
    dotPos = k;

// Characters, charAt, and char constants are not in the AP subset

return dotPos;
```

Method II works a bit faster:

```
for (int k = email.length() - 1; k >= 0; k--)
  if (email.charAt(k) == '.')
    return k;
```

The description of Method III tries to confuse you with a binary system which has no relation to Binary Search. The latter won't work here because the string is not sorted and dots are scattered among alphanumeric characters. The answer is D.

5.3. Selection and Insertion Sorts

Sorting means arranging a list of items in ascending or descending order, according to the values of the items or some key that is part of an item. Sorting algorithms are usually discussed for lists represented as arrays.

> **Selection Sort** and **Insertion Sort** are called *quadratic sorts* because they use two straightforward nested loops and the number of required comparisons is approximately proportional to n^2.

Selection Sort

In *Selection Sort* we iterate for k from n down to 2: we find the largest among the first k elements and swap it with the k-th element.

```
// sorts n values in a in ascending order
// precondition: array a contains a[0], ..., a[n-1] (n >= 1)
public void selectionSort(int[] a, int n)
{
  int maxPos;

  for (int k = n; k >= 2; k--)
  {
    maxPos = 0;
    for (int i = 1; i < k; i++)
    {
      if (a[i] > a[maxPos])
        maxPos = i;
    }
    // Swap a[maxPos], a[k-1]
    int temp = a[maxPos]; a[maxPos] = a[k-1]; a[k-1] = temp;
  }
}
```

In the above method, the inner loop runs $k-1$ times, for $k = n, n-1, ..., 2$.

> **The total number of comparisons in Selection Sort is always the same:**
>
> $$(n-1)+(n-2)+...+1 = \frac{n(n-1)}{2}$$

In another variation of *Selection Sort* we find the smallest among the elements a[k], ..., a[n-1] and swap it with a[k] (for $k = 0, ..., n-2$).

Insertion Sort

In *Insertion Sort*, we iterate for k from 2 up to n. We keep the first $(k-1)$ elements sorted and insert the k-th element among them where it belongs:

```
// sorts n values in a in ascending order
// precondition: array a contains a[0], ..., a[n-1] (n >= 1)
public void insertionSort(int[] a, int n)
{
  for (int k = 2; k <= n; k++)
  {
    int temp = a[k-1];
    int i;
    for (i = k-1; i > 0; i--)
    {
      if (a[i-1] <= temp)
        break;
      else
        a[i] = a[i-1];
    }
    a[i] = temp;
  }
}
```

In this version of Insertion Sort, if the array is already sorted, then the inner loop runs just one comparison and we immediately break out of it. Then the method needs a total of $n-1$ comparisons. This is the best case: instead of *quadratic* time, the method executes in *linear* time.

The worst case for this implementation of Insertion Sort is when the array is sorted in reverse order. Then the inner loop runs $k-1$ times and the whole method will need as many comparisons as Selection Sort:

$$1 + 2 + \ldots + (n-1) = \frac{n(n-1)}{2}$$

The average case is about half that number, still approximately proportional to n^2.

The methods above are just examples of how Selection and Insertion Sorts can be implemented. Other variations are possible.

38

Consider the task of sorting the elements of an array in ascending order. Which of the following statements are true?

    I.   Selection Sort always requires more comparisons than Insertion Sort.
    II. Insertion Sort always requires more moves than Selection Sort.
    III. Insertion Sort, on average, requires more moves than Selection Sort.

(A)   I only
(B)   II only
(C)   III only
(D)   I and II
(E)   II and III

☞   This question gives us a chance to review the properties of the two quadratic sorts. As we have seen, Statement I is false: although, on average, Selection Sort requires more comparisons, Insertion Sort in the worst case (an array sorted in reverse order) will take as many comparisons as Selection Sort. Statement II is false, too: in the best case, when the array is already sorted, Insertion Sort does not require any moves at all. (Selection Sort, too, with a slight modification, can avoid any moves when the array is already sorted.) Statement III is the vague part: what do we mean, "on average"? First, our array must be large enough to support some conclusions. Sorting an array of three elements will not be representative. Let's assume that we set up an experiment where we generate a fairly large array of random numbers, sort it using each of the two algorithms, and count the number of moves. Intuition tells us that Insertion Sort, on average, needs more moves. Indeed, the k-th iteration through the outer loop may require anywhere from 0 to k moves, $k/2$ moves on average. In Selection Sort, each iteration through the outer loop requires one swap, which can be counted as three moves. The answer is C. ☜

5.4. Recursion

You may find recursion pleasant or difficult, depending on your taste. If you happen to hate it, you can still take a stab at the multiple-choice questions on recursion.

39

Consider the following method:

```java
public void mystery(int n)
{
  if ( n <= 0)
    return;

  for (int i = 0; i < n; i++)
  {
    System.out.print("-");
  }

  for (int i = 0; i < n; i++)
  {
    System.out.print("+");
  }

  System.out.println();

  mystery(n-1);              // Recursive call
}
```

What is the output when `mystery(4)` is called?

(A)
```
----++++
```

(B)
```
----++++
----++++
----++++
----++++
```

(C)
```
----+
----++
----+++
----++++
```

(D)
```
-+
--++
---+++
----++++
```

(E)
```
----++++
---+++
--++
-+
```

This method calls itself — that's what recursion is. Note two things about it. First, if n <= 0, the method doesn't do anything. An exit from a recursive method, perhaps after some work but without recursive calls, is called the *base case* (or the *stopping case*). In this method the base case does nothing. Second, when the method calls itself, it calls itself with an argument that is less by one than the original. The argument has to change, usually decrease in some way in the direction of the base case, if the recursion is to terminate at some point.

Instead of trying to unwrap and trace all the recursive calls in this method, first try to reason more formally about its properties. The method prints some minuses followed by <u>the same number</u> of pluses. When called with *n* = 4, the method right away prints one line with 4 minuses and 4 pluses. But that is not all: after printing the first line, the method calls mystery(3), which must do the same thing as mystery(4) but on a smaller scale. The answer is E.

Now suppose we change the mystery method in the previous question, placing the recursive call <u>above</u> the for loops:

40

Consider the following method:

```
public void mystery(int n)
{
  if (n <= 0)
    return;

  mystery(n-1);              // Recursive call

  for (int i = 0; i < n; i++)
  {
    System.out.print("-");
  }

  for (int i = 0; i < n; i++)
  {
    System.out.print("+");
  }

  System.out.println();
}
```

What is the output when mystery(4) is called?

< Same answer choices as in Question 39 >

This question is a bit trickier, but D and E are still the only plausible answers:

```
(D)                    (E)
-+                     ----++++
--++                   ---+++
---+++                 --++
----++++               -+
```

We have to choose D because the last thing `mystery(4)` does is print `----++++`.

(If you are more mathematically inclined, you can reason as follows. `mystery(4)` prints a triangle pointing either up or down. Let's take a guess at this method's general behavior: say, "`mystery(n)` prints a triangle with *n* rows that points up." Suppose it's true for *n* = 3. Then `mystery(4)` first prints a triangle with 3 rows in the recursive call, then adds the longest fourth row. Our guess fits, so the answer should be D.)

41

Consider the following method:

```
public void mysteryMix(String str)
{
  int len = str.length();
  if (len >= 3)
  {
    mysteryMix (str.substring(0, len / 3));
    System.out.print (str.substring(len / 3, 2*len / 3));
    mysteryMix (str.substring(2*len / 3));
  }
}
```

What is the output when `mysteryMix("la-la-la!")` is called?

(A) `la-la-la!`
(B) ~~a~~l~~a~~-a
(C) `ala-la-la-l`
(D) `lla-l`
(E) ~~a-la-a~~!

☞   Many AP questions mix unrelated subjects. This tough question tests both recursion and strings. We start with a string of nine characters, but immediately call `mysteryMix` recursively for a string of three characters. So it makes sense to see first what happens when we call, say, `mysteryMix("xyz")`. This call just prints the middle character, `"y"`, and does nothing else: when `len` is 3 the two recursive calls do nothing. Now back to the original string of nine characters. The two recursive calls print one character each and `System.out.print` prints three characters, so the output must have five characters. This eliminates A, C, and E. The first character printed is the middle character in the first one-third of the string, which is `"a"`. The answer is B. ⚐

Recursive implementation of Binary Search

The description of the Binary Search algorithm is recursive in nature, and it can be implemented recursively with ease.

42

Consider the following incomplete recursive implementation of Binary Search:

```
// returns the position of the element equal to target or -1,
// if target is not among the values a[left], ..., a[right]
// precondition: array a contains values stored from a[left]
//               to a[right], sorted in ascending order
public int binarySearch(int[] a, int left, int right, int target)
{
  int targetPos = -1;
  int middle;

  < statement 1 >
  {
    middle = (left + right) / 2;
    if (target == a[middle])
      < statement 2 >
    else if (target < a[middle])
      targetPos = binarySearch(a, left, middle - 1, target);
    else
      targetPos = binarySearch(a, middle + 1, right, target);
  }

  return targetPos;
}
```

Which of the following could be used to replace *< statement 1 >* and *< statement 2 >* so that the `binarySearch` method works as intended?

	< *statement 1* >	< *statement 2* >
(A)	`while (left <= right)`	`return targetPos;`
(B)	`while (left <= right)`	`return middle;`
(C)	`while (left < right)`	`targetPos = middle;`
(D)	`if (left <= right)`	`targetPos = middle;`
(E)	`if (left < right)`	`return middle;`

In the choice between `while` and `if`, `if` wins, because this is a <u>recursive</u> solution and recursion <u>replaces</u> iterations. This eliminates A, B, and C. In D and E either choice works for Statement 2, but Statement 1 in E misses the case when `left == right`. The answer is D.

5.5. Mergesort

Mergesort is a recursive sorting algorithm based on the "divide and conquer" principle. It takes, on average, $n \log n$ comparisons, as opposed to n^2 comparisons in quadratic sorts. This difference can be very significant for large arrays. For example, for 1024 elements, Mergesort may run 100 times faster than Selection Sort and Insertion Sort.

 *Mergesort*

The idea of *Mergesort* is simple: divide the array into two approximately equal halves; sort (recursively) each half, then merge them together into one sorted array (Figure 5-2). Mergesort usually requires a temporary array for holding the two sorted halves before they are merged back into the original space.

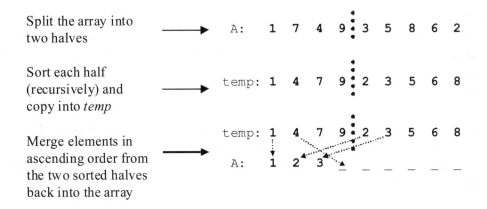

Figure 5-2. Mergesort

43

Consider the following implementation of Mergesort:

```
// sorts values a[n1], ..., a[n2] in ascending order
// precondition: 0 <= n1 <= n2 < a.length
public void sort(int[] a, int n1, int n2)
{
  if (n1 == n2)
    return;

  int m = (n1 + n2) / 2;
  sort(a, n1, m);
  sort(a, m+1, n2);
  if (a[m] > a[m+1])        // Optional line
    merge(a, n1, m, n2);
}
```

Compare it with a more conventional version with the `if` statement on the "optional line" removed. Suppose a has 8 elements and `sort(a, 0, 7)` is called. For which of the following values in a will the version with `if` work faster than the version without?

   I. 1 2 3 4 5 6 7 8
  II. 5 6 7 8 2 1 4 3
 III. 2 1 4 3 6 5 8 7

(A) I only
(B) I and II
(C) I and III
(D) I, II, and III
(E) None of the three

A typical implementation of Mergesort doesn't skip the work even when the array is already sorted. The slight change proposed in this question allows Mergesort to skip all the merging and quickly establish that an array is already sorted, as in Array I. This version also avoids merging when the array is partially sorted, namely when all the values in the left half of the array are smaller than any value in the right half, as in Array III. In that case, after the two recursive calls to sort the array becomes sorted and the call to merge is skipped.

Since the algorithm is recursive, it will also save time when some portions of the array have these properties — are either sorted or partially sorted — even when the whole array isn't. In Array II, for example, the left half is sorted and the right half is partially sorted. The answer is D.

5.6. Data Organization Questions

AP CS exam may contain multiple-choice questions on appropriate ways of representing data for specific tasks. Below are a few examples of such questions.

44

Consider designing a data structure that represents information about subscribers in an e-mail server system. Among other attributes, a subscriber has an ID and a number of unread new messages. Information about all subscribers who have unread mail will be stored in an array of `Subscriber` objects. Two possible implementations are being considered:

Method A: Store the array entries in arbitrary order.
Method B: Store the array entries in sorted order by subscriber ID.

Consider the following operations:

Operation 1:   Increment the number of messages for a subscriber with a specified ID.
Operation 2:   Add a new subscriber with a given number of messages to the list of subscribers.

Which of the following is true?

(A)   Both Operation 1 and Operation 2 can be implemented more efficiently using Method A than Method B.
(B)   Both Operation 1 and Operation 2 can be implemented more efficiently using Method B than Method A.
(C)   Operation 1 can be implemented more efficiently using Method A; Operation 2 can be implemented more efficiently using Method B.
(D)   Operation 1 can be implemented more efficiently using Method B; Operation 2 can be implemented more efficiently using Method A.
(E)   Operation 1 and Operation 2 can be implemented equally efficiently using either method.

☞ Such questions may test your reading comprehension skills, but in terms of real technical difficulty they don't go too far beyond common sense. It certainly helps if you have a good understanding of various data structures and their uses in different algorithms. Here, for example, we have to deal with finding an element with a given key (subscriber ID) in an array and inserting a new value into an array. The relevant ideas that come to mind are Sequential and Binary Search, inserting a value in order, and inserting at the end.

You may want to jot down a quick little table in order not to get confused in the Methods and Operations; then check the appropriate boxes (what works faster):

	A: random order	B: sorted
1. Increment # msgs — "find"		✓
2. Add a subscr — "insert".	✓	

Clearly, if you need to worry about the order, adding a subscriber to a sorted array will take more work than just slapping him on at the end of a random one. This alone eliminates choices B, C, and E. (Don't try to be too smart, thinking that you may need to reallocate and copy the array if it is not large enough. That is not what this question is about.)

Is it easier to find a value in a sorted array? Of course. If you remember that you can use Binary Search on a sorted array, that's great. But even if you don't, this would be a good guess. The fact that the array is sorted probably can't hurt the search operation. This eliminates A. The answer is D. ↵

Questions 45-46 refer to the following information:

The College Board administers AP exams in N subjects ($N \geq 34$) over K days ($K \geq 14$). Each subject is offered only on one day. The subjects are represented by integers from 1 to N. Two different designs are being considered for an application that keeps track of the exam calendar:

Design 1:

The exam schedule information is held in a one-dimensional array of integers. For each of the K days there is one entry that represents the number of exams on that day, followed by a list of the subjects offered on that day. For example, if the first day has two exams in subjects 29 and 31, and the second day has no exams, the array will start with 2, 29, 31, 0, ...

Design 2:

The schedule is represented as two-dimensional array of Boolean values with N rows and K columns. The `true` value in the n-th row and k-th column indicates that the n-th subject is offered on the k-th day.

Which of the following statements about the space requirements of the implementation of the two designs in Java is true?

(A) Design 1 will require less space.
(B) Design 2 will require less space.
(C) Which design will require more space depends on the value of N.
(D) Which design will require more space depends on the value of K.
(E) Which design will require more space depends on the number of bytes it takes to represent Boolean and integer values on a particular platform.

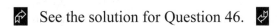

See the solution for Question 46.

46

Suppose that Design 2 is chosen and that the following method is implemented as efficiently as possible:

Given a subject number between 1 and N and a day number between 1 and K, the method returns `true` if the given subject is offered on the given day and `false` otherwise.

Which of the following statements is true?

(A)   The average time spent in the method is proportional to N.
(B)   The average time spent in the method is proportional to K.
(C)   The average time spent in the method is proportional to the total number of values in the array (N times K).
(D)   The average time spent in the method is proportional to the average number of exams per day.
(E)   The time spent in the method does not depend on N or K, nor on the distribution of exams by day.

The above two questions compare space and time requirements for the same data represented as a list (Design 1) and as a *lookup table* (Design 2). You can answer these questions right away if you are familiar with lookup tables. In a lookup table, a data item (here a valid subject/day pair) is represented as a <u>location</u> in an array. Lookup tables usually take more space but provide instantaneous (constant time) access to data regardless of the size of the table.

If you've never heard the term *lookup table*, you can still figure it out.

In Question 45 the space requirement for Design 1 is $K + N$ integers: one for each day (representing the number of exams for that day) and one for each exam (each exam has to be listed under one of the days). The space requirement for Design 2 is $N{\cdot}K$ Boolean values. Recall that in Java, an integer always takes four bytes, regardless of the particular platform. A Boolean may vary, but even if it takes only one byte, still $4{\cdot}(K + N) < N{\cdot}K$ for large enough N and K (recall that $N \geq 34$, $K \geq 14$). The answer is A.

In Question 46, you must know that you can go directly to any element of a one-dimensional or two-dimensional array,. This property is called *random access* and it's what arrays are all about. The n-th subject is offered on the k-th day if `table[n-1][k-1]` is `true`. The answer is E.

Chapter 6. GridWorld Case Study

6.1. Introduction

The GridWorld case study is a teaching and testing tool developed specifically for the AP Computer Science program. In the past, exams have had five to six multiple-choice questions and one free-response question on the case study.

The case study involves a fairly large program that manipulates various "critters" in a two-dimensional grid. The case study materials include a narrative (40 pages plus appendices); Java source code and class libraries; and javadoc documentation. All these materials are posted at the *AP Central* web site (click on <u>A Guide to AP Central</u> at www.skylit.com).

> **Only Parts 1 through 4 of the case study narrative are required for the exam. Part 5 used to be tested in the AB exam, and it is no longer required.**

The best way to prepare for the exam questions on the case study is to have the case study integrated into your course so you can work on the case study code and exercises as you go along. This chapter will help you review what you have learned. If you did not have the opportunity to work on the case study in your course, you can still answer case study questions successfully after studying the case study narrative, the required code, and this review.

> **Start by setting up the GridWorld project and running the `BugRunner` program, as described in Part 1 of the GridWorld narrative.**

The case study code includes Java files with `main` (such as `BugRunner.java` — the first project — or `BoxBugRunner.java`, `CritterRunner.java`, or `CrabRunner.java`) and the library file `gridworld.jar`. GridWorld projects are set up in the same manner as any other project in your IDE.

Figure 6-1 shows the "big picture" of the case study classes and interfaces. The code is organized into four packages: `gui`, `world`, `actor`, and `grid`. Of these four you are responsible for only two, `actor` and `grid`, and even these two you need to know to a limited extent.

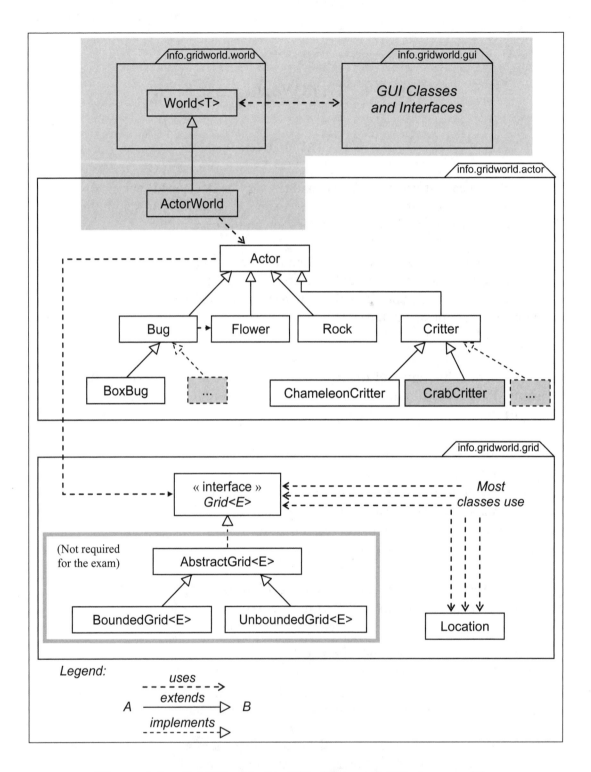

**Figure 6-1.   GridWorld: the "Big Picture."   The boxes with
dotted-line borders indicate the natural places for extension.**

> **You are not required to know what a package is or how the GridWorld classes are split into packages. However, to get practice projects to compile, you'll need to `import` classes from the correct packages.**

For example, if your class uses `Grid` and `Location`, you need

```
import info.gridworld.grid.Grid;
import info.gridworld.grid.Location;
```

If your class uses `ActorWorld`, `Actor`, or `Bug`, you need

```
import info.gridworld.actor.ActorWorld;
import info.gridworld.actor.Actor;
import info.gridworld.actor.Bug;
```

respectively.

Table 6-1 and Figure 6-2 summarize the classes and interfaces you need to learn. You need to be very comfortable with the code of four classes: `Bug`, `BoxBug`, `Critter`, and `ChameleonCritter`. You need to know only the API (specifications for using constructors and public methods) for the `Grid` interface, the `Location` class, and the `Actor`, `Flower`, and `Rock` classes.

API (documentation only)	Implementation (testable code)
Location	Bug
Grid	BoxBug
Actor	Critter
Flower	ChameleonCritter
Rock	

Table 6-1. GridWorld classes tested on the AP exam

The case study also includes a few "runner" classes. A runner class configures the grid and supplies a `main` method for a particular project.

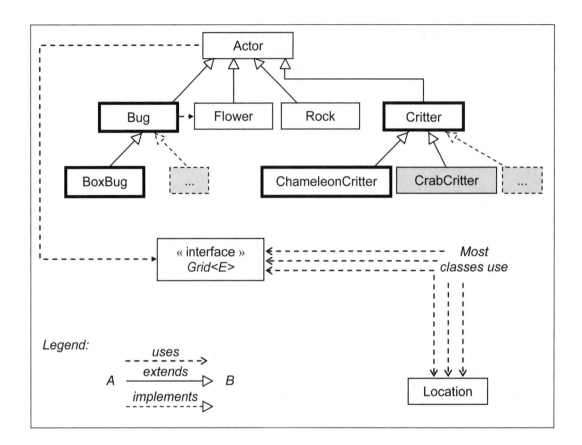

**Figure 6-2. GridWorld classes required for the AP exam.
A bold border indicates that the knowledge of the
implementation code is required; otherwise the API only is
required. Grayed classes are examples (not required but
useful) and places for likely extensions.**

▌ **The "runner" classes are not tested on the exam.**

The class `CrabCritter` is only an example — it won't be tested on the exam — but
you should get familiar with it to know what to expect.

▌ **At the exam, you will receive a booklet with the required case study code
and API.**

The booklet will contain the complete code for the classes whose implementation you
are supposed to know, in a format similar to Appendix C in the case study narrative.
The booklet will also contain a *Quick Reference*, similar to Appendix E, that lists all
the constructors and methods for the "testable-code" classes and the "API-only"
classes and interfaces. Get used to referring to these materials while practicing.

6.2. The `Location` Class and the `Grid` Interface

Location

A `Location` object represents a (*row*, *col*) location (with integer coordinates) on a two-dimensional grid.

The `Location` class has one constructor —

```
public Location(int row, int col)
```

— and two accessor methods:

```
public int getRow()            //  Returns the row for this location
public int getCol()            //  Returns the column for this location
```

> **Location objects are *immutable*: once created, a `Location` object cannot change.**

`Location` implements `Comparable` and provides a `compareTo` method that compares locations first by row and then, if equal, by column. `Location` also overrides `Object`'s `equals` method in a manner consistent with `compareTo`.

`Location`'s `toString` method converts a location into a string:

```
public String toString()
{
  return "(" + getRow() + ", " + getCol() + ")";
}
```

The `Location` class also helps to handle directions on the grid. It defines eight public constants —

```
public static final int NORTH = 0;
public static final int NORTHEAST = 45;
public static final int EAST = 90;
public static final int SOUTHEAST = 135;
public static final int SOUTH = 180;
public static final int SOUTHWEST = 225;
public static final int WEST = 270;
public static final int NORTHWEST = 315;
```

— that represent compass directions (in degrees).

The row number increases in the direction from north to south. The column number increases from west to east.

Seven more constants represent turns:

```
public static final int LEFT = -90;
public static final int RIGHT = 90;
public static final int HALF_LEFT = -45;
public static final int HALF_RIGHT = 45;
public static final int FULL_CIRCLE = 360;
public static final int HALF_CIRCLE = 180;
public static final int AHEAD = 0;
```

In your code, you might find it easier to just use the numbers, 360, 180, 0, instead of `Location.FULL_CIRCLE`, `Location.HALF_CIRCLE`, `Location.AHEAD`.

`Location`'s `getAdjacentLocation(int dir)` method returns the location that is adjacent to this location in the compass direction `dir`. Locations that touch in a corner are considered adjacent.

`Location`'s `getDirectionToward(Location other)` method returns the compass direction (in degrees) from this location to `other`. For example,

```
Location loc1 = new Location(3, 7);
Location loc2 = loc1.getAdjacentLocation(Location.SOUTHWEST);
int dir = loc1.getDirectionToward(loc2);
```

sets `loc2` to (4, 6) and `dir` to 225 (that is, `Location.SOUTHWEST`).

Grid

The `Grid<E>` interface represents a two-dimensional grid that can hold objects of the type `E`. GridWorld uses `Grid<Actor>` to hold objects that are `Actors` (that is objects of the class `Actor` or of any of the subclasses or descendants of `Actor`).

In GridWorld, only one actor can reside at a given location in the grid.

The `Grid` interface isolates specific implementations of the grid from the rest of the GridWorld classes.

A grid can be implemented as a two-dimensional array (as in `BoundedGrid`), but it can be also implemented in other ways. The particular implementations are not tested.

```
public interface Grid<E>
{
  // General grid methods:
  // ======================

  int numRows();                     // Returns the number of rows for a
                                     //    bounded grid; -1 for an unbounded
                                     //    grid

  int numCols();                     // Returns the number of columns for a
                                     //    bounded grid; -1 for an unbounded
                                     //    grid

  boolean isValid(Location loc);     // Returns true if loc is valid in this
                                     //    grid (always true for an
                                     //    unbounded grid)

  E get(Location loc);               // Returns the object at loc (or null
                                     //    if loc is empty)

  E put(Location loc, E obj);        // Puts obj at loc and returns the
                                     //    object previously at loc (or null
                                     //    if loc was empty)

  E remove(Location loc);            // Removes the object at loc and
                                     //    returns that object (or null
                                     //    if loc was empty)
  ArrayList<Location>
      getOccupiedLocations();        // Returns the list of all occupied
                                     //    locations in the grid


  // "Local neighborhood" methods:
  // =============================

  ArrayList<Location> getValidAdjacentLocations(Location loc);
                             // Returns a list of all valid locations
                             //    adjacent to loc

  ArrayList<Location> getEmptyAdjacentLocations(Location loc);
                             // Returns a list of all valid empty
                             //    locations adjacent to loc

  ArrayList<Location> getOccupiedAdjacentLocations(Location loc);
                             // Returns a list of all valid occupied
                             //    locations adjacent to loc

  ArrayList<E> getNeighbors(Location loc);
                             // Returns a list of all objects in the
                             //    occupied locations adjacent to loc
}
```

Figure 6-3.   The Grid<E> interface

The Grid<*E*> interface is shown in Figure 6-3. It has eleven methods that roughly fall into two groups: "general" grid methods and "local neighborhood" methods.

> **All Grid<*E*> methods that take Location loc as a parameter, except isValid, assume that loc is a valid location in the grid. isValid assumes that loc is not null. The put method also assumes that obj is not null.**

47

Consider the following method:

```
// Returns true if loc1 and loc2 are neighbors in grid,
// false otherwise.
// Precondition: loc1 and loc2 are both valid locations in grid
public boolean areNeighbors(Grid<Actor> grid, Location loc1,
                                              Location loc2)
{
  return < expression >;
}
```

Which of the following replacements for < *expression* > will make this method work as specified?

I.   `loc1.getAdjacentLocation(loc1.getDirectionToward(loc2)) == loc2`

II. `loc1.getAdjacentLocation(loc1.getDirectionToward(loc2)).`
                                                  `equals(loc2)`

III. `grid.getNeighbors(loc1).contains(loc2)`

(A)   I only
(B)   II only
(C)   III only
(D)   I and II
(E)   II and III

   The idea in Options I and II is to first get the direction from loc1 to loc2, then create a neighboring location from loc1 in that direction and compare it to loc2. If loc2 is a neighbor, these locations must be equal. But they won't be the same object! So Option II is correct while Option I is wrong, because == compares the addresses of objects. In Option III, Grid's getNeighbors returns ArrayList<Actor>, a list of all <u>Actors</u> in neighboring locations, rather than ArrayList<Location>. (The ArrayList class does have a method contains, but it is not in the AP subset.) The answer is B.

6.3. The Actor Class

The `Actor` class serves as a base class for a hierarchy of classes that represent different kinds of "bugs," "flowers," "rocks," "critters," and so on. `Actor` is <u>not</u> an abstract class, so you can create an object of this class. However, an object of type `Actor` is not a very interesting object: when asked to "act" it just turns around 180 degrees.

An `Actor` object has four attributes: color, location, direction, and grid.

> **An actor can belong to one and only one grid at a time; its grid attribute refers to that grid, or it is `null` if the actor is currently not in any grid.**

The `Actor` class has one constructor that takes no parameters. This constructor sets the actor's color to `Color.BLUE`, the actor's direction to 0 (`Location.NORTH`), and the actor's location and grid to `null`.

The `Actor` class has four accessors for these attributes and two modifiers:

```
public Color getColor()
public Location getLocation()
public int getDirection()
public Grid<Actor> getGrid()

public void setColor(Color newColor)
public void setDirection(int newDirection)
```

It has also a `toString` method:

```
public String toString()
```

The grid attribute is not set directly. The methods `putSelfInGrid` and `removeSelfFromGrid` are used instead, because the grid as well as the actor has to be notified of the change:

```
public void putSelfInGrid(Grid<Actor> gr, Location loc)
// Puts this actor at loc in grid.
// Precondition: the actor is not in grid;
//               loc is a valid location in grid.

public void removeSelfFromGrid()
// Removes this actor from its grid.
// Precondition: the actor is in a grid.
```

Actor's `moveTo` method —

```
public void moveTo(Location newLocation)
```

— sets the current location of the actor to `loc`, but it does more: it first removes the current occupant from `loc`, if any.

Finally, an actor has the method `act`. Actor's `act` method does something just to show some action: it turns the actor by 180 degrees.

> **Actor's `act` method is usually overridden in subclasses of `Actor`.**

48

Which of the following code segments will move `Actor` andy south by one unit, assuming the new location is empty?

I.
```
loc = andy.getLocation();
loc.setRow(loc.getRow() + 1);
```

II.
```
loc = andy.getLocation();
Location newLoc = new Location(loc.getRow() + 1, loc.getCol());
andy.setLocation(newLoc);
```

III.
```
loc = andy.getLocation();
andy.moveTo(loc.getAdjacentLocation(Location.SOUTH));
```

(A) I only
(B) II only
(C) III only
(D) I and II
(E) II and III

 Option I is nonsense because `Location` objects are immutable; a `Location` does not have a `setRow` method. Option II does not work because `Actor` has no method `setLocation`. When an actor changes its location in the grid, it has to inform the grid of the change, and possibly remove the current occupant of the new location. To emphasize that, the corresponding method is called `moveTo`, not `setLocation`. The statements

```
Location newLoc = new Location(loc.getRow() + 1, loc.getCol());
andy.moveTo(newLoc);
```

would work, but it is better to write

```
andy.moveTo(loc.getAdjacentLocation(Location.SOUTH));
```

because it is more abstract: it does not rely on the knowledge of how compass directions relate to rows and columns in the grid. The answer is C.

49

Suppose a class `Checker` is defined as follows:

```
public class Checker extends Actor
{
  public Checker (Color color)
  { setColor(color); }
}
```

Another class, `CheckerBoard`, implements `Grid<Actor>`. Consider the following method in a third class, `CheckersGame`:

```
// If the checker at loc can "jump" a checker of the
// opposite color in the direction dir, then performs the jump
// and returns true; otherwise returns false.
public boolean jump(CheckerBoard board, Location loc, int dir)
{
  if (dir % 45 != 0 || dir % 90 == 0) // only diagonal jumps are allowed
    return false;
  if (!board.isValid(loc))
    return false;

  Location loc2 = loc.getAdjacentLocation(dir);

  if (!board.isValid(loc2) || board.get(loc2) == null)
    return false;

  Location loc3 = loc2.getAdjacentLocation(dir);
  if (!board.isValid(loc3) || board.get(loc3) != null)
    return false;

  Checker chk = (Checker)board.get(loc);
  Checker chk2 = (Checker)board.get(loc2);
  if (chk.getColor().equals(chk2.getColor()))
    return false;

  // loc2 is occupied by a checker of the opposite color;
  // loc3 is empty;
  // chk is moved from loc to loc3; loc2 is emptied:

  < missing statements >

  return true;
}
```

Which of the following replacements for < *missing statements* > will make this method work as specified?

(A) `chk.moveTo(loc3);`

(B) `board.remove(loc);`
     `chk.moveTo(loc3);`
     `board.remove(loc2);`

(C) `chk.moveTo(loc3);`
     `board.remove(loc2);`

(D) `chk.moveTo(loc3);`
     `chk2.removeSelfFromGrid();`

(E) `board.remove(loc2);`
     `board.remove(loc);`
     `chk3 = new Checker(chk.getColor())`
     `board.put(loc3, chk3);`

☞ This question is a little too long for a typical multiple-choice exam question. We use it here for practice in reading GridWorld-type code and using low-level GridWorld classes. Note how general and reusable the GridWorld setup is: we can use it to hold critters or to program a game of checkers.

Choices A through D attempt to move `chk` from `loc` to `loc3`, while Choice E tries to remove `chk` and create an identical object in `loc3`. The latter approach could potentially work, but it is not in the spirit of GridWorld, and you would need to use `chk.removeSelfFromGrid(...)` and `chk3.putSelfInGrid(...)`.

Choice A forgets to remove the checker from `loc2`. In Choice B, `moveTo` throws an exception because after `board.remove(loc)`, `chk` is no longer in the grid. Choice C incorrectly uses `board`'s `remove` method instead of `chk2.removeSelfFromGrid()`. Choice E has the same problem: it uses `board`'s `put` and `remove`. The answer is D. ☟

> **Grid's put and remove methods should never be used directly — use Actor's putSelfInGrid and removeSelfFromGrid instead.**

Otherwise, the actor won't know that it was put in the grid, or the actor will "think" it is still in the grid while it no longer is.

6.4. Bugs, Flowers, and Rocks

The classes `Bug`, `Flower`, and `Rock` are subclasses of `Actor`.

The `Rock` class is the simplest of the three. It has two constructors: the no-args constructor creates a black rock, and the `Rock(Color color)` constructor creates a rock of a given color. `Rock`'s act method is empty — a rock just sits there.

The `Flower` class is similar to `Rock`, but its default color is `Color.PINK`, and its act method darkens the color of the flower. You don't need to worry about the implementation of this class — just remember how to call its constructors.

The `Bug` class is more interesting. It has two constructors, similar to `Rock`'s constructors and `Flower`'s constructors, but its default color is `Color.RED`. A `Bug` has three new methods: `canMove`, `move`, and `turn`. These methods are called from `Bug`'s act method, which looks like this:

```
public void act()
{
  if (canMove())
    move();
  else
    turn();
}
```

A `Bug` tries to move forward in its current direction. A `Bug` can move if the new location is valid and empty or contains a `Flower`:

```
public boolean canMove()
{
  Grid<Actor> gr = getGrid();
  if (gr == null)
    return false;

  Location loc = getLocation();
  Location next = loc.getAdjacentLocation(getDirection());
  if (!gr.isValid(next))
    return false;

  Actor neighbor = gr.get(next);
  return (neighbor == null) || (neighbor instanceof Flower);
  // ok to move into empty location or onto flower
  // not ok to move onto any other actor
}
```

This method uses the Java `instanceof` operator, which is not part of the AP subset but is explained in the case study narrative.

The `move` method moves this `Bug` and places a `Flower` (of the same color as the bug) at its old location:

```
public void move()
{
  Grid<Actor> gr = getGrid();
  if (gr == null)
    return;

  Location loc = getLocation();
  Location next = loc.getAdjacentLocation(getDirection());

  if (gr.isValid(next))
    moveTo(next);
  else  // never happens
    removeSelfFromGrid();

  Flower flower = new Flower(getColor());
  flower.putSelfInGrid(gr, loc);
}
```

The `turn` method turns this `Bug` clockwise by 45 degrees:

```
public void turn()
{
  setDirection(getDirection() + Location.HALF_RIGHT);
}
```

> **The purpose of the `Bug` class is to give an example of an `Actor` that does something "interesting" and to provide a base class for extensions and variations (and possible AP exam questions).**

`BoxBug` is one such extension. Study its code carefully. Also do all the exercises in Part 2 (p. 12): `CircleBug`, `SpiralBug`, `ZBug`, and `DancingBug`.

50

A `Bug` is not allowed to move to a location occupied by another `Bug`. Suppose we want to define a new class `PredatorBug` as a subclass of `Bug`. A `PredatorBug` can move to a location occupied by another `Bug` and "eat" it. Otherwise, a `PredatorBug` acts like a regular `Bug`. Which methods should be redefined in `PredatorBug`?

(A)   `act` only
(B)   `canMove` only
(C)   `move` only
(D)   `act` and `move`
(E)   `canMove` and `move`

☞   Recall that when an actor moves to a new location (that is, its `moveTo` method is called) the current occupant is removed from that location. All we have to do is allow a `PredatorBug` to move to a location occupied by another `Bug`:

```
public boolean canMove()
{
  ...
  return (neighbor == null) || (neighbor instanceof Flower)
                    || (neighbor instanceof Bug);
}
```

The answer is B.   ⏎

6.5. Critters

A `Critter` is an actor that can interact with other actors in a more sophisticated way. Critters are introduced in Part 4 of the case study narrative.

The `Critter` class is designed to serve as a base class for a hierarchy of critters. `Critter`'s `act` method involves five steps:

1. Get a list of actors to interact with;
2. Process actors from that list;
3. Get a list of locations that are candidates for this critter's next move;
4. Select a location to move to from the list obtained in Step 3;
5. Move to the selected location.

Each of these steps is accomplished in a separate method, so a critter's `act` method calls five methods, which we will call "service" methods. It looks like this:

```
public void act()
{
  if (getGrid() == null)
    return;

  // Step 1:
  ArrayList<Actor> actors = getActors();

  // Step 2:
  processActors(actors);

  // Step 3:
  ArrayList<Location> moveLocs = getMoveLocations();

  // Step 4:
  Location loc = selectMoveLocation(moveLocs);

  // Step 5:
  makeMove(loc);
}
```

In the `Critter` class itself, the service methods `getActors`, `processActors`, `getMoveLocations`, `selectMoveLocation`, and `makeMove` are pretty simple:

- `getActors` returns a list of all actors in <u>neighboring locations</u> of this critter;

- `processActors` "eats" (removes from the grid) all actors from that list, except rocks and other critters;

- `getMoveLocations` returns the list of all <u>empty</u> neighboring locations (including the ones just emptied by `processActors`);

- if the list returned by `getMoveLocations` is not empty, `selectMoveLocation` selects a <u>random location</u> from that list; otherwise it returns this `Critter`'s current location;

- `makeMove` moves this `Critter` to the selected location by calling its `moveTo` method.

> **AP exam questions may ask you to reason about or to write a subclass of `Critter`.**

A critter is an actor that <u>first</u> processes some other actors, <u>then</u> moves. The case study narrative states: "It is usually not a good idea to override the `act` method in a `Critter` subclass."

> **Do not override the `act` method in `Critter` subclasses. Override one or more of the five service methods instead.**

`Critter`'s `act` method will call the correct service method(s) of a `Critter`'s subclass due to polymorphism.

`Critter`'s setup is very flexible, and you can implement many different behaviors by overriding one or more of the five service methods. You should call the superclass's methods, where appropriate, to avoid duplicating code.

> **It is very important to pay attention to the postconditions specified in `Critter`'s service methods.**

In particular, `getActors`, `getMoveLocations`, and `selectMoveLocation` must leave the state of all actors unchanged; `processActors` can only change the state of this critter and the actors in the given list, and it must leave the location of this critter unchanged; and `makeMove` can change only the state of this critter and the actor in the new location (if any). Note that `selectMoveLocation` can return only a location from a given list, a `null`, or this critter's current location.

`makeMove(Location loc)` must move this critter to `loc`, if `loc` is not `null`, or remove this critter from the grid by calling `removeSelfFromGrid` or `super.makeMove(loc)` if `loc` is null.

51

A `Bee` is an actor that acts as follows. First the `Bee` makes all the `Flower`s in neighboring locations brighten their color. After that, the `Bee` moves to a randomly picked neighboring location that contains a `Flower` or, if no adjacent `Flower`s have been found, to a randomly picked empty neighboring location. If there is nowhere to move, the `Bee` stays in its current location. If the `Bee` moves onto a `Flower`, it saves that `Flower` and restores the same `Flower` when it moves away from that location. Which of the following is the best approach to implementing the `Bee` class?

(A)   Implement `Bee` as a subclass of `Actor`, overriding the `act` method
(B)   Implement `Bee` as a subclass of `Bug`, overriding the `act` and `moveTo` methods
(C)   Implement `Bee` as a subclass of `Critter`, overriding the `act` and `moveTo` methods
(D)   Implement `Bee` as a subclass of `Critter`, overriding the `processActors`, `getMoveLocations` and `makeMove` methods
(E)   Implement `Bee` as a subclass of `Critter`, overriding the `getActors`, `processActors`, `getMoveLocations`, `selectMoveLocation`, and `makeMove` methods

☞ A `Bee` first does something to some other actors, then moves, so it falls into the general category of "critters." It is of course possible to derive `Bee` directly from `Actor` (Choice A), but why duplicate code, when the `Critter` class already exists? It is also possible to derive `Bee` from `Bug` (Choice B), but that would damage the neat hierarchy of GridWorld actors. A `Bug` moves in a particular way, and it is better to leave it alone. We wouldn't be able to reuse any of `Bug`'s code by deriving `Bee` from `Bug`.

We are left with the three "critter" choices. Choice C is totally unacceptable: we never override `Actor`'s low-level `moveTo` method, and we usually do not override `Critter`'s `act` method. The question remains: Will overriding `processActors`, `getMoveLocations`, and `makeMove` (Choice D) be sufficient to achieve `Bee`'s functionality, or do we need to override all five of `Critter`'s service methods (Choice E)? Note that `Critter`'s `getActors` method returns a list of <u>all</u> actors in neighboring locations, then `processActors` decides which ones to "eat." A `Bee` can work in a similar way: it can use `Critter`'s `getActors` and let its `processActors` test which neighbors are `Flower`s and brighten their color.

getMoveLocations can return a list of all neighboring Flowers or, if there are no flowers among the neighbors, return a list of all empty neighboring locations. No need to change Critter's selectMoveLocation, which simply selects a random location from the list. Bee's makeMove method can handle saving and/or restoring the Flower the Bee "landed on," if necessary, and call super.makeMove() to move. So Choice E is overkill. The answer is D.

_____ Subclasses of Critter _____

The case study gives two examples of subclasses of Critter: ChameleonCritter and CrabCritter. The code for ChameleonCritter may be tested on the AP exam. CrabCritter is just an example, but we recommend that you study it very carefully.

The ChameleonCritter class has no constructors — it defaults to Critter's no-args constructor. ChameleonCritter overrides two of Critter's five service methods: processActors and makeMove. processActors chooses a random neighbor and assigns its color to this ChameleonCritter:

```
public void processActors(ArrayList<Actor> actors)
{
  int n = actors.size();
  if (n == 0)
    return;

  int r = (int)(Math.random() * n);

  Actor other = actors.get(r);
  setColor(other.getColor());
}
```

Note the idiom for choosing a random object from a list:

```
int n = list.size();
if (n == 0)
  return;
int r = (int)(Math.random() * n);
Object x = list.get(r);
```

ChameleonCritter's makeMove method sets the direction of this ChameleonCritter to the direction of the move, then moves like a regular Critter:

```
public void makeMove(Location loc)
{
  setDirection(getLocation().getDirectionToward(loc));
  super.makeMove(loc);
}
```

52

Suppose we want to create a critter `Butterfly` that acts like a `ChameleonCritter` but changes color to the color of a `Flower` in a neighboring location. If there are several `Flower`s around, the `Butterfly` picks any one of them at random; if there are no `Flower`s around, the `Butterfly` does nothing. Which of the following is the best way to implement `Butterfly`?

(A) Derive `Butterfly` from `Critter` and redefine its `act` and `makeMove` methods.
(B) Derive `Butterfly` from `Critter` and redefine the `processActors` and `makeMove` methods.
(C) Derive `Butterfly` from `ChameleonCritter` and redefine the `act` method.
(D) Derive `Butterfly` from `ChameleonCritter` and redefine the `getActors` method.
(E) Derive `Butterfly` from `ChameleonCritter` and redefine the `getActors` and `processActors` methods.

☞ Since a `Butterfly` acts in a manner similar to a `ChameleonCritter`, it makes sense to derive the `Butterfly` class from `ChameleonCritter`. `Butterfly` can override `ChameleonCritter`'s `getActors` method to include only `Flower`s in the returned list. Alternatively, `Butterfly` can override `ChameleonCritter`'s `processActors` method to select a random neighbor only among `Flower`s. There is no need to override both, though. The answer is D. ☜

6.6. Tips for the Case Study Questions

To answer GridWorld case study questions successfully, you need to be familiar with both the relevant code and the concepts behind it. Look very carefully at the code for the `Bug`, `BoxBug`, `Critter`, `ChameleonCritter`, and `CrabCritter` classes. Also take a look at the `Flower` and `Rock` classes. Make sure you are very comfortable with the `Location`, `Grid`, and `Actor` APIs. Do all the exercises for Part 2 and Part 4.

Several multiple-choice questions are likely to focus on concepts: why certain design decisions were made, what the alternatives and tradeoffs are, what certain methods do, how inheritance and polymorphism work in the case study, and so on. Don't panic; most of it is common sense, especially if you have read the case study narrative.

The free-response questions will ask you to write variations on the case-study code. The key here is to find a similar code segment in the case study booklet and adapt it. Do not improvise your code from scratch. Pay attention to the following:

- `equals` vs. `==`: Use `equals` for comparing locations; use `==` for comparing actors.

- `ArrayList`s vs. arrays: `Grid` methods `getOccupiedLocations`, `getValidAdjacentLocations`, `getEmptyAdjacentLocations`, `getOccupiedAdjacentLocations` return an `ArrayList<Location>`; `getNeighbors` returns an `ArrayList<Actor>`. Use `.get(i)`, not `[i]`, on these lists.

- Call methods of the correct class. For example, `getAdjacentLocation(int direction)` and `getDirectionToward(Location target)` are in `Location`, <u>not</u> in `Grid`; `getValidAdjacentLocations(Location loc)` is in `Grid`.

- Use an actor's `getLocation` and `getGrid` methods to get hold of its location and grid, respectively.

- Use an actor's `putSelfInGrid` method to assign the actor to a given location in a given grid. Use an actor's `removeSelfFromGrid` method to remove the actor from the grid.

- To change an actor's direction, use:

  ```
  setDirection(getDirection() + ...);
  ```

  For example, to reverse the direction, write:

  ```
  setDirection(getDirection() + 180);
  ```

- `private`: it is an error to access private instance fields. Use accessor methods instead. For example:

  ```
  Grid<Actor> gr = getGrid();
  Location loc = getLocation();
  ...
  Flower flower = new Flower(getColor());
  flower.putSelfInGrid(gr, loc);
  ```

  Note that neither `Bug` nor `Critter` has instance fields, except those inherited from `Actor` (which are private in `Actor`).

- In addition to hands-on computer work, do some paper-and-pencil exercises while practicing for the case study questions. Use Appendices C and E in the case study narrative to get used to the format: the materials you will receive on the exam will be similar.

Chapter 7. Annotated Solutions to Past Free-Response Questions

The material for this chapter is on our web site:

`www.skylit.com/beprepared/fr.html`

That page includes links to free-response questions from recent years and an annotated solution for each question.

Practice Exams

Practice Exam #1

Time — 1 hour and 15 minutes
Number of questions — 40
Percent of total grade — 50

1. What is the output of the following program segment?

```
int num = 5;
while (num >= 0)
{
   num -= 2;
}
System.out.print(num);
```

   (A) -2
   (B) -1
   (C) 0
   (D) 2
   (E) 21

2. What is the output from

```
int n = 12;
System.out.print(goFigure(n));
System.out.print(" " + n);
```

where the method goFigure is defined as follows:

```
public double goFigure(int n)
{
   n = n % 7;
   return (double)(12 / n);
}
```

   (A) 2.4 12
   (B) 2.4 6
   (C) 2.4 5
   (D) 2.0 12
   (E) 2.0 5

3. Which of the following expressions will evaluate to `true` when x and y are `boolean` variables with different values?

```
 I.   (x || y) && (!x || !y)
 II.  (x || y) && !(x && y)
 III. (x && !y) || (!x && y)
```

- (A) I only
- (B) II only
- (C) I and II
- (D) II and III
- (E) I, II, and III

4. What is the result when the following code segment is compiled and executed?

```
int m = 4, n = 5;
double d = Math.sqrt((m + n)/2);
System.out.println(d);
```

- (A) Syntax error "sqrt(double) in java.lang.Math cannot be applied to int"
- (B) `1.5` is displayed
- (C) `2.0` is displayed
- (D) `2.1213203435596424` is displayed
- (E) `ClassCastException`

5. Consider the following method of the class `Test`:

```
public static List<String> doNothing(List<String> list)
{
  return list;
}
```

Which of the following program segments in a `Test`'s client class will compile with no errors?

```
 I.     ArrayList<String> nums = new ArrayList<String>();
        nums = Test.doNothing(nums);

 II.    List<String> nums = new ArrayList<String>();
        nums = Test.doNothing(nums);

 III.   ArrayList<String> nums1 = new ArrayList<String>();
        List<String> nums2 = Test.doNothing(nums1);
```

- (A) I only
- (B) II only
- (C) I and II only
- (D) II and III only
- (E) I, II, and III

Questions 6-7 refer to the following method:

```
public void printVals(String[] items, int k)
{
  if (k > 1)
  {
    printVals(items, k - 1);
    System.out.print(items[k] + " ");
    printVals(items, k - 2);
  }
}
```

Suppose the following code segment has been executed:

```
String[] names = {"Pat", "Joe", "Ann", "Cal", "Amy"};
printVals(names, names.length - 1);
```

6.   What is the output?

    (A)   Ann Cal Amy Ann
    (B)   Ann Cal Amy Cal Ann
    (C)   Ann Cal Joe Amy Joe Ann
    (D)   Joe Ann Cal Joe Amy Joe Ann
    (E)   Joe Ann Pat Cal Joe Amy Joe Ann Pat

7.   How many calls to `printVals` have been made, including the original call?

    (A)   3
    (B)   5
    (C)   7
    (D)   8
    (E)   9

8.   In OOP, programmers often arrange classes into inheritance hierarchies as opposed to implementing isolated classes. Which of the following is NOT a valid reason for doing so?

    (A)   Abstract classes at the top of the hierarchy can easily be extended in the project or reused in other projects.
    (B)   Methods from a superclass can often be reused in its subclasses without duplication of code.
    (C)   Objects from different subclasses can be passed as arguments to a method designed to accept objects of a superclass.
    (D)   Objects from different subclasses can be stored in the same array.
    (E)   All of the above are valid reasons for using inheritance hierarchies.

9. At the county fair, prizes are awarded to the five heaviest cows. More than 2000 cows are entered, and their records are stored in an array. Which of the following algorithms provides the most efficient way of finding the records of the five heaviest cows?

    (A)   Selection Sort
    (B)   Selection Sort terminated after the first five iterations
    (C)   Insertion Sort
    (D)   Insertion Sort terminated after the first five iterations
    (E)   Mergesort

10. Which of the following recommendations for testing software is NOT good advice?

    (A)   Test a program with all possible values of input data.
    (B)   When testing a large program, test the smaller pieces individually before testing the entire program.
    (C)   If possible, use automated testing procedures or read test data from files so that you can re-run the tests after corrections have been made.
    (D)   Design test data that exercises as many different paths through the code as is practical.
    (E)   Test on data that is at the boundary of program conditionals to check for "off by one" errors.

11. Which of the following statements about interfaces and abstract classes is TRUE?

    (A)   An abstract class cannot extend another abstract class.
    (B)   If an abstract class has no implemented constructors or methods, it is better to make it an interface.
    (C)   An abstract class cannot implement an interface.
    (D)   You can declare an array of objects of an abstract class type, but not of an interface type.
    (E)   A method can take a parameter of an interface type, but not of an abstract class type.

12. The two versions of the `search` method shown below are both intended to return `true` if `ArrayList list` contains the target value, `false` otherwise.

Version 1:

```
public boolean search(ArrayList<Object> list, Object target)
{
  for (Object x : list)
  {
    if (target.equals(x))
      return true;
  }
  return false;
}
```

Version 2:

```
public boolean search(ArrayList<Object> list, Object target)
{
  boolean found = false;

  for (Object x : list)
  {
    if (target.equals(x))
      found = true;
  }
  return found;
}
```

Which of the following statements about the two versions of `search` is true?

(A) Only Version 1 works as intended.
(B) Only Version 2 works as intended.
(C) Both versions work as intended; Version 1 is often more efficient than Version 2.
(D) Both versions work as intended; Version 2 is often more efficient than Version 1.
(E) Both versions work as intended; the two versions are always equally efficient.

13. Which of the following statements displays `1234`?

```
    I.      System.out.print(12 * 100 + 34);
    II.     System.out.print("12" + 34);
    III.    System.out.print(12 + "34");
```

(A) None of the above
(B) I only
(C) I and II only
(D) II and III only
(E) I, II, and III

14. Which of the following statements about overloaded methods is FALSE?

    (A)   Overloaded methods must be made either all public or all private.
    (B)   Overloaded methods are defined in the same class and have the same name.
    (C)   Overloaded methods may have the same number of parameters.
    (D)   One of the overloaded methods may take no parameters.
    (E)   Overloaded methods cannot be differentiated based only on the names chosen for
           their parameters.

15. Consider the following class:

```
public class BuddyList
{
  /** Contains the names of buddies */
  private ArrayList<String> buddies;

  < Constructors and other methods and variables not shown >

  public ArrayList<String> getBuddies()
  { return buddies; }
}
```

If `BuddyList myFriends` is declared and initialized in some other class, a client of
`BuddyList`, which of the following correctly assigns to `name` the name of the first
buddy in the `myFriends` list?

    I.   `String name = myFriends.buddies[0];`

    II.   `String name = myFriends.buddies.get(0);`

    III. `String name = myFriends.getBuddies().get(0);`

    (A)   I only
    (B)   II only
    (C)   III only
    (D)   I and II
    (E)   II and III

16. Which of the following code segments correctly traverses a two-dimensional `int` array m, row by row?

(A)
```
for (int x : m)
{
    ...
}
```

(B)
```
for (int[] r : m)
{
  for (int x : r)
  {
      ...
  }
}
```

(C)
```
for (int r : m)
{
  for (int[] x : r)
  {
      ...
  }
}
```

(D)
```
for (int r : m)
{
  for (c = 0; c < m.length; c++)
  {
    int x = m[r][c];
    ...
  }
}
```

(E)
```
for (int c = 0; c < m.length; c++)
{
  for (int r = 0; r < m[c].length; r++)
  {
    int x = m[r][c];
    ...
  }
}
```

17. Given the declaration

```
Object obj = new String("This is a test!");
```

which of the following expressions will compile with no errors?

I. `System.out.println(obj.substring(2,7));`

II. `if (obj.equals("This is a test!"))`
    `System.out.println("Yes");`

III. `if (obj.compareTo("This is a test!") == 0)`
     `System.out.println("Yes");`

(A) I only
(B) II only
(C) I and II only
(D) II and III only
(E) I, II, and III

18. Consider the following method:

```
public void change(double[] nums, int n)
{
  for (int k = 0; k < n; k++)
  {
    nums[k] = 5.4;
  }
  n = 2;
}
```

What will be stored in `samples` and `len` after the following statements are executed?

```
double[] samples = {1.0, 2.1, 3.2, 4.3};
int len = samples.length;
change(samples, len);
```

(A) `samples` contains `5.4, 5.4, 5.4, 5.4` and `len` is 4
(B) `samples` contains `5.4, 5.4, 5.4, 5.4` and `len` is 2
(C) `samples` contains `1.0, 2.1, 3.2, 4.3` and `len` is 4
(D) `samples` contains `5.4, 5.4` and `len` is 2
(E) `samples` contains `1.0, 2.1` and `len` is 2

19. What is the output of the following code segment?

```
List<Integer> list = new ArrayList<Integer>();

for (int i = 1; i <= 8; i++)
{
   list.add(new Integer(i));
}

for (int i = 0; i < list.size(); i++)
{
   list.remove(i);
}

for (Integer x : list)
{
   System.out.print(x + " ");
}
```

   (A)   IndexOutOfBoundsException
   (B)   No output because the resulting list is empty
   (C)   1 3 5 7
   (D)   2 4 6 8
   (E)   1 2 3 4 5 6 7 8

20. What will array `arr` contain after the following code segment has been executed?

```
int[] arr = {4, 3, 2, 1, 0};
for (int i = 1; i < arr.length; i++)
{
   arr[i-1] += arr[i];
}
```

   (A)   4, 7, 5, 3, 1
   (B)   4, 7, 9, 10, 10
   (C)   7, 3, 2, 1, 0
   (D)   7, 5, 3, 1, 0
   (E)   10, 6, 3, 1, 0

21. Suppose `mat` is declared as

```
int[][] mat = new int[3][4];
```

If `mat` initially contains

```
2 1 3 4
9 7 2 1
0 2 5 6
```

what is the output of the following code segment?

```
for (int r = 1; r < mat.length; r++)
{
  for (int c = 1; c < mat[0].length; c++)
  {
    if ((r + c) % 2 == 0)
      mat[r][c] = 2 * mat[r - 1][c - 1] + c;
  }
}
System.out.println(mat[2][2]);
```

(A) 5
(B) 11
(C) 12
(D) 15
(E) 16

22. Consider the following code segment:

```
List<String> list = new ArrayList<String>();
list.add("A");
list.add("B");
list.add("C");
for (String s : list)
{
  String t = list.get(list.size() - 1);
  list.set(list.size() - 1, s);
  s = t;
}
```

What will `list` contain after the above code segment has been executed?

(A) ["A", "B", "C"]
(B) ["A", "B", "B"]
(C) ["C", "B", "A"]
(D) ["C", "A", "B"]
(E) ["C", "C", "C"]

23. Consider the following class `Athlete`:

```
public class Athlete
{
  private int numMedals;

  public int getRank() { return numMedals; }

  public int compareTo(Athlete other)
  {
    // return numMedals - other.numMedals;
    return getRank() - other.getRank();
  }

  < Constructors and other methods not shown >
}
```

As you can see, the programmer has commented out direct references to `Athlete`'s instance variable `numMedals` in the `compareTo` code and replaced them with calls to the `getRank` method. What is the most compelling reason for doing this?

(A) To correct a syntax error: being private, neither `numMedals` nor `other.numMedals` are directly accessible in the method's code

(B) To correct a syntax error: being private, `other.numMedals` is not directly accessible in the method's code (`numMedals` is replaced with `getRank()` for consistency)

(C) To avoid possible problems later: if `other` happens to be an object of a subclass of `Athlete` in which `numMedals` is not used in calculating the rank, the original code would fail

(D) To improve run-time efficiency

(E) To achieve better encapsulation

Questions 24-29 refer to the code from the GridWorld case study.

24. How does a `Bug` act if it is located in the northeast corner of a bounded grid and is facing north?

   (A)   The `Bug` turns west
   (B)   The `Bug` turns south
   (C)   The `Bug` turns northeast
   (D)   The `Bug` turns northwest
   (E)   The `Bug` is removed from the grid

25. Consider the following method:

```
/** Moves bug to the neighboring location to the west,
  * leaving bug's current location empty and bug's
  * direction unchanged.
  * Precondition: (1) this actor is contained in a grid
  *               (2) adjacent location to the west is valid
  *                   and empty in the grid of this bug
  */
public void moveWest(Bug bug)
{
  Location loc = bug.getLocation();
  Location next = loc.getAdjacentLocation(Location.WEST);
  < missing code >
}
```

Which of the following code segments could replace < *missing code* > for the method to work as specified?

   I.   `bug.moveTo(next);`

   II.   `Grid<Actor> gr = bug.getGrid();`
                    `bug.removeSelfFromGrid();`
                    `bug.putSelfInGrid(gr, next);`

   III.   `int dir = bug.getDirection();`
                    `bug.setDirection(Location.WEST);`
                    `bug.move();`
                    `bug.setDirection(dir);`

   (A)   I only
   (B)   II only
   (C)   I and II only
   (D)   II and III only
   (E)   I, II, and III

26. Which of the following code segments sets n equal to the number of occupied locations adjacent to the `Location loc` in the `Grid<Actor> gr`?

    I.
```
ArrayList<Location> neighbors =
        gr.getOccupiedAdjacentLocations(loc);
int n = neighbors.size();
```

    II.
```
ArrayList<Actor> neighbors = gr.getNeighbors(loc);
int n = neighbors.size();
```

    III.
```
ArrayList<Location> neighbors =
        gr.getValidAdjacentLocations(loc);
ArrayList<Location> emptyNeighbors =
        gr.getEmptyAdjacentLocations(loc);
int n = neighbors.size() - emptyNeighbors.size();
```

(A) I only
(B) II only
(C) I and II only
(D) II and III only
(E) I, II, and III

27. In the GridWorld design, why is the `Actor` class not made abstract, with the `act` method abstract?

(A) To enable polymorphism for instances of `Actor`
(B) To be able to override the `act` method in `Actor`'s subclasses
(C) To avoid duplication of code in constructors of `Actor`'s subclasses
(D) To avoid duplication of the `setColor` method in `Actor`'s subclasses
(E) To be able to create `Actor` objects in GridWorld applications and explore their attributes and behavior

28. A `Caterpillar` actor has some features of `Bug` and some of `Critter`. A `Caterpillar` first "eats" all the flowers in the adjacent locations (except the one just behind it), then, if possible, moves ahead to the adjacent location and leaves a flower in its wake. If the location in front is occupied, the `Caterpillar` stays in place and turns 45 degrees to the right. `Caterpillar` has two constructors similar to `Bug`'s constructors. `Caterpillar` can be implemented as a subclass of `Bug` or as a subclass of `Critter`. Approximately how many lines of code would each of these two implementations require (not counting braces, comments, and `import` statements)?

	extends Bug	extends Critter
(A)	10	10
(B)	10	30
(C)	20	30
(D)	30	50
(E)	50	50

29. Suppose we modify the `act` and `makeMove` methods in `Critter`. We place the calls to `getMoveLocations` and `selectMoveLocation` into `makeMove`, rather than into `act`, as follows:

```
public void act()
{
  if (getGrid() == null)
    return;
  ArrayList<Actor> actors = getActors();
  processActors(actors);
  makeMove();
}

public void makeMove()
{
  ArrayList<Location> moveLocs = getMoveLocations();
  Location loc = selectMoveLocation(moveLocs);

  if (loc == null)
    removeSelfFromGrid();
  else
    moveTo(loc);
}
```

Then all subclasses of `Critter` that override `makeMove` will need to be modified, too. Which other subclasses of `Critter` will need to be modified?

(A) None
(B) All subclasses that override `getMoveLocations`
(C) All subclasses that override `selectMoveLocation`
(D) All subclasses that override both `getMoveLocations` and `selectMoveLocation`
(E) All subclasses that override either `getMoveLocations` or `selectMoveLocation` (or both)

30. Consider the following method:

```
public int locate(String str, String oneLetter)
{
  j = 0;
  while (j < str.length() &&
         str.substring(j, j + 1).compareTo(oneLetter) < 0)
  {
    j++;
  }
  return j;
}
```

Which of the following must be true when the `while` loop terminates?

(A) `j == str.length()`
(B) `str.substring(j, j + 1) >= 0`
(C) `j <= str.length() ||`
          `str.substring(j, j + 1).compareTo(oneLetter) > 0`
(D) `j == str.length() ||`
          `str.substring(j, j + 1).compareTo(oneLetter) >= 0`
(E) `j == str.length() &&`
          `str.substring(j, j + 1).compareTo(oneLetter) >= 0`

31. Suppose an array `arr` contains 127 different random values arranged in ascending order, and a most efficient searching algorithm is used to find a target value. How many elements of the array will be examined when the target equals `arr[39]`?

(A) 4
(B) 5
(C) 7
(D) 63
(E) 64

32. What is the value of `product` after the following code segment is executed?

```
int[] factors = {2, 3, 4, 7, 2, 5};
int product = 1;
for (int i = 1; i < factors.length; i += 2)
{
  product *= (factors[i] % factors[i - 1]);
}
```

(A) 0
(B) 1
(C) 2
(D) 3
(E) 5

Questions 33-36 refer to the following classes:

```
public class Party
{
  private List<String> theGuests;

  public Party() { theGuests = null; }

  public Party(List<String> guests) { theGuests = guests; }

  public void setGuests(List<String> guests) { theGuests = guests; }

  public String toString()
  { /* implementation not shown */ }
}

public class BDayParty extends Party
{
  private String theName;

  public BDayParty(String name, List<String> guests)
  { /* implementation not shown */ }

  public String getName() { return theName; }

  < Other methods not shown >
}
```

33. Given

    ```
    List<String> guests = new ArrayList<String>();
    guests.add("Alice");
    guests.add("Ben");
    guests.add("Candy");
    ```

    which of the following declarations is NOT valid?

    (A) `Party[] celebrations = new Party[2];`

    (B) `Party[] celebrations =`
         `{new Party(guests), new Party()};`

    (C) `BDayParty[] celebrations =`
         `{new BDayParty("Malika", guests), new Party(guests)};`

    (D) `BDayParty[] celebrations =`
         `{new BDayParty("Lee", guests),`
         `new BDayParty("Henry", guests)};`

    (E) All of the above are valid.

34. Which of the following statements can replace < *missing statement* > in the following `BDayParty` constructor?

```
public BDayParty(String name, List guests)
{
  < missing statement >
  theName = name;
}
```

   I.   `theGuests = guests;`

   II.   `super(guests);`

   III.   `setGuests(guests);`

(A) I only
(B) II only
(C) I and II
(D) II and III
(E) I, II, and III

35. Suppose we have decided to make the `Party` class `abstract` and have added the following methods to it:

```
public abstract String getOccasion();
public String getMessage() { return "Happy"; }
public String greetings() { return getMessage() + " "
                                      + getOccasion(); }
```

Which of the following is the smallest set of `Party` methods that would have to be overridden in the `BDayParty` class to make

```
BDayParty birthday = new BDayParty("Aaron", guests);
System.out.println(birthday.greetings());
```

display

```
Happy Birthday Aaron
```

(A) None
(B) `getOccasion`
(C) `getMessage`
(D) `getOccasion` and `getMessage`
(E) `getOccasion`, `getMessage`, and `greetings`

36. `Party`'s `toString` method lists all the entries in the `theGuests` list. Should the programmer use a "for-each" loop or the list's `get(i)` method within a loop to traverse the list?

    (A) `get(i)`, because it is always more efficient
    (B) `get(i)`, because "for-each" loops are available only for arrays
    (C) A "for-each" loop, because `get(i)` may be not available in the implementation of `List` passed to the constructor
    (D) A "for-each" loop, because it is more efficient when `theGuests` happens to be an `ArrayList`
    (E) Either method works and is equally efficient when the `List` passed to the constructor is an `ArrayList`.

37. Consider the following classes:

```
public class A
{
  private int myNum;

  public A (int x) { myNum = x; }
  public int getNumber() { return myNum; }
  public String getLetters() { return "A"; }
  public String getMessage()
          { return getLetters() + "-" + getNumber(); }
}

public class B extends A
{
  public B (int x) { super(x + 1); }
  public int getNumber() { return super.getNumber() + 1; }
  public String getLetters() { return "B"; }
}
```

What is the output of the following code segment?

```
A test = new B(0);
System.out.print(test.getMessage());
```

    (A) `A-0`
    (B) `A-1`
    (C) `A-2`
    (D) `B-1`
    (E) `B-2`

Questions 38-39 refer to the following method:

```
private int product(int n)
{
  if (n <= 1)
    return 1;
  else
    return n * product(n-2);
}
```

38. What is the output when `product(6)` is called?

    (A) 1
    (B) 8
    (C) 12
    (D) 48
    (E) 720

39. `product(25)` returns −1181211311, a negative number. Which of the following accounts for this result?

    (A) Logic error that shows up for odd values of n
    (B) Stack overflow error in recursive calls
    (C) Small range of integers in the Java Virtual Machine installed on your computer
    (D) Integer arithmetic overflow
    (E) A loss of precision in calculations

40. Consider the following interface and class:

```
public interface Student
{
  double getGPA();
  int getSemesterUnits();
}

public class FullTimeStudent implements Student
{
  < required methods go here >
}
```

What is the minimum set of methods that a developer must implement in order to successfully compile the FullTimeStudent class?

(A)   No methods would need to be implemented
(B)   getGPA(), getSemesterUnits()
(C)   getGPA(), getSemesterUnits(), equals(Object s)
(D)   getGPA(), getSemesterUnits(), equals(Object s), toString()
(E)   getGPA(), getSemesterUnits(), compareTo(Object s),
                                    equals(Object s), toString()

Practice Exam #1

Time — 1 hour and 45 minutes
Number of questions — 4
Percent of total grade — 50

1. All emails received by the Office of Complaints in Appaloosa County are assigned a priority rank from 0 to 9 and answered in the order of priority; emails with a higher rank are answered first; emails with the same rank are answered in the order in which they were received. In the Java application that handles email in Appaloosa, each message is represented by an object of some class that implements the following interface `Message`:

```
public interface Message
{
  /** Returns the priority of this message, an int value
   *  in the range from 0 to 9
   */
  int getPriority();
}
```

In this question you will design and write a class `AppaloosaPriorityQueue`, which helps to store all incoming messages and retrieve them in order of priority. Your class must implement the following interface `Queue`:

```
public interface Queue
{
  boolean isEmpty();
  int size();
  void add(Message msg);
  Message remove();
}
```

(a)   Design the `AppaloosaPriorityQueue` class according to the above description. Your class should maintain a list `messageQueues` of 10 elements. This is a list of lists: each element in `messageQueues` (with an index 0 through 9) is the list of messages that have the corresponding priority rank. Use `ArrayList`s for implementing all lists. `AppaloosaPriorityQueue` must also keep track of the total number of messages currently in the system.

Define the necessary instance variables in a manner consistent with the principle of encapsulation. Write only the header for one constructor, which takes no arguments, and the headers of all the necessary methods. <u>Do not implement any constructors or methods</u> in this part of the question.

(b)   Write the constructor of the `AppaloosaPriorityQueue` class, and the `size` and `isEmpty` methods. Your constructor must create the `messageQueues` list of 10 elements, with each element initialized to an empty list of messages.

The `size` method returns the total number of messages in the system. The `isEmpty` method checks whether there are any messages and returns `true` or `false`, appropriately.

(c)   Write the `add` and `remove` methods of the `AppaloosaPriorityQueue` class. The `add` method adds a new message to the appropriate message queue, according to this message's priority. The `remove` method removes and returns the earliest message of the highest priority. Assume that `remove` is never called when `isEmpty()` is `true`.

2. This question involves reasoning about the code from the GridWorld case study. A copy of the code is provided as part of this exam.

`Twister` is a subclass of `Actor`. A `Twister` always stays in the same row in which it was created: on each step it moves to an adjacent location, choosing randomly between east or west, with equal probabilities. If the location of the intended move contains another actor, that actor is removed from the grid. If the location of the intended move is invalid, the `Twister` removes itself from the grid. Before moving, a `Twister` destroys all the actors in its column that are below (to the south of) the `Twister`. For example:

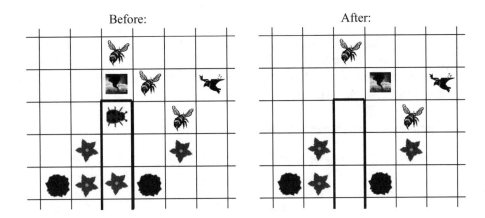

A partial definition of the `Twister` class is shown below:

```
public class Twister extends Actor
{
    public Twister()
    {
        setColor(Color.BLACK);
    }

    public void act()
    {
        destroy();
        move();
    }

    /** Removes from the grid all the actors in its column
     *  that are below (to the south of) this Twister
     */
    public void destroy()
    {   /* to be implemented in part (a) */  }

    public void move()
    {   /* to be implemented in part (b) */  }
}
```

(a) Write the `destroy` method of the `Twister` class. The method should destroy (remove from the grid) all the actors that are in the same column as this `Twister` to the south of it.

Complete the `destroy` method below.

```
/** Removes from the grid all the actors in its column
 *  that are below (to the south of) this Twister
 */
public void destroy()
```

(b) Write the `move` method of the `Twister` class. A `Twister` moves to an adjacent location in the same row, choosing randomly between east or west, with equal probabilities. If the location of the intended move contains another actor, that actor is removed from the grid. If the location of the intended move is invalid, the `Twister` disappears (removes itself from the grid).

Complete the `move` method below.

```
/** Moves this Twister east or west, with equal
 *  probabilities; if the location of the intended move
 *  contains another actor, that actor is removed from the
 *  grid; if the location of the intended move is invalid,
 *  this Twister removes itself from the grid
 */
public void move()
```

3.   E*Theater recommends movies to customers based on their previous selections. Clearly some movie matching mechanism is employed. A movie is represented by an object of the following partially defined class `Movie`:

```
public class Movie
{
   /** Describes the features of this movie */
   private String features;

   /** Returns the match coefficient between this movie
    *  and other
    *  Precondition: The length of the features string is
    *                the same in this and other Movie;
    *                it is not 0 and is evenly divisible by 3
    */
   public double getMatchCoeff(Movie other)
   {   /* to be implemented in part (a) */   }

   < Other fields, constructors, and methods not shown >
}
```

A movie is described by a set of predefined features, such as genre, rating, director, lead actress, lead actor, and so on. A feature is coded by a three-letter code. For example, the genre of a movie may be COM for comedy, DRA for drama, ADV for adventure. The three-letter codes are concatenated to form one string `features`. The lengths of the `features` strings are the same for all movies, and that length is evenly divisible by 3. A particular feature may have different values for different movies, but its code always occurs at the same position in the respective `features` strings.

The match coefficient of two movies is defined as the number of matching features, divided by the total number of features. For example:

Movie1 features	`"COMROMPALAFF_R_"`
Movie2 features	`"DRAROMPALHOP_R_"`
Total number of features	5
Number of matching features	3
Match coefficient	3/5 = 0.6

(a)   Write the `getMatchCoeff` method of the `Movie` class that returns the match coefficient between this movie and another movie. Complete the `getMatchCoeff` method below.

```
/** Returns the match coefficient between this movie
 *   and other
 *   Precondition: The length of the features string
 *                 is the same in this and other;
 *                 it is positive and evenly divisible
 *                 by 3
 */
public double getMatchCoeff(Movie other)
```

(b)   E*Theater's software maintains the list of movies previously ordered by a customer. Some of the movies in that list may not fit well with the rest (for example, a movie may have been ordered for a friend or family member). The fit coefficient for a movie M is defined as the average of match coefficients between M and all the other movies in the list.

Write a method `getFitCoefficients` that takes a list of movies and returns an array of values that describe how well each movie fits with the rest. The size of the returned array is the same as the size of the movie list. The k-th element in the returned array is equal to the fit coefficient for the k-th movie in the list. Assume that the `getMatchCoeff` method from Part (a) works as specified, regardless of what you wrote there. To receive full credit, your `getFitCoefficients` method must work in such a way that the match between any two movies in the list is computed only once. Complete `getFitCoefficients` below.

```
/** Returns an array of values that measure how well each
 *   movie in the movies list fits with the rest
 *   @return    an array whose size is equal to the size
 *             of the movies list; the value of the k-th
 *             element holds the average of the match
 *             coefficients between the k-th movie in movies
 *             and the rest of the movies in the list.
 *   Precondition:  The size of the movies list is
 *                 not less than 2
 *   Postcondition: movies remains unchanged
 */
public double[] getFitCoefficients(List<Movie> movies)
```

(c) E*Theater's marketing department wishes to detect and remove all "outliers" from each customer's movies list. An "outlier" is defined as a movie whose measure of fit with the rest of the movies is less than a half of the average fit of all the movies. Your task is to write the method `removeOutliers`. Assume that the `getFitCoefficients` method from Part (b) works as specified and avoid duplication of code. Complete `removeOutliers` below.

```
/** Obtains the fit coefficients for the movies in the
 *  given list, calculates their average, and removes
 *  from the movies list all the elements whose fit
 *  coefficient is less than half the average.
 *  Precondition:  The size of the movies list is
 *                 not less than 2
 */
public void removeOutliers(List<Movie> movies)
```

4. The goal of a Sudoku puzzle is to complete a 9-by-9 grid with numbers from 1 to 9 in
    such a way that each row, each column, and each of the nine 3-by-3 squares contain all
    the numbers from 1 to 9 (without repetition). This is an example of an initial Sudoku grid
    and the correctly completed grid:

	3				1			
		6					5	
5						9	8	3
	8				6	3		2
			5					
9		3	8				6	
7	1	4						9
	2					8		
			4				3	

8	3	2	5	9	1	6	7	4
4	9	6	3	8	7	2	5	1
5	7	1	2	6	4	9	8	3
1	8	5	7	4	6	3	9	2
2	6	7	9	5	3	4	1	8
9	4	3	8	1	2	7	6	5
7	1	4	6	3	8	5	2	9
3	2	9	1	7	5	8	4	6
6	5	8	4	2	9	1	3	7

The class `Sudoku` helps solve a Sudoku puzzle by computer; its partial definition is
shown below. Empty spots in the grid are represented by zero values.

```
public class Sudoku
{
  /** Holds a 9-by-9 Sudoku grid */
  private int[][] grid;

  /** Returns the number of times a given digit occurs
   *   within a given row in grid
   *   @param row - the row to look in
   *   @param d - the digit to look for
   *          Precondition: 0 <= row < 9
   *   @return - the number of times d occurs in row
   */
  private int countOccurrencesInRow(int row, int d)
  {  /* implementation not shown */  }

  /** Returns the number of times a given digit occurs
   *   within a given column in grid
   *   @param col - the column to look in
   *   @param d - the digit to look for
   *          Precondition: 0 <= col <= 8
   *   @return - the number of times d occurs in col
   */
  private int countOccurrencesInCol(int col, int d)
  {  /* to be implemented in part (a) */  }
```

```
/** Returns the number of times a given digit occurs
 *   within a given 3-by-3 square in grid
 *   @param row - the uppermost row of the 3-by-3 square
 *   @param col - the leftmost column of the 3-by-3 square
 *   @param d - the digit to look for
 *           Precondition: row == 0, 3, or 6;
 *                         col == 0, 3, or 6
 *   @return - the number of times d occurs in this square
 */
private int countOccurrencesIn3by3(int row, int col, int d)
{  /* implementation not shown */  }

/** Returns the number of places in a given column in grid
 *   where a given digit can be placed without a conflict;
 *   the digit can be placed into a spot if that spot is
 *   empty (holds 0) and the digit does not yet occur in the
 *   same row, column, or 3-by-3 square
 *   @param col - the column to be examined
 *   @param d - the digit to be placed in col
 *           Precondition: 0 <= col < 9; 1 <= d <= 9
 *   @return the number of spots where d can be placed
 */
private int countPossiblePlacementsInCol(int col, int d)
{  /* to be implemented in part (b) */  }

/** Returns true if grid is completely and correctly filled;
 *   otherwise returns false
 */
public boolean isSolved()
{  /* to be implemented in part (c) */  }

< Constructors and other methods not shown >
}
```

(a) Write the method `countOccurrencesInCol` below. The method returns the number of times a given digit occurs in a given column.

```
/** Returns the number of times a given digit occurs
 *   within a given column in grid
 *   @param col - the column to look in
 *   @param d - the digit to look for
 *           Precondition: 0 <= col <= 8
 *   @return - the number of times d occurs in col
 */
private int countOccurrencesInCol(int col, int d)
```

(b) Write the method `countPossiblePlacementsInCol`. The method returns the number of spots in a given column where a given digit d can be placed. If d already occurs in this column, the method returns 0. d can be placed in a particular spot if that spot is empty (its current value is 0) and d does not occur in the same row or the same 3-by-3 square.

```
/** Returns the number of places in a given column in grid
 *   where a given digit can be placed without a conflict;
 *   the digit can be placed into a spot if that spot is
 *   empty (holds 0) and the digit does not yet occur in the
 *   same row, column, or 3-by-3 square
 *   @param col - the column to be examined
 *   @param d - the digit to be placed in col
 *          Precondition: 0 <= col < 9; 1 <= d <= 9
 *   @return the number of spots where d can be placed
 */
private int countPossiblePlacementsInCol(int col, int d)
```

(c) Write the method `isSolved` that checks whether or not the Sudoku grid is filled completely and correctly. Assume that all the other methods in the `Sudoku` class work as specified and avoid duplication of code.

```
/** Returns true if grid is completely and correctly filled;
 *   otherwise returns false
 */
public boolean isSolved()
```

Practice Exam #2

SECTION I

Time — 1 hour and 15 minutes
Number of questions — 40
Percent of total grade — 50

1. Given the declarations

   ```
   int p = 5, q = 3;
   ```

   which of the following expressions evaluate to 7.5?

   I.   `(double)p * (double)q / 2;`
   II. `(double)p * (double)(q / 2);`
   III. `(double)(p * q / 2);`

   (A)   I only
   (B)   II only
   (C)   I and II
   (D)   I, II, and III
   (E)   None of the above

2. Consider the following method:

   ```java
   public void mystery(int a, int b)
   {
     System.out.print(a + " ");
     if (a <= b)
       mystery(a + 5, b - 1);
   }
   ```

   What is the output when `mystery(0, 16)` is called?

   (A)   0
   (B)   0 5
   (C)   0 5 10
   (D)   0 5 10 15
   (E)   0 5 10 15 20

3.   Suppose the method `fun2` is defined as:

```
public int fun2(int x, int y)
{
  y -= x;
  return y;
}
```

What are the values of the variables a and b after the following code is executed?

```
int a = 3, b = 7;
b = fun2(a, b);
a = fun2(b, a);
```

(A)   -1 and 4
(B)   -4 and 7
(C)   -4 and 4
(D)   3 and 7
(E)   3 and 4

4.   Assuming that a and b are Boolean variables, when is the following expression true?

```
!(!a || b) || (!a && b)
```

(A)   If and only if a and b have different values
(B)   If and only if a and b have the same value
(C)   If and only if both a and b are true
(D)   If and only if both a and b are false
(E)   Never

5.   A project needs two related classes, *X* and *Y*. A programmer has decided to provide an abstract class *A* and derive both *X* and *Y* from *A* rather than implementing *X* and *Y* completely independently of each other. Which of the following is NOT a valid rationale for this design decision?

(A)   Being able to use some common code accessible in classes *X* and *Y* without duplication
(B)   Being able to cast objects of type *X* into *Y* and vice-versa
(C)   Being able to pass as a parameter an object of either type, *X* or *Y*, to the same constructor or method in place of a parameter of the type *A*
(D)   Being able to place objects of both types, *X* and *Y*, into the same array of type `A[]`
(E)   Making it easier to implement in the future another class that reuses some code from *A*

6.   The method

```
private void transpose(int[][] m)
{
    < implementation not shown >
}
```

flips the elements of m symmetrically over the diagonal. For example:

```
1 2 3                1 4 7
4 5 6   transpose     2 5 8
7 8 9      ------>    3 6 9
```

Which of the following implementations of transpose will work as specified?

I.
```
for (int r = 0; r < m.length; r++)
{
    for (int c = 0; c < m[0].length; c++)
    {
        int temp = m[r][c];
        m[r][c] = m[c][r];
        m[c][r] = temp;
    }
}
```

II.
```
for (int c = m[0].length - 1; c > 0; c--)
{
    for (int r = c-1; r >= 0; r--)
    {
        int temp = m[r][c];
        m[r][c] = m[c][r];
        m[c][r] = temp;
    }
}
```

III.
```
for (int c = 0; c < m[0].length - 1; c++)
{
    for (int r = c + 1; r < m.length; r++)
    {
        int temp = m[r][c];
        m[r][c] = m[c][r];
        m[c][r] = temp;
    }
}
```

(A)   I only
(B)   II only
(C)   I and II only
(D)   II and III only
(E)   I, II, and III

7. What is the value of `v[4]` after the following code is executed?

```
int d = 1;
int[] v = {1, 1, 1, 1, 1};

for (int i = 0; i < v.length; i++)
{
  d *= 2;
  v[i] += d;
}
```

(A) 16
(B) 32
(C) 33
(D) 64
(E) 65

8. Which of the following is NOT a good reason to use comments in programs?

(A) To describe parameters of a method
(B) To explain a convoluted piece of code
(C) To document which methods of a class are private
(D) To document requirements for correct operation of a method
(E) To document the names of the programmers and the date of the last change

9. Suppose we have the following interface `Game`:

```
public interface Game
{
  void playWith(Fun other);
}
```

We have found a compiled Java class, `Fun.class`. We do not have its source code, but we have discovered that a statement

```
Fun fun = new Fun(100);
```

compiles with no errors. Which of the following statements, if it compiles correctly, will convince us that `Fun` implements `Game`?

```
  I.   Game game = fun;
 II.   System.out.print(fun.playWith(new Fun(99)));
III.   System.out.print(fun.playWith(fun));
```

(A) I only
(B) II only
(C) I and II only
(D) II and III only
(E) I, II, and III

10. What is the result from the following code segment?

```
List<String> xyz = new ArrayList<String>();
xyz.add("X");
xyz.add("Y");
xyz.add("Z");

int count = 0;
for (String s1 : xyz)
{
  for (String s2 : xyz)
  {
    if (s1.equals(s2))
    {
      count++;
    }
  }
}

System.out.print(count);
```

(A) Syntax error
(B) 0 is displayed
(C) 1 is displayed
(D) 3 is displayed
(E) `NullPointerException`

11. Which of the following statements about Java's platform independence are true?

    I.   The value of the `MAX_VALUE` constant in the `java.lang.Integer` class is the same on any computer.

    II.   Java source code is compiled into bytecodes, which may then be run on any computer that has a Java Virtual Machine installed.

    III.   Overflow in arithmetic operations occurs at the same values regardless of the platform on which the Java program is running.

(A) I only
(B) II only
(C) I and II
(D) II and III
(E) I, II, and III

12. Suppose a class `Particle` has the following variables defined:

```
public class Particle
{
  public static final int START_POS = 100;
  private double velocity;

  < Other code not shown >
}
```

Which of the following is true?

(A) `velocity` can be passed as an argument to one of `Particle`'s methods, but `START_POS` cannot.

(B) Java syntax rules wouldn't allow us to use the name `startPos` instead of `START_POS`.

(C) A statement

```
double pos = START_POS + velocity;
```

in one of `Particle`'s methods would result in a syntax error.

(D) Java syntax rules wouldn't allow us to make `velocity` public.

(E) A statement

```
START_POS += velocity;
```

in one of `Particle`'s methods would result in a syntax error.

13. What is the output of the following code segment?

```
String s = "ban";
ArrayList<String> words = new ArrayList<String>();
words.add(s);
words.add(s.substring(1));
words.add(s.substring(1,2));
String total = "";
for (String w : words)
{
  total += w;
}
System.out.print(total.indexOf("an"));
```

(A) 1
(B) 2
(C) 3
(D) ana
(E) banana

Questions 14-15 refer to the method `smile` below:

```java
public static void smile(int n)
{
  if (n == 0)
    return;
  for (int k = 1; k <= n; k++)
  {
    System.out.print("smile!");
  }
  smile(n-1);
}
```

14. What is the output when `smile(4)` is called?

    (A) `smile!`
    (B) `smile!smile!`
    (C) `smile!smile!smile!`
    (D) `smile!smile!smile!smile!`
    (E) `smile!smile!smile!smile!smile!smile!smile!smile!smile!smile!`

15. When `smile(4)` is called, how many times will `smile` actually be called, including the initial call?

    (A) 2
    (B) 3
    (C) 4
    (D) 5
    (E) 10

16. Consider the following code segment, intended to find the position of an integer `targetValue` in `int[] a`:

```java
int i = 0;
while (a[i] != targetValue)
{
  i++;
}
int position = i;
```

When will this code work as intended?

    (A) Always
    (B) Only when `targetValue == a[0]`
    (C) Only when `0 <= targetValue < a.length`
    (D) Only when `targetValue` equals `a[i]` for some i, `0 <= i < a.length`
    (E) Only when `targetValue` is not equal to `a[i]` for any i, `0 <= i < a.length`

17. Given two initialized `String` variables, `str1` and `str2`, which of the following conditions correctly tests whether the value of `str1` is greater than or equal to the value of `str2` (in lexicographical order)?

    (A) `str1 >= str2`
    (B) `str1.compareTo(str2) >= 0`
    (C) `str1.compareTo(str2) == true`
    (D) `str1.length() > str2.length() || str1 >= str2`
    (E) `str1.equals(str2) || str1.compareTo(str2) == 1`

18. Consider the following method from `ClassX`:

    ```
    private int modXY(int x, int y)
    {
      r = x / y;
      return x % y;
    }
    ```

    If `ClassX` compiles with no errors, which of the following must be true?

    I.   `r` must have the type `double`.
    II. `modXY` has a side effect since `r` is not a local variable in `modXY`.
    III. `r` must be a static variable in `ClassX`.

    (A) I only
    (B) II only
    (D) I and II
    (C) II and III
    (E) I, II, and III

19. What is the output from the following code segment?

    ```
    double pi = 3.14159;
    int r = 100;
    int area = (int)(pi * Math.pow(r, 2));
    System.out.println(area);
    ```

    (A) `30000`
    (B) `31415`
    (C) `31416`
    (D) `314159`
    (E) Depends on the particular computer system

20. Consider the following three code segments:

    I.
    ```
    int  i = 1;
    while (i <= 10)
    {
       System.out.print(i);
       i += 2;
    }
    ```

    II.
    ```
    for (int i = 0;  i < 5;  i++)
    {
       System.out.print(2*i + 1);
    }
    ```

    III.
    ```
    for (int i = 0;  i < 10;  i++)
    {
       i++;
       System.out.print(i);
    }
    ```

    Which of the three segments produce the same output?

    (A)   I and II only
    (B)   II and III only
    (C)   I and III only
    (D)   I, II, and III
    (E)   All three outputs are different.

21. Suppose a, b, and c are positive integers under 1000 and x satisfies the formula

    $$\frac{a}{b} = \frac{c}{x}$$

    The integer value d is obtained by truncating x to an integer. Which of the following code segments correctly calculates d?

    I.
    ```
    d = c * b / a;
    ```

    II.
    ```
    int temp = c * b;
    d = temp / a;
    ```

    III.
    ```
    int temp = b / a;
    d = c * temp;
    ```

    (A)   I only
    (B)   II only
    (C)   I and II
    (D)   II and III
    (E)   I, II, and III

22. Consider the following class:

```
public class Question
{
  private static String no = "No";
  private String answer;

  public static void flip(Question q)
  {
    < Code not shown >
  }

  < Constructors and other methods not shown >

}
```

Which of the following statements in the method `flip` will compile with no errors?

    I.   `answer = "Yes";`

    II.   `q.no = "Yes";`

    III.   `q.answer = "Yes";`

(A)   None
(B)   I only
(C)   II only
(D)   I and II only
(E)   All three

23. Which of the following statements will compile with no errors?

    I.   `ArrayList<Integer> nums = new ArrayList<Integer>();`
    II.   `List<Integer> nums = new ArrayList<Integer>();`
    III. `ArrayList<Integer> nums = new List<Integer>();`

(A)   I only
(B)   II only
(C)   I and II only
(D)   II and III only
(E)   I, II, and III

24. Consider the following method with two missing statements:

```
/** Returns the sum of all positive odd values
 *   among the first n elements of arr
 *   Precondition: 1 <= n <= arr.length
 */
public static int addPositiveOddValues(int[] arr, int n)
{
  int sum = 0;
  < statement1 >
  {
    < statement2 >
      sum += arr[i];
  }
  return sum;
}
```

Which of the following are appropriate replacements for < *statement1* > and < *statement2* > so that the method works as specified?

	< *statement1* >	< *statement2* >
(A)	`for (int i = 1; i < n; i += 2)`	`if (arr[i] > 0)`
(B)	`for (int i = 0; i < n; i++)`	`if (arr[i] > 0 && arr[i] % 2 != 0)`
(C)	`for (int i = 1; i <= n; i += 2)`	`if (arr[i] > 0)`
(D)	`for (int i = 0; i <= n; i++)`	`if (arr[i] % 2 != 0)`
(E)	None of the above	

25. Brad has derived his class from the library class `JPanel`. `JPanel`'s `paintComponent` method displays a blank picture in a panel. Brad has redefined `JPanel`'s `paintComponent` to display his own picture. Brad's class compiles with no errors, but when he runs the program, only a blank background is displayed. Which of the following hypotheses CANNOT be true in this situation?

(A) Brad misspelled "paintComponent" in his method's name.
(B) Brad specified an incorrect return type for his `paintComponent` method.
(C) Brad chose the wrong type for a parameter in his `paintComponent` method.
(D) Brad specified two parameters for his `paintComponent` method, while `JPanel`'s `paintComponent` takes only one parameter.
(E) Brad has a logic error in his `paintComponent` code which prevents it from generating the picture.

Questions 26-31 refer to the code from the GridWorld case study.

26. How does a `Bug` act if there is a `Flower` directly in front of it in the grid?

   (A)   The `Bug` is removed from the grid.
   (B)   The `Bug` remains in its current state — no action is taken.
   (C)   The `Flower` is removed, and the `Bug` moves forward, putting into its old location a new `Flower`.
   (D)   The `Bug` turns 180 degrees.
   (E)   The `Bug` turns 45 degrees to the right.

27. Consider the following method:

```
/** Returns true if location in front of bug contains
 *  a Rock; otherwise returns false.
 */
public boolean rockInFront(Bug bug)
{
  Grid<Actor> gr = bug.getGrid();
  if (gr == null)
    return false;
  Location loc = bug.getLocation();
  Location next = < expression1 >;
  if (!gr.isValid(next))
    return false;
  return < expression2 >;
}
```

Which of the following could replace < *expression1* > and < *expression2* > for the method to work as specified?

   (A)   < *expression1* >:   `loc.getAdjacentLocation(Location.AHEAD)`
         < *expression2* >:   `gr.get(next).equals(Rock)`

   (B)   < *expression1* >:   `loc.getLocationToward(Location.AHEAD)`
         < *expression2* >:   `gr.get(next).equals(Rock)`

   (C)   < *expression1* >:   `loc.getLocationToward(bug.getDirection())`
         < *expression2* >:   `gr.get(next).equals(Rock)`

   (D)   < *expression1* >:   `loc.getAdjacentLocation(Location.AHEAD)`
         < *expression2* >:   `gr.get(next) instanceof Rock`

   (E)   < *expression1* >:   `loc.getAdjacentLocation(bug.getDirection())`
         < *expression2* >:   `gr.get(next) instanceof Rock`

28. `grid` and `location` are instance fields in the `Actor` class. In `Actor`'s `putSelfInGrid` method —

```
public void putSelfInGrid(Grid<Actor> gr, Location loc)
{
  if (grid != null)
    throw new IllegalStateException(
          "This actor is already contained in a grid.");

  < missing code >

  grid = gr;
  location = loc;
}
```

which of the following could replace < *missing code* >?

    I.
```
Actor actor = gr.get(loc);
if (actor != null)
  actor.removeSelfFromGrid();
gr.put(loc, this);
```

    II.
```
gr.remove(loc);
gr.put(loc, this);
```

    III.
```
gr.put(loc, this);
```

(A)   I only
(B)   II only
(C)   I and II
(D)   II and III
(E)   I, II, and III

29. Suppose we replace the `act` method in `Actor` with an empty method (only braces and no code) and remove the `act` method from `Rock`. What effect will this have on the `BugRunner` program?

(A)   The program will work as before with no changes.
(B)   The program will work as before, except `Actor` objects, if added to the grid, won't flip over.
(C)   The `Rock` class won't compile.
(D)   It will become possible for a `Bug` to move to a location occupied by a `Rock`.
(E)   `Critter`'s `processActors` method will no longer work as specified.

30. Let us change the design of the `Critter` class, moving the call to `getActors` from `act` to `processActors` —

```
public void act()
{
  if (getGrid() == null)
    return;
  processActors();
  ...
}

public void processActors()
{
  ArrayList<Actor> actors = getActors();
  for (Actor a : actors)
  ...
}
```

How does the new design compare to the original design?

(A) The new design violates encapsulation.

(B) The new design is less flexible than the original design, because some of the subclasses of `Critter` that overrode only `getActors` and `processActors` now will have to override `act`, too.

(C) The new design is less flexible than the original design, because in the original design a `Critter`'s subclass can override only the `getActors` method, while in the new design that is not possible.

(D) The new design is less flexible than the original design, because in the original design methods of `Critter`'s subclasses can call `super.getActors`, while in the new design that won't work.

(E) The new design is as flexible as the original design and may be more economical, because it may eliminate the need to override `getActors` in some subclasses of `Critter`.

31. A `RockChameleonCritter` "acts" exactly like a `ChameleonCritter`, except it changes color to the color of a randomly chosen adjacent `Rock`. If there are no rocks among its neighbors, `RockChameleonCritter`'s color remains unchanged. Which of the following approaches to implementing the `RockChameleonCritter` class can work?

    I.   Derive `RockChameleonCritter` from `Critter` and override the `processActors` and `makeMove` methods

    II.   Derive `RockChameleonCritter` from `ChameleonCritter` and override only the `processActors` method

    III.   Derive `RockChameleonCritter` from `ChameleonCritter` and override only the `getActors` method

    (A)   I only
    (B)   II only
    (C)   I and II
    (D)   II and III
    (E)   I, II, and III

32. Which of the following best describes the return value for the method `propertyX` below?

```
/** Precondition: v.length >= 2
 */
public boolean propertyX(int[] v)
{
  boolean flag = false;

  for (int i = 0; i < v.length - 1; i++)
  {
    flag = flag || (v[i] == v[i+1]);
  }

  return flag;
}
```

    (A)   Returns `true` if the elements of `v` are sorted in ascending order, `false` otherwise
    (B)   Returns `true` if the elements of `v` are sorted in descending order, `false` otherwise
    (C)   Returns `true` if `v` has two adjacent elements with the same value, `false` otherwise
    (D)   Returns `true` if `v` has two elements with the same value, `false` otherwise
    (E)   Returns `true` if all elements in `v` have different values, `false` otherwise

Questions 33-35 involve reasoning about classes and objects used in an implementation of a library catalog system.

An object of the class `BookInfo` represents information about a particular book, and an object of the class `LibraryBook` represents copies of a book on the library's shelves:

```
public class BookInfo
{
  private String title;
  private String author;
  private int numPages;

  < Constructors not shown >

  public String toString()
  {
    return title + " by " + author;
  }

  public String getTitle() { return title; }
  public int getNumPages() { return numPages; }
}

public class LibraryBook
{
  private BookInfo info;
  private int numCopies;   // Number of copies on shelf

  < Constructors not shown >

  public int getNumCopies() { return numCopies; }
  public void setNumCopies(int num)
                             { numCopies = num; }
  public BookInfo getInfo() { return info; }

  /** If there are copies on shelf, decrements
   *  the number of copies left and returns true;
   *  otherwise returns false
   */
  public boolean checkOut() { /* code not shown */ }
}
```

33. If `catalog` is declared in a client class as

    ```
    LibraryBook[] catalog;
    ```

    which of the following statements will correctly display *title* by *author* of the third book in `catalog`?

    I.   `System.out.println(catalog[2]);`

    II.   `System.out.println(catalog[2].getInfo());`

    III. `System.out.println(catalog[2].getInfo().toString());`

    (A) I only
    (B) II only
    (C) I and II
    (D) II and III
    (E) I, II and III

34. Consider the following method from another class, a client of `LibraryBook`:

    ```
    /** Returns the total number of pages in all
      *  books in catalog that are on the shelves
      */
    public int totalPages(LibraryBook[] catalog)
    {
      int count = 0;

      for (LibraryBook bk : catalog)
      {
        < statement >
      }
      return count;
    }
    ```

    Which of the following replacements for *< statement >* completes the method as specified?

    (A) `count += bk.numCopies * bk.info.numPages;`
    (B) `count += bk.getNumCopies() * bk.getNumPages();`
    (C) `count += bk.(numCopies * info.getNumPages());`
    (D) `count += bk.getNumCopies() * bk.getInfo().getNumPages();`
    (E) None of the above

35. Which of the following code segments will correctly complete the `checkOut()` method of the `LibraryBook` class?

I.
```
if (getNumCopies() == 0)
{
  return false;
}
else
{
  setNumCopies(getNumCopies() - 1);
  return true;
}
```

II.
```
int n = getNumCopies();
if (n == 0)
{
  return false;
}
else
{
  setNumCopies(n - 1);
  return true;
}
```

III.
```
if (numCopies == 0)
{
  return false;
}
else
{
  numCopies--;
  return true;
}
```

(A) I only
(B) II only
(C) I and II
(D) I and III
(E) I, II, and III

36. The following method is intended to remove from List<Integer> list all elements whose value is less than zero:

```
public void removeNegatives(List<Integer> list)
{
  int i = 0, n = list.size();

  while (i < n)
  {
    if (list.get(i) < 0)
    {
      list.remove(i);
      n--;
    }
    i++;
  }
}
```

For which lists of Integer values does this method work as intended?

(A)   Only an empty list
(B)   All lists that do not contain negative values in consecutive positions
(C)   All lists where all the negative values occur before all the positive values
(D)   All lists where all the positive values occur before all the negative values
(E)   All lists

37. Consider the following method:

```
/** Returns the location of the target value
 *   in the array a, or -1 if not found
 *   Precondition: a[0] ... a[a.length - 1] are
 *                 sorted in ascending order
 */
public static int search(int[] a, int target)
{
  int first = 0;
  int middle;
  int last = a.length - 1;

  while (first <= last)
  {
    middle = (first + last) / 2;
    if (target == a[middle])
      return middle;
    else if (target < a[middle])
      last = middle;
    else
      first = middle;
  }
  return -1;
}
```

This method fails to work as expected under certain conditions. If the array has five elements with values 3 4 35 42 51, which of the following values of `target` would make this method fail?

(A)   3
(B)   4
(C)   35
(D)   42
(E)   51

Questions 38-40 refer to the following class `SortX`:

```
public class SortX
{
  public static void sort(String[] items)
  {
    int n = items.length;
    while (n > 1)
    {
      sortHelper(items, n - 1);
      n--;
    }
  }

  private static void sortHelper(String[] items, int last)
  {
    int m = last;
    for (int k = 0; k < last; k++)
    {
      if (items[k].compareTo(items[m]) > 0)
        m = k;
    }
    String temp = items[m];
    items[m] = items[last];
    items[last] = temp;
  }
}
```

38. The sorting algorithm implemented in the `sort` method can be best described as:

    (A)   Selection Sort
    (B)   Insertion Sort
    (C)   Binary Sort
    (D)   Mergesort
    (E)   Incorrect implementation of a sorting algorithm

39. Suppose `names` is an array of `String` objects:

    ```
    String[] names =
            {"Dan", "Alice", "Claire", "Evan", "Boris"};
    ```

    If `SortX.sort(names)` is running, what is the order of the values in `names` after two complete iterations through the `while` loop in the `sort` method?

    (A)   `"Boris", "Alice", "Claire", "Dan", "Evan"`
    (B)   `"Alice", "Claire", "Boris", "Dan", "Evan"`
    (C)   `"Alice", "Boris", "Claire", "Evan", "Dan"`
    (D)   `"Alice", "Claire", "Dan", "Evan", "Boris"`
    (E)   None of the above

40. If `items` contains five values and `SortX.sort(items)` is called, how many times, total, will `items[k].compareTo(items[m])` be called in the `sortHelper` method?

   (A)   5
   (B)   10
   (C)   15
   (D)   25
   (E)   Depends on the values in `items`

Practice Exam #2

SECTION II

Time — 1 hour and 45 minutes
Number of questions — 4
Percent of total grade — 50

1. Consider the class `APExam` that represents an AP exam taken by a student:

```
public class APExam
{
  /** Exam subject name */
  private String subject;

  /** Exam grade: from 1 to 5 */
  private int grade;

  public APExam(String subj, int gr)
  {
    subject = subj;
    grade = gr;
  }

  public String getSubject() { return subject; }
  public int getGrade() { return grade; }
}
```

The class `APStudent` represents a student's participation in the AP program. An `APStudent` object holds the name of the student and a list of all the AP exams taken by that student. The list of exams is represented by an `ArrayList<APExam>`. The `APStudent` class should have a constructor that takes a student name as a parameter and initializes the list of exams to an empty list. The class provides accessor methods for the name and the list of exams, a method that adds an AP exam to the list, and a method that returns the student's average grade on all exams.

(a) Write a class definition for `APStudent`, putting only "..." in the bodies of its constructor and methods. In writing this definition you must:

   • choose appropriate names for methods, data fields, and parameters;

   • provide the functionality specified above;

   • make data representation consistent with the above specification;

   • make design decisions that are consistent with information-hiding principles.

   DO NOT write the implementations of the constructors or the methods of the `APStudent` class.

(b)   The College Board offers an AP Scholar award to students who earned grades of 3 or higher on three or more AP Exams. The College Board also grants an AP Scholar with Honor award to students with grades of 3 or higher on four or more exams and an average AP Exam grade of at least 3.25 on all exams taken. Students may have low grades on some AP exams and still meet the requirements for either award. This is summarized in the table below:

	AP Scholar	AP Scholar with Honor
Minimum grade that counts	3	3
Required number of exams not below the minimum grade	3	4
Average grade on <u>all</u> AP exams taken	no effect	3.25
Number of exams below min grade	no effect	no effect

Write a complete definition of a class `APScholar` as a subclass of `APStudent`. `APScholar` has the same features as `APStudent`. It should have one constructor that takes one parameter, student's name. The `APScholar` class also has a method `getAwardLevel` that returns the level of award earned by this student: 0 for no award, 1 for the AP Scholar award, and 2 for the AP Scholar with Honor award. You may assume that all the methods of the `APStudent` class that you have designed in Part (a) work as specified.

(c)   Suppose the class `APStats` keeps track of the AP exam statistics. Write a method `getStats` of the `APStats` class that takes a non-empty list of `APScholar` objects and calculates the percentages of students with no award, AP Scholars, and AP Scholars with Honor. For example, if a list holds 10 AP students of whom 6 received no award, 3 are AP Scholars, and 1 is an AP Scholar with Honor, then `getStats` returns an array with values 60.0, 30.0, and 10.0. In writing `getStats`, assume that the classes from Part (a) and Part (b) work as specified.

Complete the method `getStats` below.

```
/** Returns an array percents of length 3;
 *   percents[0], percents[1], and percents[2]
 *   are set to percentages of all students from list with
 *   no award, AP Scholars, and AP Scholars with Honor,
 *   respectively
 *   Precondition: list.size() > 0
 public static double[] getStats(ArrayList<APScholar> list)
```

2. Millions of web pages on the Internet are formatted in HTML, the HyperText Markup Language. HTML text contains embedded tags — formatting instructions enclosed in angle brackets < and >. The formatting tags often come in pairs where the opening tag indicates the beginning of some formatting (for example, italics, bold, underline) and the closing tag indicates the end of the formatting. The closing tag contains the same keyword or instruction as the opening tag, but preceded by a slash (the "/" character). The following example shows a line of HTML text and illustrates the way it might be displayed on the screen:

```
The <i>quick</i> <b>brown</b> fox <b>jumps
<u>over</b> the lazy</u> dog
```

> The *quick* **brown** fox **jumps** <u>**over**</u> the lazy dog

Processing HTML text may involve such tasks as removing HTML tags from the text or verifying that opening and closing tags come in matching pairs.

In this question we deal with text represented as a `String` object. We assume that this HTML text contains only complete tags: all "<" and ">" characters properly delimit tags and do not otherwise occur inside tags or anywhere else in the text. Segments of text formatted with different tags may overlap. In the above example, the word "**<u>over</u>**" falls into the overlapping bold and underlined segments. You will write a few methods of the `HTMLProcessor` class for processing HTML text.

(a) Write the `findFirstTag` method of the `HTMLProcessor` class as started below. The method finds and returns the first tag in a given HTML text string. The method returns `null` if no tags were found.

```
/** Returns the first HTML tag found in text
 * (including the < and > brackets) or null if no tags
 *   are found
 * Precondition: text is a segment of HTML text which may
 *                contain complete HTML tags; a tag is any
 *                substring starting with < and ending with
 *                the closest > character
public static String findFirstTag(String text)
```

(b) Write a method `remove` for the `HTMLProcessor` class, as started below. The method finds the first occurrence of a given substring in a given `String text` and returns `text` with that substring removed. If the given substring is not found, the method returns `text` unchanged.

```
/** If str is found in text, its first occurrence is
 *   removed from text and the new text is returned;
 *   otherwise the original text is returned
 * Precondition: str is a non-empty string
public static String remove(String text, String str)
```

(c) Write a method `removeAllTags` for the `HTMLProcessor` class. The method deals only with a subset of HTML tags: it assumes that a given text contains only complete simple tags, such as `<u>` and `</u>` or `<cite>` and `</cite>`, where a closing tag differs from the corresponding opening tag only by the `"/"` character after `"<"`. The closing tag must come after the opening tag. The method returns the text with all tags removed (or the original text if no tags were found). However, the method should return the string `"Error"` if the tags in `text` do not match (no closing tag found after an opening tag). You can assume that the methods `remove` and `findFirstTag` work as specified, regardless of what you wrote in Parts (a) and (b).

Complete method `removeAllTags` below.

```
/** If all HTML tags in text come in matching opening-
 *   closing pairs, then returns a new text string with
 *   all the tags removed from text; returns the original
 *   string if text has no tags; returns "Error" if the
 *   tags do not match
 *   Precondition: text is a segment of HTML text which may
 *                 contain complete HTML tags
public static String removeAllTags(String text)
```

3. This question involves reasoning about the code from the GridWorld case study. A copy of the code is provided as part of this exam.

In Part (a) you will design a class Dahlia, which is a subclass of Flower. In Parts (b) and (c) you will implement Dahlia's constructors and act method. A Dahlia at first acts like a regular Flower, but at some point, when mature, it produces seeds for new Dahlias and dies. Dahlias can have different colors. A Dahlia of a particular color produces seeds that later "grow" into Dahlias of the same color. Your implementation of the Dahlia class must be such that any later change in the details of implementation of the Flower class (such as the default color or the formula for darkening the color) automatically apply to Dahlia, without changes to its source code.

(a) Design the class Dahlia as a subclass of Flower. Define the necessary instance fields and write headers for the constructors and method(s) but DO NOT implement them in this part of the question. A Dahlia keeps track of its age (the number of times the act method has been called). It also saves its initial color when constructed in order to be able to pass that color on to its seeds. Provide the following features:

- Instance fields to hold Dahlia's age and initial color.

- Two constructors, similar to Flower's constructors (to be implemented in Part (b)).

- The act method (to be implemented in Part (c)).

- Make your design consistent with the principles of encapsulation and code reuse.

Write a sketch of the class Dahlia, including the fields and the header lines for the constructors and method(s). You DO NOT need to write any import statements.

(b) Write two constructors for the Dahlia class. A Dahlia constructed with a "no-args" constructor (the constructor that takes no parameters) should get the same color as Flower's default color. (Pretend you do not know how that color is defined in Flower.) The constructor that takes one parameter of the type Color should set the initial color of this Dahlia to the given color. Both Dahlia constructors should save the initial color in an instance field to be used later for generating seeds.

(c) Write the act method of the Dahlia class. For the first three "weeks" (first three calls to act) a Dahlia acts like a regular Flower. On the fourth call, the Dahlia produces three seeds and attempts to place each of them into the grid. Then it dies. A Dahlia attempts to place each seed (a DahliaSeed object) into a randomly chosen adjacent location. If the location is occupied by any other actor (including a previously placed seed), the attempt is wasted, and the seed is not placed. Assume that the class DahliaSeed is provided and that it has one constructor, which takes a color as a parameter. The Dahlia should pass its initial color to that constructor.

4. Bill is planning a U.S. tour for the Bolshoi Ballet. He has made a list of cities where the Bolshoi will perform. His plan is to always proceed to the nearest city that has not been visited yet. The tour will begin in the "remotest" city; Bill defines the "remotest" city as the one for which the sum of distances to all other cities is the largest.

Bill uses a distance chart to plan the trip. It is a square table with the cities listed horizontally and vertically in the same order; the intersection of the *i*-th row and *j*-th column shows the distance between the *i*-th and *j*-th cities. The table has zero values on the diagonal and is symmetrical with respect to the diagonal. For example:

	Atlanta	Boston	Cleveland	Dallas	Washington
Atlanta	0	936	550	719	540
Boston	936	0	554	1547	396
Cleveland	550	554	0	1018	309
Dallas	719	1547	1018	0	1181
Washington	540	396	309	1181	0

In this example, Dallas is the remotest city, because for Dallas the sum of the distances to the other cities — 4465 miles — is greater than for any other city. So the tour would begin in Dallas and then proceed to Atlanta, then Washington, then Cleveland, then Boston.

The distance chart is represented by the class `DistanceChart`, partially defined below:

```
public class DistanceChart
{
  /** The list of cities in the chart */
  private List<String> cityNames;

  /** The table of distances between cities */
  private int[][] distances;

  /** Returns the index of the city for which the sum of
   *   the distances to all other cities is the largest;
   *   (if there is more than one candidate, returns
   *   any one of them)
   *   Precondition: cityNames is not empty;
   *                 distances[i][j] holds the distance
   *                 between the i-th and the j-th cities
   */
  public int findRemotestCity()
  {  /* to be implemented in part (a) */  }

  /** Returns the index of the city from cityNames to be
   *   visited next, that is, the city nearest to the i-th
   *   city among those cities that have not been visited yet
   *   @param i  the index of a given city, already visited
   *   @param visited  indicates which cities have been
   *                 visited: visited[j] == true if the
   *                 j-th city has been visited
   *   Precondition:  0 <= i < cityNames.size();
   *                 visited[i] == true
   *   Postcondition: visited remains unchanged
   */
  public int findNearestCity(int i, boolean[] visited)
  {  /* to be implemented in part (b) */  }

  /** Returns the itinerary (an ArrayList of city names)
   *   starting from the remotest city and going through
   *   all the cities in cityNames, always proceeding to the
   *   nearest city that has not been visited yet
   *   Precondition: cityNames is not empty;
   *                 distances[i][j] holds the distance
   *                 between the i-th and the j-th cities
   */
  public List<String> makeItinerary()
  {  /* to be implemented in part (c) */  }
}
```

(a) Write the method `findRemotestCity` as started below. The method returns the index of the city in `cityNames` that has the largest sum of distances to all other cities. If the same largest sum is found for more than one city, `findRemotestCity` returns the index of any one of them.

```
/** Returns the index of the city for which the sum of
 *   the distances to all other cities is the largest;
 *   (if there is more than one candidate, returns
 *   any one of them)
 *   Precondition: cityNames is not empty;
 *                 distances[i][j] holds the distance
 *                 between the i-th and the j-th cities
 */
public int findRemotestCity()
```

(b) Write the method `findNearestCity`. This method finds the index of the city that is nearest to th *i*-th city and has not been visited yet. The `boolean` array `visited`, passed to `findNearestCity` as a parameter, indicates which cities have already been visited: `visited[j] == true` indicates that the *j*-th city has been visited. It is assumed that the *i*-th city has been visited, so when `findNearestCity(i, visited)` is called, the value of `visited[i]` is true.

```
/** Returns the index of the city from cityNames to be
 *   visited next, that is, the city nearest to the i-th
 *   city among those cities that have not been visited yet
 *   @param i  the index of a given city, already visited
 *   @param visited  indicates which cities have been
 *                 visited: visited[j] == true if the
 *                 j-th city has been visited
 *   Precondition:  0 <= i < cityNames.size();
 *                  visited[i] == true
 *   Postcondition: visited remains unchanged
 */
public int findNearestCity(int i, boolean[] visited)
```

(c) Write the method `makeItinerary` that generates and returns a list of cities, starting with the remotest one and visiting each city in the `cityNames` list once. The itinerary proceeds from a city to the nearest one that has not been visited yet. Assume that the `findRemotestCity` and `findNearestCity` work as specified, regardless of what you wrote in Parts (a) and (b).

```
/** Returns the itinerary (an ArrayList of city names)
 *   starting from the remotest city and going through
 *   all the cities in cityNames, always proceeding to the
 *   nearest city that has not been visited yet
 *   Precondition: cityNames is not empty;
 *                 distances[i][j] holds the distance
 *                 between the i-th and the j-th cities
 */
public List<String> makeItinerary()
```

Practice Exam #3

SECTION I

Time — 1 hour and 15 minutes
Number of questions — 40
Percent of total grade — 50

1. Assuming that x and y are int variables, the expression

    ```
    !(x > y && y <= 0)
    ```

    is equivalent to which of the following?

    (A)   `!(x <= y) || (y > 0)`
    (B)   `x > y && y <= 0`
    (C)   `x <= y || y > 0`
    (D)   `x > y || y < 0`
    (E)   `x <= y && y <= 0`

2. Which of the following describes the return value of the following method?

    ```
    /** Precondition: amt represents a positive value in dollars
     *               and cents (for example, 1.15 represents
     *               one dollar and fifteen cents)
     */
    private int process(double amt)
    {
      return (int)(amt * 100 + 0.5) % 100;
    }
    ```

    (A)   the cent portion in amt
    (B)   the number of whole dollars in amt
    (C)   amt converted into cents
    (D)   amt rounded to the nearest integer
    (E)   amt truncated to the nearest integer

3.   What is the output of the following code segment?

```
int sum = 0, d = -1;

for (int count = 10; count > 0; count--)
{
  sum += d;
  if (d > 0)
  {
    d++;
  }
  else
  {
    d--;
  }
  d = -d;
}

System.out.println(sum);
```

(A)   0
(B)   5
(C)   -5
(D)   10
(E)   -10

4.   The following code segment is supposed to calculate and display the sum $1 + 2 + ... + 20$:

```
int count = 0, sum = 0;
while (count < 20)
{
  sum += count;
}
System.out.println(sum);
```

Which statement best describes the result:

(A)   The total displayed will be correct.
(B)   The total displayed will be 20 too small.
(C)   The output will be the number 0.
(D)   The output will be the number 20.
(E)   There will be no output because the program goes into an infinite loop.

5.   What is the result when the following code segment is compiled/executed?

```
Integer n = new Integer(Integer.MIN_VALUE); // Line 1
Double x = new Double(n.intValue());        // Line 2
System.out.print(x);
```

(A)   0 is displayed
(B)   -2147483648 is displayed
(C)   -2147483648.0 is displayed
(D)   Syntax error on Line 1
(E)   Syntax error on Line 2

6.   Which of the following Boolean expressions properly implement a comparison for equality of two String objects str1 and str2 and evaluate to true if and only if str1 and str2 hold the same values?

   I.   str1 == str2

   II. str1.equals(str2)

   III. str1.compareTo(str2) == 0

(A)   I only
(B)   II only
(C)   I and II
(D)   II and III
(E)   I, II, and III

7.   Consider the following class:

```
public class Sphere
{
  public static final double pi = 3.14159;

  public static double volume(int r)
  {
    return 4 / 3 * pi * Math.pow(r, 3);
  }
}
```

Which of the following statements about this code is true?

(A)   The class will not compile because no constructors are defined.
(B)   The class will not compile because pi cannot be declared public.
(C)   The class will not compile because the volume method is declared static.
(D)   Math.pow(r, 3) cannot be used because r is an int.
(E)   The class compiles with no errors but the volume method returns a smaller value than the expected $\frac{4}{3}\pi r^3$.

8. Consider the following code segment:

```
int n = IO.readInt();    // read an int value
n = Math.abs(n);

while (n >= 2)
{
   n = n/2 - 1;
}
System.out.println(n);
```

Which of the following is the list of all possible outputs?

(A) 0
(B) -1, 0
(C) 0, 1
(D) -1, 1
(E) -1, 0, 1

9.   Consider the following class:

```
public class Rectangle
{
  private int width, height;

  public Rectangle(int w, int h) { width = w; height = h; }
  public int getArea() { return width * height; }

  < Other methods not shown >
}
```

Suppose this class also overrides `Object`'s `equals` method in such a way that `Rectangle` objects with the same area are deemed equal. Which of the following `equals` methods will accomplish this?

(A)
```
public int equals(int area)
{
  return getArea() - area;
}
```

(B)
```
public boolean equals(int area)
{
  return getArea() == area;
}
```

(C)
```
public boolean equals(Rectangle other)
{
  return getArea() == other.getArea();
}
```

(D)
```
public boolean equals(Object other)
{
  return this.getArea() == other.getArea();
}
```

(E)
```
public boolean equals(Object other)
{
  return getArea() == ((Rectangle)other).getArea();
}
```

10. Consider the following method:

```
// Precondition: a != null; a.length > 0
private static void doIt(double[] a)
{
  double temp;

  for (int k = 0; k < a.length / 2; k++)
  {
    temp = a[k];
    a[k] = a[a.length - 1 - k];
    a[a.length - 1 - k] = temp;
  }
}
```

Which of the following best describes the task performed by this method?

(A)   Sorts an array in ascending order
(B)   Sorts an array in descending order
(C)   Swaps the first and last elements of an array
(D)   Reverses the order of elements in an array
(E)   None of the above tasks is implemented correctly.

11. Consider the following classes:

```
public class A
{
  public A() { methodOne(); }

  public void methodOne() { System.out.print("A"); }
}

public class B extends A
{
  public B() { System.out.print("*"); }

  public void methodOne() { System.out.print("B"); }
}
```

What is the output when the following code statement is executed?

```
A obj = new B();
```

(A)   *
(B)   *A
(C)   *B
(D)   A*
(E)   B*

12. Consider the following method:

```
public String filter(String str, String pattern)
{
  int pos = str.indexOf(pattern);
  if (pos == -1)
    return str;
  else
    return filter(str.substring(0, pos) +
        str.substring(pos + pattern.length()), pattern);
}
```

What is the output of

```
System.out.println(filter("papaya", "pa"));
```

(A)   p
(B)   pa
(C)   ya
(D)   aya
(E)   paya

13. Consider the following method, intended to use Binary Search to find the location of `target` within an `ArrayList a`:

```
public int findLocation(ArrayList<String> a, String target)
{
  int first = 0, last = a.size() - 1;
  while (first <= last)
  {
    int middle = (first + last) / 2;
    int compResult = target.compareTo(a.get(middle));
    if (compResult == 0)
      return middle;
    if (compResult < 0)
      last = middle - 1;
    else
      first = middle + 1;
  }
  return -1;
}
```

This method may fail if it is applied to a list that is not sorted. For which of the following lists will `findLocation(a, "C")` return -1?

(A)   "A", "B", "C", "D", "E", "F", "G"
(B)   "G", "F", "E", "D", "C", "B", "A"
(C)   "A", "C", "D", "G", "E", "B", "F"
(D)   "B", "A", "D", "C", "F", "E", "G"
(E)   "D", "F", "B", "A", "G", "C", "E"

Questions 14-15 refer to the following `sortX` method:

```
public void sortX(int[] a)
{
  for (int i = 1; i < a.length; i++)  // Line 1
  {
    int current = a[i];                 // Line 2
    int j = 0;                          // Line 3

    while (a[j] < current)              // Line 4
    {
       j++;                             // Line 5
    }

    for (int k = i; k > j; k--)         // Line 6
    {
       a[k] = a[k-1];                   // Line 7
    }

    a[j] = current;                     // Line 8
  }
}
```

14. The sorting algorithm implemented in the `sortX` method can be best described as:

   (A)   Selection Sort
   (B)   Insertion Sort
   (C)   Quicksort
   (D)   Mergesort
   (E)   Incorrect implementation of a sorting algorithm

15. Given

```
int[] a = {24, 16, 68, 56, 32};
```

   what will be the result after the statement on Line 8 in `sortX` completes for the second time?

   (A)   The values in a are 16, 24, 68, 56, 32
   (B)   The values in a are 16, 24, 32, 56, 68
   (C)   The values in a are 24, 16, 32, 56, 68
   (D)   The code has failed with an `ArrayIndexOutOfBoundsException` on Line 4
   (E)   The code has failed with an `ArrayIndexOutOfBoundsException` on Line 8

16. The class `PlayList` provides methods that allow you to represent and manipulate a list of tunes, but you are not concerned with how these operations work or how the list is stored in memory. You only know how to initialize and use `PlayList` objects and have no direct access to the implementation of the `PlayList` class or its private data fields. This is an example of:

    (A)   encapsulation
    (B)   overriding
    (C)   inheritance
    (D)   polymorphism
    (E)   method overloading

17. Which of the following statements about constructors is NOT true?

    (A)   All constructors must have the same name as the class they are in.
    (B)   Constructors' return type must be declared `void`.
    (C)   A class may have a constructor that takes no parameters.
    (D)   A constructor is invoked when a program creates an object with the `new` operator.
    (E)   A constructor of a subclass can call a constructor of its superclass using the Java reserved word `super`.

18. Consider the following method:

```
public void splat(String s)
{
  if (s.length() < 8)
    splat(s + s);
  System.out.println(s);
}
```

What is displayed when `splat("**")` is called?

    (A)   `**`

    (B)   `****`

    (C)   `********`

    (D)   `********`
                `**`

    (E)   `********`
                `****`
                `**`

Questions 19 and 20 refer to the following class:

```
public class Sample
{
  private double[][] amps;

  public Sample(int n) { < missing statements > }
  public double get(int j, int k) { return amps[j][k]; }
}
```

19. Which of the following code segments can replace < *missing statements* > in `Sample`'s constructor so that it initializes `amps` to hold a table of values with n rows and n columns and fills them with random values $0.0 \leq$ `amps[i][j]` < 1.0?

       I.
```
amps = new double[n][n];
```

       II.
```
amps = new double[n][n];
for (int j = 0; j < n; j++)
{
  for (int k = 0; k < n; k++)
  {
    amps[j][k] = Math.random();
  }
}
```

       III.
```
amps = new double[n][n];
for (int j = 0; j < n; j++)
{
  for (int k = j; k < n; k++)
  {
    amps[j][k] = Math.random();
    amps[k][j] = Math.random();
  }
}
```

    (A) I only
    (B) II only
    (C) I and II only
    (D) II and III only
    (E) I, II, and III

20. Given

```
int size = 100;
Sample s = new Sample(size);
```

which of the following statements assigns to x the value in the last row and the first column of amps in s?

(A)   `double x = s.amps[amps.length - 1][0];`
(B)   `double x = s.get(amps.length - 1, 0);`
(C)   `double x = s.get[s.length - 1, 0];`
(D)   `double x = s.get(size - 1, 0);`
(E)   `double x = s[99][0];`

21. Suppose `ArrayList<Integer> numbers` and `ArrayList<String> names` are created as follows:

```
ArrayList<Integer> numbers = new ArrayList<Integer>();
Integer x = new Integer(1);
numbers.add(x);
numbers.add(x);

ArrayList<String> names = new ArrayList<String>();
names.add(0, "Anya");
names.add(0, "Ben");
names.add(0, "Cathy");
```

What is the result of the following code segment?

```
for (Integer i : numbers)
{
  names.remove(i.intValue());
}
for (String name : names)
{
  System.out.print(name + " ");
}
```

(A)   `Cathy`
(B)   `Cathy Anya`
(C)   `Anya Cathy`
(D)   `IndexOutOfBoundsException`
(E)   `NoSuchElementException`

22. Consider the following class definitions:

```
public class Airplane
{
  private int fuel;

  public Airplane() { fuel = 0; }
  public Airplane(int g) { fuel = g; }

  public void addFuel() { fuel++; }
  public String toString() { return fuel + " "; }
}

public class Jet extends Airplane
{
  public Jet(int g) { super(2*g); }
}
```

What is the result when the following code is compiled and run?

```
Airplane plane = new Airplane(4);
Airplane jet = new Jet(4);

System.out.print(plane);
plane.addFuel();
System.out.print(plane);

System.out.print(jet);
jet.addFuel();
System.out.print(jet);
```

(A)   A syntax error, "undefined addFuel," is reported for the `jet.addFuel();` statement.
(B)   A run-time error, `ClassCastException`, occurs when `jet.addFuel()` is attempted.
(C)   The code compiles and runs with no errors; the output is 4 5 5 6
(D)   The code compiles and runs with no errors; the output is 4 5 8 9
(E)   The code compiles and runs with no errors; the output is 8 9 9 10

23. When does a class have to be declared `abstract`?

(A)   When it has no constructors
(B)   When it has no public methods
(C)   When the class has no public or private instance variables
(D)   When you need to derive another class from this class
(E)   When one or more methods in the class are declared abstract

24. Which of the situations below would allow the following statement to compile with no errors?

```
Animal a = new Mammal("Elephant");
```

(A)   `Mammal` is a class with a constructor that takes one parameter of the `String` type, and `Animal` is its subclass.

(B)   `Mammal` is a class with a constructor that takes one parameter of the `String` type, `Animal` is an interface, and `Mammal` implements `Animal`.

(C)   `Animal` is a class with a constructor that takes one parameter of the `String` type, `Mammal` is its subclass that has only the default constructor.

(D)   `Animal` has a public static data field `String Mammal`.

(E)   None of the above

25. Consider the following interface `TV` and class `MyTV`:

```
public interface TV
{
    void tuneTo(String channel);
}

public class MyTV implements TV
{
    private ArrayList<String> myFavoriteChannels;

    public MyTV(ArrayList<String> channels)
    { /* implementation not shown */ }

    public void tuneTo(int k)
    { /* implementation not shown */ }

    public void tuneTo(int k, String name)
    { /* implementation not shown */ }
}
```

One of them has one or more errors and won't compile properly. Which of the following best describes the compiler errors reported for the code that is shown?

(A)   In the `TV` interface, the `tuneTo` declaration is missing the keyword `public`

(B)   `MyTV` should be declared abstract; it does not define `tuneTo(String)`

(C)   `tuneTo` is defined more than once in `MyTV`

(D)   Cannot convert `int` to `String` in the `tuneTo` method in `MyTV`

(E)   Two errors: (1) `tuneTo` is defined more than once and (2) cannot convert `int` to `String` in the `tuneTo(int)` method in `MyTV`

Questions 26-31 **refer to the code from the GridWorld case study.**

26. Which of the following code segments will compile with no errors?

    I.
    ```
    BoxBug bb = new BoxBug();
    if (!bb.canMove())
    {
      bb.turn();
    }
    ```

    II.
    ```
    BoxBug bb = new BoxBug(5);
    bb.setColor(Color.BLUE);
    ```

    III.
    ```
    BoxBug bb = new BoxBug(Color.BLUE);
    bb.move();
    ```

    (A) I only
    (B) II only
    (C) I and II
    (D) II and III
    (E) I, II, and III

27. Assuming that `loc1` and `loc2` are `Location` objects that represent valid locations in a grid, which of the following conditions verifies that `loc2` lies to the north of `loc1`?

    (A) `Grid.getDirection(loc1, loc2).equals(Location.NORTH)`
    (B) `loc1.getAdjacentLocation(Location.NORTH)).equals(loc2)`
    (C) `loc1.getDirectionToward(loc2) == Location.NORTH`
    (D) `loc1.getDirectionToward(loc2).equals(Location.NORTH)`
    (E) `loc1.getDirection(loc2).equals(new Location(Location.NORTH, 0))`

28. Suppose we want to create a variation of `Bug` that acts like a regular `Bug` but turns 45 degrees randomly left or right after each move. Which of the following is the most economical approach, in terms of the amount of code to be written?

    (A) Extend `Actor` and override the `act` method
    (B) Extend `Bug` and override the `move` method
    (C) Extend `Bug` and override the `turn` method
    (D) Extend `Bug` and override both `move` and `turn` methods
    (E) Extend `Bug` and override both `move` and `canMove` methods

29. The diagram below shows the interactions between some of the GridWorld classes and interfaces.

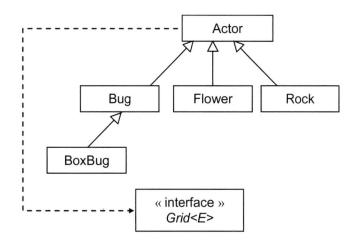

An ⟶▷ arrow from *A* to *B* indicates that *A* extends *B*. An ⇢ arrow from *A* to *B* indicates that *A* uses *B*; that is, *A* refers directly to variables of the type *B*. Two "uses" arrows can be added to the diagram to make it more accurate. Which ones?

(A) Bug uses Grid and Bug uses Flower
(B) Bug uses Flower and Bug uses Rock
(C) Bug uses Grid and Flower uses Grid
(D) Bug uses Grid and BoxBug uses Grid
(E) Bug uses Grid and BoxBug uses Flower

30. Given

```
Rock rock = new Rock();
```

and assuming that all the necessary import statements are present, which of the following statements will cause a syntax error?

(A) rock.moveTo(null);
(B) rock.setDirection(0);
(C) rock.setColor(Color.GRAY);
(D) rock.setGrid(null);
(E) Grid<Actor> gr = rock.getGrid();

31. Which of Critter's methods calls selectMoveLocation?

(A) act
(B) processActors
(C) makeMove
(D) moveTo
(E) None of the above

Questions 32-35 use the classes `Track` and `CD`:

```
public class Track
{
  private String name;
  private int duration;

  public Track(String nm, int dur)
  { name = nm; duration = dur; }

  public String getName() { return name; }
  public int getDuration() { return duration; }
}

public class CD
{
  private String title;
  private String band;
  private int numTracks;
  private ArrayList<Track> tracks;

  public CD(String t, int n)
  { title = t; numTracks = n; }

  /** Initializes all the instance variables and copies
   *   all the data from songs into tracks
   */
  public CD(String t, String b, int n, ArrayList<Track> songs)
  {
    title = t; band = b; numTracks = n;

    < missing code >
  }

  public int totalPlayTime()
  { /* implementation not shown */ }

  /** Returns duration of the k-th track
   *   Precondition:  1 <= k <= numTracks
   */
  public int getDuration(int k)
  { /* implementation not shown */

  < Other methods not shown >
}
```

32. Which one of the following declarations is INVALID?

   (A)   `Track tune = new Track();`
   (B)   `Track tune = new Track("Help", 305);`
   (C)   `Track[] playList = new Track[20];`
   (D)   `CD top = new CD("throwing copper", 13);`
   (E)   `CD[][] rack = new CD[3][40];`

33. Which of the following expressions correctly refers to the duration of the *k*-th track inside CD's `totalPlayTime` method?

    (A)   `getDuration(k);`
    (B)   `tracks[k-1].duration;`
    (C)   `tracks.getDuration(k);`
    (D)   `tracks.get(k-1).duration;`
    (E)   `getDuration(tracks[k-1]);`

34. What is the result of the following code?

```
Track t = new Track("lightning crashes", 200);
ArrayList<Track> tracks = new ArrayList<Track>();  // Line **
for (int count = 1; count <= 13; count++)
{
   tracks.add(t);
}
CD live = new CD("throwing copper", "live", 13, tracks);
System.out.println(live.totalPlayTime());
```

    (A)   Syntax error on Line **
    (B)   Run-time `IndexOutOfBoundsException`
    (C)   0 is displayed
    (D)   200 is displayed
    (E)   2600 is displayed

35. Which of the following can replace missing code in the CD class's constructor?

    I.
```
for (Track t : songs)
{
   tracks.add(t);
}
```

    II.
```
tracks = new ArrayList<Track>();
for (Track t : songs)
{
   tracks.add(t);
}
```

    III.
```
tracks = new ArrayList<Track>();
for (int i = 0; i < songs.size(); i++)
{
   tracks.set(i, songs.get(i));
}
```

    (A)   I only
    (B)   II only
    (C)   I or II only
    (D)   II or III only
    (E)   I, II, or III

36. Consider the following code segment:

```
if (!somethingIsFalse())
  return false;
else
  return true;
```

Which of the following replacements for this code will produce the same result?

(A)   `return true;`
(B)   `return false;`
(C)   `return !somethingIsFalse();`
(D)   `return somethingIsFalse();`
(E)   none of the above

37. A programmer wants to create a swap method that swaps two integer values. Which of the following three ways of representing the values and corresponding methods successfully swap the values?

I.
```
// a and b are Integer objects that represent the values
// to be swapped
public static void swap(Integer a, Integer b)
{
   Integer temp = a; a = b; b = temp;
}
```

II.
```
// a[0] and a[1] contain the values to be swapped
public static void swap(int[] a)
{
   int temp = a[0]; a[0] = a[1]; a[1] = temp;
}
```

III.
```
// a[0] and b[0] contain the values to be swapped
public static void swap(int[] a, int[] b)
{
   int temp = a[0]; a[0] = b[0]; b[0] = temp;
}
```

(A)   I only
(B)   II only
(C)   I and II
(D)   II and III
(E)   I, II, and III

38. Suppose an interface `Solid` specifies the `getVolume()` method. Two classes, `Cube` and `Pyramid`, implement `Solid`. Which Java feature makes it possible for the following code segment to print the correct values for the volume of a pyramid and a cube?

```
Solid[] solids = new Solid[2];
solids[0] = new Cube(100);
solids[1] = new Pyramid(150, 100);
System.out.println("Cube: " + solids[0].getVolume());
System.out.println("Pyramid: " + solids[1].getVolume());
```

(A) abstraction
(B) encapsulation
(C) polymorphism
(D) platform-independence
(E) method overloading

39. Consider the following code segment:

```
List<String> list = new ArrayList<String>();
list.add("One");
list.add("Two");
String[] msg = new String[2];
list.add(msg[0]);
< another statement >
```

Which of the following choices for < *another statement* > will cause a `NullPointerException`?

(A) `msg[0] = "Three";`
(B) `msg[0] = list.get(list.size());`
(C) `if (!"Three".equals(list.get(2))) msg[0] = "Three";`
(D) `list.add(2, msg[0]);`
(E) `msg[1] = msg[0].substring(0, 2);`

40. A programmer is trying to choose between an `ArrayList` and a standard one-dimensional array for representing data. Which of the following is NOT a correct statement?

   (A) Both an `ArrayList` and a standard array allow direct access to the *k*-th element.

   (B) A standard array may hold elements of a primitive data type, such as `int` or `double`; an `ArrayList` may only hold objects.

   (C) An `ArrayList` may hold objects of different types, such as `Integer` and `Double`, simultaneously.

   (D) An `ArrayList` has a convenient method for inserting a value at a specified location in the middle.

   (E) Both an `ArrayList` and a standard array are expanded automatically when the number of values stored exceeds their size.

Practice Exam #3

SECTION II

Time — 1 hour and 45 minutes
Number of questions — 4
Percent of total grade — 50

1. The diagram below shows a hierarchy of classes used in a telephone billing system:

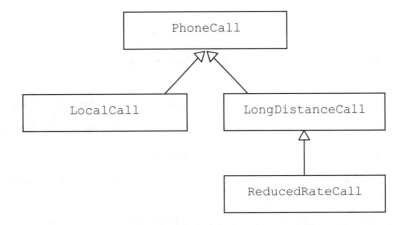

PhoneCall is an abstract class. A PhoneCall object holds information about the call duration (in minutes) and the methods necessary to calculate the total cost of the call, based on its duration and rate. PhoneCall's constructor assigns a unique sequential number to the call.

The PhoneCall class does not deal directly with per-minute rates; instead it relies on an abstract method getRate that is defined in concrete classes lower in the hierarchy. The rate for a local call is defined in a parameter to LocalCall's constructor. The rate for a long distance call is for now set to a constant, 6.0. The rate for a reduced-rate call is one half of the rate for a regular long distance call.

Your task is to write the PhoneCall, LongDistanceCall and ReducedRateCall classes. In writing these classes you must avoid duplication of code: the classes should, whenever possible, reuse the code from the classes higher in the hierarchy.

Your classes should support text output. For example, the following code segment —

```
List<PhoneCall> calls = new ArrayList<PhoneCall>();
calls.add(new LocalCall(10, 2.5));
calls.add(new LongDistanceCall(3));
calls.add(new ReducedRateCall(8));
for (PhoneCall call : calls)
{
   System.out.println(call);
}
```

— should display

```
Duration 10 Rate 2.5 Total 25
Duration 3 Rate 6.0 Total 18 LD
Duration 8 Rate 3.0 Total 24 LDRR
```

(a) Write the complete definition of the abstract class `PhoneCall`. Your class must have the following features:

- An instance variable that holds the call duration, an integer (in minutes);

- A constructor that initializes that instance variable to a given integer value;

- An accessor method for the call duration;

- An abstract method `getRate` that takes no parameters and returns a `double` value (in cents per minute);

- A private method that calculates the total cost of the call as the product of the call duration and rate, rounded to the nearest integer;
- A `toString` method that displays the duration, rate, and total cost of the call on one line, as in the following example:

```
Duration 10 Rate 2.5 Total 25
```

(b) Write the class `LongDistanceCall`. The rate for all long distance calls is set to 6.0. Provide other necessary features, so that the `LongDistanceCall` objects can generate text output. For example, the statement

```
System.out.println(new LongDistanceCall(3));
```

must generate the following output:

```
Duration 3 Rate 6.0 Total 18 LD
```

(c) Write the class `ReducedRateCall` as a subclass of `LongDistanceCall`. The rate for a reduced rate call is one half of the rate of a long distance call. Provide other necessary features so that the `ReducedRateCall` objects can generate appropriate text output. For example, the statement

```
System.out.println(new ReducedRateCall(8));
```

must generate the following output:

```
Duration 8 Rate 3.0 Total 24 LDRR
```

2.   This question involves reasoning about the code from the GridWorld case study. A copy
     of the code is provided as part of this exam.

     A `Bee` is a `Critter` that interacts with `Clover` objects in the grid. A `Clover` is a kind
     of `Flower` that can be pollinated. Partial code of the `Clover` class is shown below:

```
public class Clover extends Flower
{
  /** Pollinates this clover (typically called by a Bee)
   */
  public void pollinate()
  { /* implementation not shown */ }

  /** Returns true if this clover has been pollinated;
   *   otherwise returns false
   */
  public boolean hasBeenPollinated()
  { /* implementation not shown */ }

  < Fields, constructors, and other methods not shown >
}
```

A `Bee` first pollinates all `Clover` flowers in the adjacent locations, then moves toward the nearest clover that has not been pollinated yet. A partial definition of the `Bee` class is shown below:

```java
public class Bee extends Critter
{
  /** Creates a yellow bee
   */
  public Bee()
  {
    setColor(Color.YELLOW);
  }

  /** Processes the elements of actors; pollinates all
   *  Clover objects among them
   */
  public void processActors(ArrayList<Actor> actors)
  {  /* to be implemented in part (a) */  }

  /** Returns the location chosen among locs and the current
   *   location that is nearest to an unpollinated clover;
   *   if several locations are at the same distance
   *   from an unpollinated clover, returns any one of them;
   *   if the grid does not have any unpollinated clovers,
   *   returns the current location
   */
  public Location selectMoveLocation(ArrayList<Location> locs)
  {  /* to be implemented in part (b) */  }

  /** Turns towards loc, then moves into loc like a
   *   regular Critter
   */
  public void makeMove(Location loc)
  {  /* to be implemented in part (c) */  }

  /** Returns the distance between loc1 and loc2
   *  Precondition: loc1 != null and loc2 != null
   */
  private int distance(Location loc1, Location loc2)
  { /* implementation not shown */ }

  /** Returns the location of a Clover that has not
   *   yet been pollinated and that is nearest to loc;
   *   if the grid does not contain any unpollinated clovers,
   *   returns null
   *  Precondition: loc != null
   */
  private Location findNearestClover(Location loc)
  { /* implementation not shown */ }
}
```

(a)   Write the `processActors` method. This method pollinates each `Clover` in the `actors` list passed to it.

Complete the `processActors` method below.

```
/** Processes the elements of actors; pollinates all
 *  Clover objects among them
 */
public void processActors(ArrayList<Actor> actors)
```

(b)   Write the `selectMoveLocation` method. This method takes the current location plus all the locations in the given list and finds among them the one that is nearest to any unpollinated clover. (If several locations are at the same minimal distance to an unpollinated clover, any one of them can be selected.) If the grid contains no unpollinated clovers, `selectMoveLocation` should return this `Bee`'s current location.

Complete the `selectMoveLocation` method below.

```
/** Returns the location chosen among locs and the current
 *  location that is nearest to an unpollinated clover;
 *  if several locations are at the same distance
 *  from an unpollinated clover, returns any one of them;
 *  if the grid does not have any unpollinated clovers,
 *  returns the current location
 */
public Location selectMoveLocation(ArrayList<Location> locs)
```

(c)   Write the `makeMove` method. A `Bee` turns towards `loc`, then moves like a regular `Critter`.

Complete the `makeMove` method below.

```
/** Turns towards loc, then moves into loc like a
 *  regular Critter
 */
public void makeMove(Location loc)
```

3.   In the Chain Words game, a player builds a chain of linked words. We say that *Word2* is linked to *Word1* if the beginning of *Word2* (or the whole word *Word2*) contains the same letters in the same order as the end of *Word1* (or the whole word *Word1*). The strength of a link is equal to the number of letters matched. For example:

Word1	*Word2*	*Link strength*
wheat	toast	1
ripe	peach	2
wheat	eat	3
sand	sandwich	4
take	cake	0

(a)   Write a method `linkStrength` as started below. The method returns the link strength from *word2* to *word1*. If *word2* is not linked to *word1*, the method returns 0.

```
/** Returns the link strength from word2 to word1,
 *  which is defined as the length of the longest substring
 *  at the end of word1 that matches a substring at the
 *  beginning of word2; returns 0 if there is no match
 */
public static int linkStrength(String word1, String word2)
```

(b)   Write a method `keepFirstChain`, which takes a list of words and keeps only the first chain of words, in which each word (except the first one) is linked to the previous word. All the words beyond the first chain are removed. For example, if the list `words` contains

```
["stop", "top", "place", "wheat", "eat", "cake"]
```

after a call `keepFirstChain(words)` the list `words` should contain

```
["stop", "top", "place"]
```

Any subsequent calls to `keepFirstChain(words)` should leave the list `words` unchanged.

```
/** Modifies a list of words, keeping only the first
 *  chain of words (in which each word, after the first one,
 *  is linked to the previous word with a non-zero link
 *  strength) and removes all words beyond
 *  the first chain
 *  @param words - a list of words
 *  Precondition: words is not empty
 */
public static void keepFirstChain(List<String> words)
```

4. OCR software interprets images of letters or digits scanned from documents. An image is represented by a two-dimensional array of "pixels" (picture elements). Each pixel has an intensity, represented by an integer value. Here high intensity represents "ink" and low intensity represents "white space."

    A simple OCR method is called "template matching." A template is a rectangular numeric mask that has positive numbers (weights) in those places where the picture of the character is likely to have "ink" and negative weights where the picture is likely to have white space. The template for each character in the font is superimposed on the digitized image at the approximate location where the picture of a letter or a digit is found and the "fit ratio" is computed for each template. The template that gives the best fit determines the recognition result.

    The picture below shows an example of a template for the letter "A". To simplify things, we assume that a template is always placed at the top row of the image.

Template for "A"
9 rows by 11 columns

```
-1  -1  -1  -1  -1   0  -1  -1  -1  -1  -1
-1  -1  -1  -1   0   5   0  -1  -1  -1  -1
-1  -1  -1   0   5   0   5  -1  -1  -1  -1
-1  -1   0   5   0  -5   0   5   0  -1  -1
-1   0   5   0   0   0   0   0   5  -1  -1
-1   0   5   5   8   8   8   5   5  -1  -1
 0   5   5   0   0   0   0   0   5   5   0
 0   0  -1  -1  -1  -1  -1  -1  -1   0   0
-1  -1  -1  -1  -5  -5  -5  -1  -1  -1  -1
```

A digitized image of a character
x — high intensity pixels
. — low intensity pixels
A template is superimposed at
row = 0 and *col* = 3 .

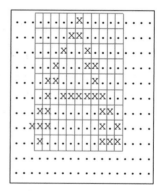

The following class `Template` represents a template for a character in the font:

```
public class Template
{
  /** Returns the name of the character */
  public String getCharName()
  {  < implementation not shown >  }

  /** Returns the number of rows in this template */
  public int numRows()
  {  < implementation not shown >  }

  /** Returns the number of columns in this template */
  public int numCols()
  {  < implementation not shown >  }

  /** Returns the weight at row, col position */
  public double getWeight(int row, int col)
  {  < implementation not shown >  }

  < Constructors, fields, and other methods not shown >
}
```

You will write three methods that help perform OCR on a given image. Assume that all these methods belong to the same class `OCR`.

(a) To find the horizontal position of the character in an image, we find the contiguous block of *h* columns (where *h* is the width of the template) with the largest amount of black "ink" in it. Write a method `findLeftCol`, which returns the leftmost position `col` such that the total cumulative intensity of pixels in all rows and in the columns from `col` to `col + charWidth - 1` is the largest. (If several column positions result in the same maximum intensity, the one with the smallest index is returned.) For example, for the image in the picture above, `findLeftCol` should return 3. Complete the method `findLeftCol` below.

```
  /** Returns col such that the total sum of pixel intensities
   *   in all rows and in columns from col to
   *   col + charWidth - 1 is the largest; if several col
   *   values give the same maximum intensity, returns the
   *   leftmost one of them (the one with the smallest index)
   *   Precondition:  charWidth <= the number of columns
   *                  in image
   */
  public int findLeftCol(int[][] image, int charWidth)
```

(b) Write the `calculateFitRatio` method of the `OCR` class. The fit ratio is computed by multiplying the intensity of each image pixel covered by the template by the corresponding template weight and adding all the results. For a 9-by-11 template, for example, 99 individual products contribute to the sum. The sum is then divided by the total number of pixels covered by the template, and that number is returned as the fit ratio.

Complete the `calculateFitRatio` method below.

```
/** Returns the fit ratio when Template t is superimposed
 *   on this image with the template's top at the image top
 *   and the template's left column at leftCol
 *   Precondition: t.numRows() <= image height
 *                 leftCol + t.numCols() <= image width
 */
public double calculateFitRatio(int[][] image,
                                       Template t, int leftCol)
```

(c) Write the `ocr` method of the `OCR` class, as started below. Given an image and a list of templates that represent a font, for each template in the list `ocr` obtains the leftmost column of the character and calculates the fit ratio for that position. The method identifies the template in the list that gives the best fit ratio and returns the name of the character in that template. The method returns `null` if none of the templates produces a positive fit ratio. Assume that the methods from Part (a) and Part (b) work as specified, regardless of what you wrote there.

```
/** Returns a String that corresponds to the name of the
 *   best-fitting template (or any one of the best-fitting
 *   templates) from the font, or null if none of
 *   the templates produces a positive fit
 */
public String ocr(int[][] image, List<Template> templates)
```

Practice Exam #4

SECTION I

Time — 1 hour and 15 minutes
Number of questions — 40
Percent of total grade — 50

1. Consider the following method:

```
public void reduce(int[] arr, int len)
{
  for (int i = 0; i < len; i++)
  {
    arr[i]--;
  }
  len--;
}
```

What is the output of the following code segment?

```
int[] counts = {3, 2, 1, 0};
int len = 3;
reduce(counts, len);

for (int k : counts)
{
  System.out.print(k + " ");
}
System.out.println(len);
```

(A) 1 2 1 2
(B) 2 1 0 2
(C) 2 1 1 3
(D) 2 1 0 3
(E) 2 1 0 -1 2

2. Which of the following statements will result in a syntax error?

(A) `String x = "123";`
(B) `Integer x = "123";`
(C) `Object x = "123";`
(D) `String[] x = {"123"};`
(E) All of the above will compile with no errors.

3. Consider the following method:

```
public String encrypt(String word)
{
  int pos = word.length() / 2;
  if (pos >= 1)
  {
    word = encrypt(word.substring(pos)) +
           encrypt(word.substring(0, pos));
  }
  return word;
}
```

What is the contents of the string returned by `encrypt("SECRET")`?

(A) TERCES
(B) TSECRE
(C) RETSEC
(D) CESTER
(E) ETRECS

4. Given that x is `true`, y is `true`, and z is `false`, which of the following expressions will evaluate to `false`?

(A) `(x && y) || z`
(B) `(x || y) && z`
(C) `y || (x && z)`
(D) `x || (y && z)`
(E) `x && (y || z)`

5. What values are stored in `arr` after the following code segment has been executed?

```
int[] arr = {1, 2, 3, 4, 5, 6, 7, 8};
for (int k = 1; k <= 6; k += 2)
{
  arr[7] = arr[k];
  arr[k] = arr[k+1];
  arr[k+1] = arr[7];
}
```

(A) 1 3 2 5 4 7 6 6
(B) 1 3 2 5 4 7 6 8
(C) 2 1 4 3 6 5 8 7
(D) 2 1 4 3 6 5 7 8
(E) 2 1 4 3 6 5 7 5

6. A two-dimensional array `image` holds brightness values for pixels (picture elements) in an image. The brightness values range from 0 to 255. Consider the following method:

```java
public int findMax(int[][] image)
{
  int[] count = new int[256];
  int i, iMax = 0;

  for (int r = 0; r < image.length; r++)
  {
    for (int c = 0; c < image[0].length; c++)
    {
      i = image[r][c];
      count[i]++;
    }
  }
  for (i = 1; i < 256; i++)
  {
    if (count[i] > count[iMax])
      iMax = i;
  }
  return iMax;
}
```

What does this method compute?

(A)   The column with the highest sum of brightness values in `image`
(B)   The maximum brightness value for all pixels in `image`
(C)   The most frequent brightness value in `image`
(D)   The maximum sum of brightness values in any 256 by 256 square in `image`
(E)   The maximum sum of brightness values in any 256 consecutive rows in `image`

7. What is the output of the following code segment?

```java
String url = "http://www.usa.gov";
int pos = url.indexOf("http://");
if (pos >= 0)
{
  System.out.println("<" + url.substring(0, pos) + ">");
}
else
{
  System.out.println("not found");
}
```

(A)   `<>`
(B)   `<www.usa.gov>`
(C)   `<http://www.usa.gov>`
(D)   `not found`
(E)   `IndexOutOfBoundsException`

8. Consider the following method:

```
/** Returns the index of searchVal, if found in list;
 *  otherwise returns -1
 */
public int binarySearch(ArrayList<String> list,
                                      String searchVal)
{
  int first = 0, last = list.size() - 1;
  while (first <= last)
  {
    int mid = (first + last) / 2;

    if (searchVal.compareTo(list.get(mid)) < 0)
      last = mid - 1;
    else if (searchVal.compareTo(list.get(mid)) > 0)
      first = mid + 1;
    else
      return mid;     // Statement 1
  }
  return -1;          // Statement 2
}
```

We want to modify this method: if `searchVal` is not already in the list, we want `binarySearch` to return the position where it can be inserted keeping the list sorted. Which of the following could be used for *Statement 1* and *Statement 2*?

	Statement 1	*Statement 2*
(A)	return mid;	return mid;
(B)	return mid;	return first;
(C)	return mid;	return last;
(D)	return mid - 1;	return first;
(E)	return mid - 1;	return last;

9. What is printed as a result of executing the following code segment?

```
int i = 2;
for (int k = 0; k <= 12; k += i)
{
  System.out.print(k + " ");
  i++;
}
```

(A)   0 3 7
(B)   0 3 7 12
(C)   2 5 8 11
(D)   0 3 6 9 12
(E)   0 2 4 6 8 10

10. Consider the following method:

```
/** Returns the number of times the digit d occurs in the
 *   decimal representation of n
 *   Precondition: n and d are non-negative integers
 */
private int findDigit(int n, int d)
{
  int count = 0;
  < statement1 >

  while (n > 0)
  {
    if (n % 10 == d)
    {
      count++;
    }
    < statement2 >
  }

  return count;
}
```

Which of the following could replace < *statement1* > and < *statement2* > to make findDigit work as specified?

	< *statement1* >	< *statement2* >
(A)	if (n == 0) return 1;	n /= 10;
(B)	if (n == 0) return 1;	d *= 10;
(C)	if (d == 0) count++;	n -= n % 10;
(D)	if (n == 0 && d == 0) count++;	n /= 10;
(E)	if (n == 0 && d != 0) return 0;	n *= 10;

11. What is printed when the following code segment is executed?

```
List<Integer> list = new ArrayList<Integer>();
list.add(new Integer(1));
list.add(new Integer(2));
for (int i = 1; i <= 3; i++)
{
  list.add(i, new Integer(i));
}
System.out.println(list);
```

(A) [1, 1, 2, 2, 3]
(B) [1, 1, 2, 3, 2]
(C) [1, 2, 1, 2, 3]
(D) [1, 2, 3, 1, 2]
(E) IndexOutOfBoundsException

12. Classes `Salsa` and `Swing` implement an interface `Dance`. If both of the calls

```
perform(new Salsa());
perform(new Swing());
```

are valid, which of the following could serve as definitions of the `perform` method(s) in the class `Dancer`?

    I.   Two methods:

```
public void perform(Salsa dance) { /* code not shown */ }
public void perform(Swing dance) { /* code not shown */ }
```

    II.   `public void perform(Dance dance) { /* code not shown */ }`

    III.   `public void perform(Object dance) { /* code not shown */ }`

(A)   I only
(B)   II only
(C)   I and II only
(D)   II and III only
(E)   I, II, and III

13. Suppose class `C` has a private `int` data field `value`:

```
public class C
{
  private int value;
  < Other fields, constructors, and methods not shown >
}
```

Suppose we have a method

```
public static int compare(C x, C y)
{ return x.value - y.value; }
```

and we need to find "home" for it: place it into some class. Where can we place this method so that it compiles with no errors?

(A)   Only into `C`
(B)   Only into `C` or any subclass of `C`
(C)   Only into `C` or any superclass of `C`
(D)   Into any class
(E)   This method will always cause a syntax error, no matter what class we place it in.

14. Consider the following code segment:

```
int[][] t = new int[2][3];
for (int i = 0; i < t.length; i++)
{
   for (int j = 0; j < t[0].length; j++)
   {
      t[i][j] = i + j + 1;
   }
}
```

What is the result when the code segment is executed?

(A)   t holds the values

```
1 2 3
4 5 6
```

(B)   t holds the values

```
1 2 0
2 3 0
```

(C)   t holds the values

```
1 2 3
2 3 4
```

(D)   t holds the values

```
3 4 5
4 5 6
```

(E)   `ArrayIndexOutOfBoundsException`

15. Which of the following tasks is made easier when information hiding is practiced?

   I.   Implementing IS-A relationships for classes

   II. Making changes to the implementation of one of the classes in a project

   III. Producing specifications for individual programmers working on the same project

(A)   I only
(B)   II only
(C)   I and II
(D)   II and III
(E)   I, II, and III

16. Consider the following classes:

```
public class APTestResult
{
  private String subject;
  private int score;

  public int getScore() { return score; }

  < Constructors and other methods not shown >
}

public class APScholar
{
  private String name;
  private int id;
  private ArrayList<APTestResult> exams;

  public ArrayList<APTestResult> getExams() { return exams; }

  < Constructors and other methods not shown >
}
```

Given

```
APScholar[] list = new APScholar[100];
```

which of the following expressions correctly represents the third AP score of the sixth AP Scholar in `list`?

(A)   `list[5].exams[2].score`
(B)   `list[5].exams.getScore(2)`
(C)   `list[5].exams[2].getScore()`
(D)   `list[5].getExams(2).getScore()`
(E)   `list[5].getExams().get(2).getScore()`

17. In a regular pentagon, the ratio of the length of a diagonal to the length of a side is equal to the Golden Ratio (defined as $\dfrac{1+\sqrt{5}}{2} \approx 1.618$). Consider the following class `Pentagon`, which represents a regular pentagon:

```
public class Pentagon
{
  public static final double goldenRatio =
                              (1 + Math.sqrt(5.0)) / 2;
  private double side;

  public Pentagon (double x)
  {
    side = x;
  }

  public double getDiagonalLength()
  {
    return side * goldenRatio;
  }
}
```

Which of the following code segments will compile with no errors and display the correct length of a diagonal in a regular pentagon with side 3.0?

I.   `System.out.println(3/2 * (1 + Math.sqrt(5.0)));`

II.   `System.out.println(3.0 * Pentagon.goldenRatio);`

III.   `Pentagon p = new Pentagon(3);`
        `System.out.println(p.getDiagonalLength());`

(A)   I only
(B)   II only
(C)   III only
(D)   I and II
(E)   II and III

Questions 18-19 refer to the following implementation of Mergesort:

```
public class Mergesort
{
  /** Returns a new array which holds the values
   *  arr[m], arr[m+1], ... arr[n] arranged in ascending order
   *  Precondition: 0 <= m <= n
   */
  public static int[] sort(int[] arr, int m, int n)
  {
    int[] result = new int[n - m + 1];

    if (m == n)
    {
      result[0] = arr[m];
    }
    else
    {
      int mid = (n + m) / 2;
      int[] result1 = sort(arr, m, mid);
      int[] result2 = sort(arr, mid + 1, n);
      result = merge(result1, result2);
    }

    return result;
  }

  /** Merges arr1 and arr2 in ascending order and returns the
   *  resulting array
   */
  private static int[] merge(int[] arr1, int[] arr2)
  { /* implementation not shown */ }
}
```

18. If `int[] arr` holds eight values and `Mergesort(arr, 0, 7)` is called, how many times in total will `Mergesort`'s `merge` method will be called?

    (A)   1
    (B)   3
    (C)   7
    (D)   8
    (E)   15

19. If `Mergesort.sort(arr, 0, 999)` takes on average 40 ms and
    `Mergesort.merge(arr1, arr2)` takes on average
    `0.01*(arr1.length + arr2.length)`, what is the average run time for
    `Mergesort.sort(arr, 0, 1999)`?

    (A) 50 ms
    (B) 100 ms
    (C) 160 ms
    (D) 170 ms
    (E) 180 ms

20. Consider the following method:

```
private double compute(int x, int y)
{
  double r = 0;
  if (!(y == 0 || x / y <= 2))
  {
    r = 1 / ((x - 2*y) * (2*x - y));
  }
  return r;
}
```

    For which of the following values of x and y will `compute(x, y)` throw an exception?

    (A) x = 0, y = 0
    (B) x = 1, y = 2
    (C) x = 2, y = 1
    (D) x = 3, y = 5
    (E) None of the above

21. The Binary Search algorithm is designed to work with an array sorted in ascending order. Under which of the following circumstances will the algorithm find a given target value even if the array is not sorted?

    I.   The array has an odd number of elements and the target value is located exactly in the middle of the array.

    II. The array is partially sorted: the left third of the array has values all in ascending order and the target value is among them.

    III. The array is partially sorted: all the values to the left of the target are smaller than the target and all the values to the right of the target are larger than the target.

    (A) I only
    (B) I and II
    (C) I and III
    (D) II and III
    (E) I, II, and III

Questions 22-25 refer to the class `House` and its subclass `HouseForSale`:

```
public class House
{
  private int mySize;

  public House(int size) { mySize = size; }
  public int getSize() { return mySize; }
  public void setSize(int size) { mySize = size; }

  public int compareToOther(House other)
  {
    return getSize() - other.getSize();
  }
}

public class HouseForSale extends House
{
  private int myPrice;

  public HouseForSale(int size, int price)
  {
    < missing statement >
    myPrice = price;
  }

  public int getPrice() { return myPrice; }

  public int compareToOther(House other)
  {
    return getPrice() - ((HouseForSale)other).getPrice();
  }

  < Other constructors, methods, and fields not shown >
}
```

22. Which of the following is the most appropriate replacement for *< missing statement >* in `HouseForSale`'s constructor?

    (A) `mySize = size;`
    (B) `setSize(size);`
    (C) `super.setSize(size);`
    (D) `super(size);`
    (E) `super = new House(size);`

23. Suppose that while coding `HouseForSale` the programmer accidentally misspelled "compareToOther" in his class. What will happen when he tries to compile and run his class and the following statements in a client class?

```
HouseForSale house1 = new HouseForSale(2000, 129000);
HouseForSale house2 = new HouseForSale(1800, 149000);
System.out.println(house1.compareToOther(house2));
```

(A) A syntax error "undefined compareToOther method"
(B) A syntax error "HouseForSale should be declared abstract"
(C) The code compiles with no errors and displays `200`.
(D) The code compiles with no errors but throws a `NoSuchMethodException`.
(E) The code compiles with no errors but throws a `ClassCastException`.

24. If the classes `House` and `HouseForSale` compile with no problems, which of the following declarations will result in a syntax error?

(A) `House[] houses = new House[2];`

(B) `HouseForSale[] houses = {new House(2000), new House(1800)};`

(C) `House[] houses = {new HouseForSale(2000, 129000),`
    `new HouseForSale(1800, 149000)};`

(D) `HouseForSale[] houses = {new HouseForSale(2000, 129000),`
    `new HouseForSale(1800, 149000)};`

(E) All of the above compile with no errors.

25. Which of the following is the most appropriate way to define the `getSize` method in `HouseForSale`?

(A) `public int getSize() { return mySize; }`
(B) `public int getSize() { return super.mySize; }`
(C) `public int getSize() { return super(mySize); }`
(D) `public int getSize() { return super.getSize(); }`
(E) No definition is necessary because the same code is already written in `House`.

Questions 26-31 refer to the code from the GridWorld case study.

26. How does a `Bug` act if there is a `Rock` directly in front of it in the grid?

   (A) The `Bug` is removed from the grid.
   (B) The `Bug` remains in its current state — no action is taken.
   (C) The `Rock` is removed, and the `Bug` moves forward, leaving a new `Flower` in its old location.
   (D) The `Bug` turns 45 degrees to the right.
   (E) The `Bug` turns 180 degrees.

27. Consider the following subclass of `Bug`:

```
public class SpinningBug extends Bug
{
  public void act()
  {
    super.act();
    turn();
  }

  public void turn()
  {
    setDirection(getDirection() + Location.LEFT);
  }
}
```

If a `SpinningBug` is put into a grid, among other actors, how does it act?

   (A) The `SpinningBug` throws a `NoSuchMethodException`, because the `canMove` and `move` methods are undefined.
   (B) The `SpinningBug` acts like a regular `Bug` but turns 90 degrees to the left after each move.
   (C) If the `SpinningBug` can move, it moves forward, then turns 90 degrees to the left; otherwise the bug turns 180 degrees.
   (D) If the `SpinningBug` can move, it moves forward, then turns 90 degrees to the left; otherwise the bug turns 45 degrees to the left.
   (E) If the `SpinningBug` can move (that is, the location in front is valid and empty), it moves forward, then turns 90 degrees to the left; otherwise the bug turns 45 degrees to the right.

28. Which of the following code segments will compile with no errors?

     I.
```
Actor a = new Actor();
a.setColor(Color.RED);
```

     II.
```
Actor a = new Bug(Color.GREEN);
```

     III.
```
Actor a = new Bug();
a.setColor(Color.BLUE);
```

(A) I only
(B) II only
(C) I and II
(D) II and III
(E) I, II, and III

29. When a `ChameleonCritter` object is first created, what are its initial color and direction?

(A) blue color and north
(B) red color and north
(C) blue color and random direction
(D) random color and random direction
(E) The color passed to `ChameleonCritter`'s constructor as a parameter and random direction

30. Which of the following is NOT an example of polymorphism?

(A) The appropriate `act` method is called for `Rocks`, `Bugs`, `Flowers`, and `Critters`
(B) `BoxBug`'s `act` method calls `move` and `turn` inherited from `Bug`
(C) `ChameleonCritter`'s `act` method, inherited from `Critter`, calls `ChameleonCritter`'s `processActors` and `makeMove`
(D) `Bug`'s `canMove` method calls the appropriate `Grid`'s `isValid` for different implementations of `Grid`
(E) All of the above are examples of polymorphism.

31. Consider the following class:

```
public class IntGrid extends BoundedGrid<Integer>
{
  < Constructors not shown >

  /** Increments by 1 Integer objects in all occupied
   *  locations
   */
  public void increment()
  {
    < missing code >
  }
}
```

Which of the following code segments could replace < *missing code* > so that the method
increment works as specified?

(A)
```
for (Location loc : getOccupiedLocations())
{
  Integer i = get(loc);
  i = new Integer(i.intValue() + 1);
}
```

(B)
```
for (Location loc : grid.getOccupiedLocations())
{
  Integer i = grid.get(loc);
  i.setValue(i.intValue() + 1);
}
```

(C)
```
for (Location loc : getOccupiedLocations())
{
  Integer i = get(loc);
  i.setValue(i.intValue() + 1);
  put(loc, i);
}
```

(D)
```
for (Location loc : getOccupiedLocations())
{
  put(loc, new Integer(get(loc).intValue() + 1));
}
```

(E)
```
for (Location loc : grid.getOccupiedLocations())
{
  grid.put(loc,
           new Integer(grid.get(loc).intValue() + 1));
}
```

32. Consider the following code segment with a missing "for" loop:

```
List<String> letters = new ArrayList<String>();

letters.add("A");
letters.add("B");
letters.add("C");

< missing "for" loop >

System.out.println(letters);
```

Suppose, when executed, the above code segment displays

```
[A*, B*, C*]
```

Which of the following could replace < *missing "for" loop* >?

I.
```
for (int i = 0; i < letters.size(); i++)
{
   letters.set(i, letters.get(i) + "*");
}
```

II.
```
for (int i = 0; i < letters.size(); i++)
{
   String s = letters.get(i);
   s = s + "*";
}
```

III.
```
for (String s : letters)
{
   s = s + "*";
}
```

(A) I only
(B) II only
(C) I and II
(D) II and III
(E) I, II, and III

33. Consider the following method:

```
public int guess(int num1, int num2)
{
  if (num1 % num2 == 0)
    return num2;
  return guess(num2, num1 % num2);
}
```

What is the value of num after the following code segment is executed?

```
int num = (6 * 14) / guess(6, 14);
```

(A) 6
(B) 12
(C) 14
(D) 28
(E) 42

34. Consider the following class:

```
public class Game
{
  private static int bestScore;
  private int score;
  private String player;

  < Constructors and methods not shown >
}
```

Which of the following constructors or methods in Game will cause a syntax error?

I.
```
public static void resetScore()
{ score = 0; bestScore = 0; }
```

II.
```
public Game()
{ score = 0; bestScore = 0; }
```

III.
```
public void setPlayer(String name)
{ score = 0; bestScore = 0; }
```

(A) I only
(B) II only
(C) I and II only
(D) II and III only
(E) I, II, and III

35. Consider two different designs for a data structure to hold the total number of home runs hit in a season by baseball players. There are *n* players (n > 1000), and each total is in the range from 0 to 80.

Design A: Use an array of length 81. Each index into the array corresponds to a number of home runs, and each element of the array is a reference to a list containing the names of the players who hit that many home runs, in no particular order.

Design B: Use an array of length *n* so that each element of the array corresponds to one player. Each element of the array is an object that represents a player, holding his name and the number of home runs he has hit. The elements of the array are sorted alphabetically by player name.

This data structure will be used to support three operations:

Operation 1: Print the names of all players who hit over 50 home runs.

Operation 2: Given a player's name, look up that player's home run total.

Operation 3: Given the names of two players, determine whether they hit the same number of home runs.

Which of the three operations could be performed more efficiently using Design A rather than Design B?

(A)   Operation 1 only
(B)   Operation 2 only
(C)   Operation 3 only
(D)   Operations 1 and 2
(E)   Operations 2 and 3

36. Suppose a programmer has written a method that implements Insertion Sort for an array of integers. The method has no preconditions. Which of the following is NOT a useful test for this method?

(A)   An array of length 5 with random values
(B)   An array of length 5 with values sorted in ascending order
(C)   An empty array (length 0)
(D)   An array of length 1
(E)   All of the above are useful tests.

Questions 37-38 refer to a project that includes the following classes:

```java
public class OrderItem
{
  private String itemName;
  private int price, quantity;

  public OrderItem (String name, int pr, int qty)
  { itemName = name; price = pr; quantity = qty; }

  public int getExtendedPrice() { return price * quantity; }

  < Other constructors and methods not shown >
}

public class Order
{
  private ArrayList<OrderItem> items;

  public Order() { items = new ArrayList<OrderItem>(); }

  public int getTotal()
  {
    int total = 0;

    for (OrderItem item : items)
    {
      total += item.getExtendedPrice();
    }
    return total;
  }

  public void add(OrderItem item) { items.add(item); }
}
```

The project designer has instructed the programmer to modify the code as follows: to introduce

```java
public interface Priced
{
  int getExtendedPrice();
}
```

into the project, add `implements Priced` to the `OrderItem` class header, and replace `OrderItem` with `Priced` everywhere in the `Order` class.

37. Which design principle is applied here, and which Java feature makes it possible for the modified code to work?

    (A) Encapsulation and polymorphism
    (B) Abstraction and encapsulation
    (C) Abstraction and polymorphism
    (D) Information hiding and encapsulation
    (E) Information hiding and Java Virtual Machine

38. Which of the following are good reasons for this change?

    I. In some future version of the project, the `items` list in an `Order` object may hold items of the type of a subclass of `OrderItem`.

    II. In some future version of the project, different types of `Priced` objects can be intermixed in the `items` list in an `Order` object.

    III. The `Order` class can be reused in other projects dealing with a different type of `Priced` items.

    (A) I only
    (B) II only
    (C) I and II
    (D) II and III
    (E) I, II, and III

39. Consider the following classes:

```
public class MyList1 extends ArrayList<Double>
{
  public MyList1() { }
  < Other constructors, methods and data fields not shown >
}

public class MyList2 implements List<Double>
{
  public MyList2() { }
  < Other constructors, methods and data fields not shown >
}
```

Which of the following statements will cause a compile-time error?

    (A) `MyList1 list = new MyList1();`
    (B) `ArrayList<Double> list = new MyList1();`
    (C) `List<Double> list = new MyList1();`
    (D) `List<Double> list = new MyList2();`
    (E) All of the above will compile with no errors.

40. Consider the following class:

```
public class ArrayProcessor
{
  public static void run(int[] arr)
  {
    for (int i = 0; i < arr.length; i++)
    {
      for (int j = arr.length - 1; j > i; j--)
      {
        if (arr[j] < arr[i])
        {
          swap(arr, i, j);
        }
      }
    }
  }

  private static void swap(int[] arr, int i, int j)
  {
    int temp = arr[i];
    arr[i] = arr[j];
    arr[j] = temp;
  }
}
```

How many times will `ArrayProcessor`'s `swap` method be called when the following code segment is executed?

```
int[] counts = {1, 2, 3, 4, 5, 0};
ArrayProcessor.run(counts);
```

(A) 1
(B) 5
(C) 15
(D) 30
(E) 35

Practice Exam #4

SECTION II

Time — 1 hour and 45 minutes
Number of questions — 4
Percent of total grade — 50

1. This question is concerned with the design and implementation of classes for a school bus transportation system. In this system, a `Student` object represents a student in a given school. A student has a name and address, represented as a street name (a string) and a house number on the street:

```
public class Student
{
  < Data fields and constructors not shown >

  /** Returns the name of this student
   */
  private String getName() { /* implementation not shown */ }

  /** Returns the street where this student lives
   */
  private String getStreet()
  { /* implementation not shown */ }

  /** Returns the house number in the street where
   */ this student lives
  private int getNumber() { /* implementation not shown */ }

  /** Returns a string that represents this student in
   *  the format "name: number street"
   *  for example,
   *  Maria Litvin: 15 River St
   */
  public String toString()
  { /* implementation not shown */ }

  /** If this student and other live on the same street,
   *  returns the absolute value of the difference in their
   *  house numbers; otherwise returns 99999
   *  Precondition: other is not null
   */
  public int distance(Student other)
  { /* to be implemented in part (a) */ }
}
```

A `SchoolBus` object corresponds to one bus route and holds a list of students assigned to that bus. The `SchoolBus` class has a constructor that creates a bus with a given number of seats, and methods `getNumStudents` that returns the number of students currently assigned to this bus, `isFull` that indicates whether there are vacant seats on this bus, and other methods that help handle the list of students on this bus. You will design and implement this class in Part (b).

A `SchoolTransport` object handles bus assignments for a given school. It has an `ArrayList` of `SchoolBus` objects and a method to enroll a new student into this school's transportation system. The new student is added to the bus that already carries a student from the same street who lives closest to the new student:

```
public class SchoolTransport
{
  /** List of all bus routes for this school */
  private List<SchoolBus> buses;

  /** Looks in all buses for someone whose bus is not
   *  yet full and who lives the closest to student
   *  (in terms of distance defined for Student objects);
   *  if found, adds student to the same bus and returns true;
   *  otherwise returns false
   */
  boolean enroll(Student student)
  { /* to be implemented in Part (c) */ }

  < Constructors and other methods not shown >
}
```

(a) Write the `distance` method of the `Student` class. If `this` student lives on the same street as `other`, then `distance` returns the absolute value of the difference in the numbers of their houses; otherwise it returns 99999.

Complete the method `distance` below.

```
/** If this student and other live on the same street,
 *  returns the absolute value of the difference in the
 *  numbers of their houses; otherwise returns 99999
 *  Precondition: other is not null
 */
public int distance(Student other)
```

(b) Write a class `SchoolBus` that represents a bus route and holds the list of students who ride on that bus. In writing this class:

- use an `ArrayList` of `Student` objects to hold the list of students on this bus;

- use appropriate name(s) for the data field(s);

- implement a constructor that takes one parameter, the total number of seats available on this bus;

- implement the following public methods:

`int getNumStudents()` —	returns the number of students currently on this bus's list
`boolean isFull()` —	returns true if there are no more vacant seats on this bus; false otherwise
`Student getStudent(i)` —	returns the student in the *i*-th position on this bus's list
`boolean add(Student student)` —	if seats are available, adds student to this bus's list and returns true; otherwise returns false
`void printOut()` —	displays all students on this bus, each on a separate line, in the format consistent with `Student`'s `toString` method

For example, the following code segment —

```
bus = new SchoolBus(3);
boolean result;
result = bus.add(new Student("Dave", "High St", 27));
System.out.println(result + " " + bus.isFull());
result = bus.add(new Student("Roger", "Elm St", 3));
System.out.println(result + " " + bus.isFull());
result = bus.add(new Student("Judy", "High St", 124));
System.out.println(result + " " + bus.isFull());
result = bus.add(new Student("Maria", "River St", 15));
System.out.println(result + " " + bus.isFull());
bus.printOut();
```

— should display

```
true false
true false
true true
false true
Dave: 27 High St
Roger: 3 Elm St
Judy: 124 High St
```

(c) Write the `enroll` method of the `SchoolTransport` class. This method tries to find a bus on which it makes sense to place a new student. On all the buses that are not already full, it looks for a student already enrolled, who is closest to the new student (such that the distance between that student and the new student, as defined by the `Student`'s `distance` method, is the smallest). If such a student is found, then the method places the new student on the same bus and returns `true`. Otherwise the method returns `false`, indicating that the bus placement decision is left to the school's transportation manager.

Complete the `enroll` method below.

```
/** Looks in all bus routes for someone whose bus is not
 *   yet full and who lives the closest to student
 *   (in terms of distance defined for Student objects);
 *   if found, adds student to the same bus and returns
 *   true; otherwise returns false
 */
boolean enroll(Student student)
```

2. The diagram below shows a simplified hierarchy of classes used for computing postage
    for different types of mail.

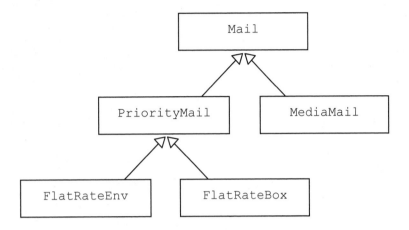

The classes `Mail` and `PriorityMail` are shown below. `Mail` is an abstract class:

```
public abstract class Mail
{
  public abstract double calculatePostage();

  /** Returns the amount of postage formatted
   *   with 2 digits after the decimal point
   */
  public String toString()
  {
    DecimalFormat money = new DecimalFormat("0.00");
    return money.format(calculatePostage());
  }
}
```

`PriorityMail` has a constructor that takes two parameters: the weight of the mail piece in pounds and the delivery zone. It also has a method to calculate postage based on the weight and zone:

```
public class PriorityMail extends Mail
{
  /** Weight of this piece of mail in pounds */
  private double weight;

  /** Delivery zone for this piece of mail */
  private int zone;

  /** Precondition: 1 <= zone <= 8
   */
  public PriorityMail(double lbs, int z)
  {
    weight = lbs;
    zone = z;
  }

  /** Returns the cost of mailing this piece of mail by
   *  priority mail: $4.05 for under one pound to any zone;
   *  plus $0.80 * zone for any pound or fraction
   *  over 1 pound
   */
  public double calculatePostage()
  { /* implementation not shown */ }
}
```

A `FlatRateEnv` object represents a Priority Mail flat-rate envelope, and a `FlatRateBox` object represents a Priority Mail flat-rate box. These two services offer a flat rate regardless of the actual weight and delivery zone.

(a)   Write the complete definitions of the `FlatRateEnv` and `FlatRateBox` classes that correspond to the inheritance hierarchy described above. In each of these classes, provide a no-args constructor (a constructor that takes no parameters). The cost of mailing a flat-rate Priority Mail envelope (regardless of its actual weight and zone) is the same as the cost of mailing a one-pound Priority Mail piece in Zone 1. A flat-rate Priority Mail box costs twice as much as a flat-rate envelope. For example, if you have

```
Mail piece1 = new PriorityMail(1.0, 1);
Mail piece2 = new FlatRateEnv();
Mail piece3 = new FlatRateBox();
```

and

```
System.out.println(piece1);
```

displays 5.15, then

```
System.out.println(piece2 + " " + piece3);
```

should display

```
 5.15 10.30
```

To receive full credit, you must reuse provided methods and avoid duplication of instance variables and methods.

(b) In this part of the question you are to write a complete definition of the
`InsuredMail` class.

The US Postal Service provides insurance for different types of mail. The cost of
insurance depends only on the amount of insurance purchased by the sender and not
on the particular type of mail. It would be too tedious to add the insurance option to
each of the classes that represent different types of mail. Instead, we can create one
"wrapper" class that will help us calculate the total cost, including insurance, for all
kinds of mail pieces. `InsuredMail` is such a class. It is somewhat unusual
because it both <u>extends</u> `Mail` and <u>has an instance variable</u> of the type `Mail`.
`InsuredMail`'s constructor sets that instance variable to a `Mail` object, passed to
the constructor as a parameter. The second parameter passed to the constructor is
the amount of insurance (in dollars):

```
public InsuredMail(Mail piece, int amount)
```

`InsuredMail`'s `calculatePostage` method returns the sum of the regular
postage for the mail piece (represented by the `Mail` instance variable of the
`InsuredMail` object) and the cost of insurance. The latter depends only on the
amount of insurance: suppose it costs $0.50 per $100 or any fraction of $100 of the
insurance amount. For example, if

```
System.out.println(piece);
```

displays 5.15, then

```
Mail insured = new InsuredMail(piece, 350);
System.out.println(insured);
```

should display 7.15 (which is 5.15 + 4 * 0.50).

Write a complete definition of the `InsuredMail` class.

3. This question involves reasoning about the code from the GridWorld case study. A copy of the code is provided as part of this exam.

MazeBug, a subclass of Bug, implements a bug that can find its way out of a maze. The walls of a maze are made of rocks (Rock objects). A MazeBug can move only in four directions: north, east, south, and west. Its strategy is to cling to the wall on its left: when the wall turns left, the bug turns left, too. The picture below shows a bug's path in a small maze.

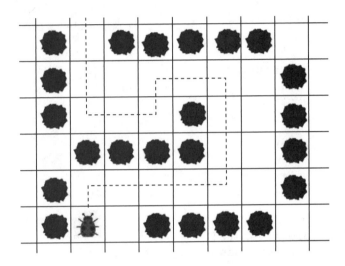

A partial definition of the `MazeBug` class is shown below:

```
public class MazeBug extends Bug
{
  /** Returns true if this bug is in a grid and all other
   *  actors in its grid are either rocks or flowers;
   *  otherwise returns false
   */
  public boolean isValidGrid()
  {  /* to be implemented in part (a) */  }

  /** Moves left if it can move left; otherwise acts
   *  like a regular bug
   */
  public void act()
  {
    if (canMoveLeft())
      moveLeft();
    else
      super.act();
  }

  /** Turns 90 degrees to the left, then moves like a
   *  regular bug
   */
  public void moveLeft()
  {  /* to be implemented in part (b) */  }

  /** Returns true if this bug is located next to a left turn
   *  of the wall, that is, the adjacent location to the
   *  left of this bug is valid and is either empty or holds
   *  a flower, while the adjacent location diagonally to the
   *  left and back is either invalid or holds a rock;
   *  otherwise returns false
   */
  public boolean canMoveLeft()
  {  /* to be implemented in part (c) */  }

  < Possibly other methods (not shown) >
  /* to be discussed in part (d) */
}
```

(a)   Write the `isValidGrid` method of the `MazeBug` class. The method should return true if this bug's grid contains only this bug, rocks, and flowers.

Complete the `isValidGrid` method below.

```
/** Returns true if this bug is in a grid and all other
 *  actors in its grid are either rocks or flowers;
 *  otherwise returns false
 */
public boolean isValidGrid()
```

(b) Write the `moveLeft` method of the `MazeBug` class. This method turns the bug 90 degrees to the left, then moves it forward to the adjacent location, putting a flower into the location it previously occupied. In other words, after turning left a `MazeBug` moves just like a regular `Bug`.

Complete the `moveLeft` method below.

```
/** Turns 90 degrees to the left, then moves like a
 *   regular bug
 */
public void moveLeft()
```

(c) Write the method `canMoveLeft`. A `MazeBug` can turn left whenever the adjacent location to the left of the bug is valid and does not hold a rock while the adjacent location diagonally to the left and back is either invalid or holds a rock. If, for example, the bug is facing east, the adjacent location to the north should be empty (or hold a flower) and the adjacent location to the northwest should hold a rock (or be invalid) for the bug to be able to turn left. The picture below illustrates such a situation:

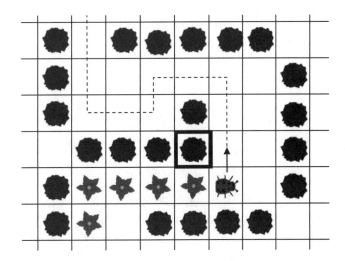

Complete the `canMoveLeft` method below.

```
/** Returns true if this bug is located next to a left turn
 *   of the wall, that is, the adjacent location to the
 *   left of this bug is valid and is either empty or holds
 *   a flower, while the adjacent location diagonally to the
 *   left and back is either invalid or holds a rock;
 *   otherwise returns false
 */
public boolean canMoveLeft()
```

(d) `MazeBug` overrides `Bug`'s `act` method. Do you need to override any other methods of `Bug` in `MazeBug` to make `MazeBug` work as specified? If so, write the needed method(s).

4. This question deals with the task of finding a value that occurs most frequently in a given list. For example, we can take a text, represented as a list of words, and look for a word that occurs in this text more often than any other word. We will use an `List<String>` to represent a list of words. Assume that all the methods discussed below belong to the same class.

    (a) Write a method `countHits` that counts the number of times a given word occurs in a list of words and returns that count.

        Complete method `countHits` below.

        ```
        /** Returns the number of times word appears in text
         */
        public static int countHits(List<String> text,
                                                  String word)
        ```

    (b) Write a method `mostFrequent` that returns the word that occurs most frequently in a given list of words. If several words occur in the list the same number of times as the most frequent word, the method may return any one of them. In writing `mostFrequent`, you must call the method `countHits` from Part (a) where appropriate. Assume `countHits` works as specified, regardless of what you wrote in your solution to Part (a).

        Complete the `mostFrequent` method below.

        ```
        /** Returns the word that occurs in text most frequently;
         *   if several words occur in text with the same maximum
         *   frequency, returns any one of them
         */
        public static String mostFrequent(List<String> text)
        ```

    (c) What is the total number of times that comparison of strings is performed when you call the `mostFrequent(text)` method that you wrote in Part (b)? Write your answer in terms of n = `text.size()`. Assume that a call `countHits(list, word)` performs `list.size()` string comparisons, regardless of what you wrote in Part (a).

Answers and Solutions

Exam #1 ~ Multiple Choice

1.	B	11.	B	21.	C	31.	A
2.	D	12.	C	22.	B	32.	D
3.	E	13.	E	23.	C	33.	C
4.	C	14.	A	24.	C	34.	D
5.	D	15.	C	25.	C	35.	B
6.	A	16.	B	26.	E	36.	E
7.	E	17.	B	27.	E	37.	E
8.	E	18.	A	28.	B	38.	D
9.	B	19.	D	29.	A	39.	D
10.	A	20.	D	30.	D	40.	B

Notes:

1. The last iteration starts with `num = 1`.
2. `(double)(12 / 5)` results in 2.0; `n` remains unchanged because it is passed to `goFigure` by value.
3. The expressions in Options I and II are identical: use De Morgan's Laws. The expression in Option III is also `true` when x ≠ y.
4. `(m + n)/2` evaluates to 4.
5. Option I doesn't work, because `doNothing` returns a `List`, not an `ArrayList`, and you can't assign a `List` object to an `ArrayList` variable.
6. `printVals(names, 0)` and `printVals(names, 1)` do nothing.
    `printVals(names, 2)` prints `"Ann"`.
    `printVals(names, 3)` prints `"Ann"`, then `"Cal"`.
    `printVals(names, 4)` prints `"Ann"`, then `"Cal"`, then `"Amy"`, then `"Ann"`.
7. `printVals(names, 2)` results in $1 + 1 + 1 = 3$ calls.
    `printVals(names, 3)` results in $1 + 3 + 1 = 5$ calls.
    `printVals(names, 4)` results in $1 + 5 + 3 = 9$ calls.
8. Indeed.
9. Selection Sort finds the largest element among 2000, then among the remaining 1999, etc.
10. It is usually impossible to test the program with all possible values of input data.
11. All the advantages of inheritance are preserved, plus a class that implements the interface can potentially extend some other class.
12. The first version quits as soon as the target value is found; the second version always scans the whole array.
13. When one of the operands in the + operator is a string, the other is converted into a string, and the two strings are concatenated.
14. Choice C is true, for example, `fun(int x, double y)` and `fun(double x, int y)`.

15. Options I and II do not work, because `buddies` is private in `BuddyList`.

16. A 2D array is implemented as a 1D array of its rows, where each row is a 1D array. Therefore, the elements of m have the type `int[]`, not `int`. In Choice E, the syntax is correct, but m is traversed column by column instead of row by row.

17. `Object` has neither `substring` nor `compareTo` method.

18. n remains unchanged because it is passed to `change` by value.

19. `list.remove(i)` shifts the subscripts of the subsequent elements down by one, so only every other element is removed.

20. Nothing unexpected happens here.

21. `mat[0][0]` remains equal to 2, `mat[1][1]` becomes 2 * 2 + 1 = 5; `mat[2][2]` becomes 2*5+2 = 12.

22. The statement `s = t;` has no effect in this code: s acts like a local variable. So the last element in the list is set in turn to the first element, then second element, etc. and at the end remains equal to the next to the last element.

23. For example, a subclass of `Athlete` may be a wrapper class for `Athlete`, which has an embedded `Athlete` object and channels all method calls to it, while `numMedals` remains 0 (this design pattern is called "Decorator").

24. If a bug cannot move, it turns to the right by 45 degrees.

25. In Option III, the bug leaves a `Flower` behind, not an empty location.

26. See `Grid`'s documentation.

27. You cannot create an object of an abstract class.

28. In a subclass of `Bug`, each of the two constructors takes a couple of lines, and the following `move` method will make it work:

```
public void move()
{
  ArrayList<Actor> actors = getGrid().getNeighbors(getLocation());
  for (Actor a : actors)
  {
    if (a instanceof Flower)
      a.removeSelfFromGrid();
  }
  super.move();
}
```

29. The change does not affect other methods.

30. Use De Morgan's Laws.

31. Binary Search will look at `arr[63]`, `arr[31]`, `arr[47]`, and `arr[39]`.

32. `product` = (3%2) * (7%4) * (5%2) = 1 * 3 * 1.

33. The second element in the array causes a problem: a `Party` is not always a `BDayParty`.

34. `theGuests` is private in `Party`.

35. The abstract method `getOccasion` must be defined, and it can return `"Birthday " + getName();`

36. Actually, a "for-each" loop is more efficient when the list happens to be a linked list.

37. Due to polymorphism, B's `getLetters` and `getNumber` will be called. `getLetters` returns `"B"` and `getNumber` returns `myNum` (which is set to 1 in the constructor) plus 1.

38. `product` returns 6·4·2.

39. When an `int` gets out of range, it is interpreted as negative because the sign bit is set.

40. Must provide the methods specified in the interface `Student` — the rest are optional.

Answers and Solutions

Exam #1 ~ Free Response

1. (a)
```
public class AppaloosaPriorityQueue implements Queue
{
  private ArrayList<ArrayList<Message>> messageLists;
  private int numMessages;

  public AppaloosaPriorityQueue() { ... }

  public int size() { ... }
  public boolean isEmpty() { ... }
  public void add(Message msg) { ... }
  public Message remove() { ... }
}
```

    (b)
```
public AppaloosaPriorityQueue()
{
  messageLists = new ArrayList<ArrayList<Message>>();

  for (int pr = 0; pr < 10; pr++)
    messageLists.add(new ArrayList<Message>());

  numMessages = 0;
}

public int size()
{
  return numMessages;
}

public boolean isEmpty()
{
  return size() == 0;
}
```

(c)

```
public void add(Message msg)
{
  messageLists.get(msg.getPriority()).add(msg);
  numMessages++;
}

public Message remove()
{
  for (int pr = 9; pr >= 0; pr--)
  {
    if (!messageLists.get(pr).isEmpty())
    {
      numMessages--;
      return messageLists.get(pr).remove(0);
    }
  }

  return null; // should never happen
}
```

2. (a)

```
public void destroy()
{
  Grid<Actor> gr = getGrid();
  ArrayList<Location> locs = gr.getOccupiedLocations();

  for (Location loc : locs)
  {
    Actor a = gr.get(loc);
    Location aLoc = a.getLocation();
    if (aLoc.getCol() == getLocation().getCol() &&
        aLoc.getRow() > getLocation().getRow())
      a.removeSelfFromGrid();
  }
}
```

(b)

```
public void move()
{
  Location next =
          getLocation().getAdjacentLocation(Location.EAST);
  if (Math.random() < 0.5)
    next = getLocation().getAdjacentLocation(Location.WEST);
  if (getGrid().isValid(next))
    moveTo(next);
  else
    removeSelfFromGrid();
}
```

3. (a)
```java
public double getMatchCoeff(Movie other)
{
  int count = 0;

  for (int k = 0; k < features.length(); k += 3)
    if (features.substring(k, k+3).equals(other.
                            features.substring(k, k+3)))
      count++;

  return (double)count / (features.length() / 3);
}
```

    (b)
```java
public double[] getFitCoefficients(List<Movie> movies)
{
  int numMovies = movies.size();
  double[] coefficients = new double[numMovies];

  for (int j = 0; j < numMovies; j++)
  {
    for (int k = j + 1; k < numMovies; k++)
    {
      double match =
            movies.get(j).getMatchCoeff(movies.get(k));
      coefficients[j] += match;
      coefficients[k] += match;
    }
  }

  for (int k = 0; k < numMovies; k++)
    coefficients[k] /= (numMovies - 1);

  return coefficients;
}
```

(c)
```
    public void removeOutliers(List<Movie> movies)
    {
      double[] coefficients = getFitCoefficients(movies);
      double avg = 0.0;

      for (double c : coefficients)
        avg += c;
      avg /= coefficients.length;

      for (int k = coefficients.length - 1; k >= 0; k--)  ¹
        if (coefficients[k] < avg / 2)
          movies.remove(k);
    }
```

Notes:

1. Traverse backwards to avoid problems with subscripts when elements are removed.

4. (a)
```
        private int countOccurrencesInCol(int col, int d)
        {
          int count = 0;

          for (int row = 0; row < 9; row++)
            if (grid[row][col] == d)
              count++;

          return count;
        }
```

(b)
```
        private int countPossiblePlacementsInCol(int col, int d)
        {
          if (countOccurrencesInCol(col, d) > 0)
            return 0;

          int count = 0;
          for (int row = 0; row < 9; row++)
          {
            int row3 = row - row % 3;
            int col3 = col - col % 3;

            if (grid[row][col] == 0 &&
                countOccurrencesInRow(row, d) == 0 &&
                countOccurrencesIn3by3(row3, col3, d) == 0)
              count++;
          }
          return count;
        }
```

(c)
```
        public boolean isSolved()
        {
          for (int d = 1; d <=9; d++)
          {
            for (int row = 0; row < 9; row++)
              if (countOccurrencesInRow(row, d) != 1)
                return false;

            for (int col = 0; col < 9; col++)
              if (countOccurrencesInCol(col, d) != 1)
                return false;

            for (int row = 0; row < 9; row += 3)
              for (int col = 0; col < 9; col += 3)
                if (countOccurrencesIn3by3(row, col, d) != 1)
                  return false;
          }
          return true;
        }
```

Answers and Solutions

Exam #2 ~ Multiple Choice

1.	A	11.	E	21.	C	31.	E
2.	D	12.	E	22.	C	32.	C
3.	A	13.	A	23.	C	33.	D
4.	A	14.	E	24.	B	34.	D
5.	B	15.	D	25.	B	35.	E
6.	D	16.	D	26.	C	36.	B
7.	C	17.	B	27.	E	37.	E
8.	C	18.	B	28.	A	38.	A
9.	A	19.	B	29.	B	39.	A
10.	D	20.	D	30.	E	40.	B

Notes:

1. In Option II, `(double)(q / 2)` evaluates to 1.0;
   in Option III, `(double)(p * q / 2)` evaluates to 7.0

2. `mystery(0, 16)` prints 0, then calls `mystery(5, 15)`; that call prints 5, then calls `mystery(10, 14)`; that call prints 10, then calls `mystery(15, 13)`; that call prints 15 and quits.

3. `b = fun2(a, b)` sets b to 4, a remains 3 (because a and b are passed to `fun2` by value); then `a = fun2(b, a)` sets a to –1, b remains 4.

4. This is equivalent to `(a && !b) || (!a && b)`.

5. Two subclasses of *A* normally cannot be cast one into another — they represent different "animals."

6. In Option I the loops go "too far," flipping `m[r][c]` and `m[c][r]` twice.

7. The code adds 2, 4, 8, 16, and 32 to the elements of v, respectively. `v[4]`, the last element, becomes 33.

8. Private methods are identified by the keyword `private`.

9. Options II and III are not convincing, because `Fun` can have a `playWith` method but not implement `Game`.

10. Each of the 3 elements equals only to itself.

11. `Integer.MAX_VALUE` is determined by the size of int, which is always 4 bytes.

12. `START_POS` is declared `final`, so it cannot be modified.

13. Before the loop, `words` contains `["ban", "an", "an"]`; the `for` loop concatenates all the elements together to make `"banana"`. The first occurrence of `"an"` in `"banana"` is at index 1.

14. `smile(4)` prints `"smile!"` 4 times, then calls `smile(3)`, etc. The total number of times `"smile!"` will be printed is 4 + 3 + 2 + 1 = 10.

15. `smile` is called in succession with parameters 4, 3, 2, 1, and 0.

16. If `targetValue` is not in a, the `while` loop eventually causes `ArrayIndexOutOfBoundsException`.

17. To compare two strings you must use `compareTo`, which returns an `int`.

18. `r` does not have to be a `double` (`x / y` results in an `int` anyway); `r` can be either a static variable or an instance variable in `ClassX`.

19. A cast to `int` truncates the `double` value 31415.9 toward zero.

20. All three print 13579. In Option III, the loop is entered with `i` = 0, 2, 4, 6, and 8.

21. Take, for instance, $a = 2$, $b = 1$, $c = 2$. The code in Option III gives 0 instead of 1.

22. In Options I and III, a static method `flip` attempts to access an instance variable `answer`. Option II has no problems, even though `no` is `private`, because the concept of privacy applies to the whole class, not to individual objects of the class.

23. In Option III, you cannot instantiate an interface.

24. Array indices start from 0; need `arr[i]` to be both positive and odd.

25. For Choice B, the compiler would report an error.

26.
```
public boolean canMove()
{
  ...
  Actor neighbor = gr.get(next);
  return (neighbor == null) || (neighbor instanceof Flower);
  // ok to move into empty location or onto flower
  // not ok to move onto any other actor
}
```

27. See `Bug`'s code for an example.

28. You must use `removeSelfFromGrid` to remove an actor from the grid; otherwise the actor won't know that it has been removed.

29. `Rock` will inherit the empty `act` method from `Actor`.

30. If, for example, both `getActors` and `processActors` must be empty methods, in the new design you need to override only `processActors`.

31. In Option I, recall that a `ChameleonCritter` turns in the direction of the move, so if you derive `RockChameleonCritter` from `Critter`, you need to override the `makeMove` method. In Option II, you can consider only rocks in `processActors`. In Option III, you can select only rocks in `getActors`.

32. The `boolean` variable `flag` "accumulates" the `v[i] == v[i+1]` conditions.

33. `LibraryBook` does not override `Object`'s `toString` method, so Option I is out.

34. Choice A does not work, because `numCopies` and `info` are private in `LibraryBook`.

35. It is your choice to use `getNumCopies` / `setNumCopies` methods or to manipulate the `numCopies` variable directly within the `LibraryBook` class.

36. `list.remove(i)` decrements all the subsequent subscripts. Therefore, it is a mistake to increment `i` when an element is removed: the following element won't be examined.

37. The code goes into an infinite loop when `first` is 3 and `last` is 4.

38. `sortHelper` finds the largest element and swaps it with the last element.

39. First `"Boris"` is swapped with `"Evan"`, then `"Boris"` is swapped with `"Dan"`.

40. $4 + 3 + 2 + 1 = 10$

Answers and Solutions

Exam #2 ~ Free Response

1. (a)
```
public class APStudent
{
  private String studentName;
  private ArrayList<APExam> exams;

  public APStudent(String name) { ... }
  public String getName() { ... }
  public ArrayList<APExam> getExams() { ... }
  public void add(APExam exam) { ... }
  public double getAverageGrade() { ... }
}
```

   (b)
```
public class APScholar extends APStudent
{
  public APScholar(String name)
  {
    super(name);
  }

  public int getAwardLevel()
  {
    int len = getExams().size();
    int exams = 0;
    int award;

    for (APExam exam : getExams())
    {
      if (exam.getGrade() >= 3)
        exams++;
    }

    if (exams >= 4 && getAverageGrade() >= 3.25)
      award = 2;
    else if (years >= 3)
      award = 1;
    else
      award = 0;

    return award;
  }
}
```

(c)

```
public static double[] getStats(ArrayList<APScholar> list)
{
  int[] counts = new int[3];

  for (APScholar scholar : list)
  {
    int award = scholar.getAwardLevel();
    counts[award]++;
  }

  double[] percents = new double[3];

  for (int award = 0; award <= 2; award++)
    percents[award] = 100.0 *
            (double)counts[award] / list.size();  [1]

  return percents;
}
```

Notes:

1. The cast to `double` is optional here.

2.   (a)

```
public static String findFirstTag(String text)
{
  int tagStart = text.indexOf("<");
  if (tagStart != -1)
  {
    int tagEnd = text.indexOf(">");
    return text.substring(tagStart, tagEnd + 1);
  }
  else
    return null;
}
```

(b)

```
public static String remove(String text, String str)
{
  int pos = text.indexOf(str);
  if (pos != -1)
    text = text.substring(0, pos) +
                        text.substring(pos + str.length());
  return text;
}
```

(c)

```
public static String removeAllTags(String text)
{
  String tag = findFirstTag(text);
  while (tag != null)
  {
    String closingTag = "</" + tag.substring(1);
    if (text.indexOf(closingTag) <= text.indexOf(tag))
      throw new IllegalArgumentException();
    text = remove(text, tag);      [1]
    text = remove(text, closingTag);
    tag = findFirstTag(text);
  }
  return text;
}
```

Notes:

1.   Not just

```
remove(text, tag);
```

— because `String` objects are immutable.

3. (a)

```
public class Dahlia extends Flower
{
  private Color initColor;
  private int age;

  public Dahlia()
  {
    ...
  }

  public Dahlia(Color color)
  {
    ...
  }

  public void act()
  {
    ...
  }
}
```

(b)

```
public Dahlia()
{
  initColor = getColor();
}

public Dahlia(Color color)
{
  super(color);  [1]
  initColor = color;
}
```

Notes:

1. Or:

    ```
    setColor(color);
    ```

(c)

```java
public void act()
{
  age++;
  if (age < 4)
  {
    super.act();
  }
  else
  {
    Grid<Actor> gr = getGrid();
    ArrayList<Location> locs =
            gr.getValidAdjacentLocations(getLocation());
    int n = locs.size();
    if (n > 0)
    {
      for (int k = 1;  k <= 3;  k++)
      {
        int r = (int)(Math.random() * n);
        Location loc = locs.get(r);
        if (gr.get(loc) == null)
        {
          DahliaSeed seed = new DahliaSeed(initColor);
          seed.putSelfInGrid(gr, loc);
        }
      }
    }
    removeSelfFromGrid();
  }
}
```

4. (a)

```
public int findRemotestCity()
{
  int iMax = -1;
  int maxSum = 0;
  for (int i = 0; i < distances.length; i++)
  {
    int sum = 0;

    for (int j = 0; j < distances.length; j++)
      sum += distances[i][j];

    if (sum > maxSum)
    {
      iMax = i;
      maxSum = sum;
    }
  }
  return iMax;
}
```

(b)

```
public int findNearestCity(int i, boolean[] visited)
{
  int jMin = -1;
  int minDistance = Integer.MAX_VALUE;
  for (int j = 0; j < cityNames.size(); j++)
  {
    if (!visited[j] && distances[i][j] < minDistance)
    {
      jMin = j;
      minDistance = distances[i][j];
    }
  }
  return jMin;
}
```

(c)

```
public List<String> makeItinerary()
{
  List<String> itinerary = new ArrayList<String>();
  boolean[] visited = new boolean[cityNames.size()];
  for (int i = 0; i < cityNames.size(); i++)
    visited[i] = false;  ¹

  int i = findRemotestCity();
  itinerary.add(cityNames.get(i));
  visited[i] = true;

  for (int count = 2; count <= cityNames.size(); count++)
  {
    i = findNearestCity(i, visited);
    itinerary.add(cityNames.get(i));
    visited[i] = true;
  }

  return itinerary;
}
```

Notes:

1.   This `for` loop is optional: the elements of `visited` are initialized to `false` by default.

Answers and Solutions

Exam #3 ~ Multiple Choice

1. C	11. E	21. A	31. A
2. A	12. C	22. D	32. A
3. B	13. B	23. E	33. A
4. E	14. B	24. B	34. E
5. C	15. A	25. B	35. B
6. D	16. A	26. B	36. D
7. E	17. B	27. C	37. D
8. C	18. E	28. B	38. C
9. E	19. D	29. A	39. E
10. D	20. D	30. D	40. E

Notes:

1. Use De Morgan's Laws.
2. `% 100` leaves the last 2 digits.
3. $0 - 1 + 2 - 3 + 4 - ... + 10 = 0 + (-1 + 2) + (-3 + 4) + ... (-9 + 10) = 5$
4. `count` is not incremented.
5. A `Double` is displayed with a decimal point.
6. In Option 1, `str1` and `str2` must refer to the same object.
7. `4 / 3` yields 1
8. `n` remains positive and eventually is reduced either to 0 or to 1.
9. The correct signature for `equals` is in Choice E and potentially in Choice D, but in D, `Object other` has no method `getArea`, and there is no cast of `other` into a `Rectangle`.
10. This is pretty standard code to reverse an array.
11. The sequence of calls: `B`'s constructor ==> `A`'s constructor ==> `B`'s methodOne (not `A`'s, due to polymorphism) ==> print "B" in `B`'s methodOne ==> print "*", finishing `B`'s constructor.
12. `filter` makes a new string from `str` with all the occurrences of `pattern` in `str` removed.
13. In Choice B, after the first comparison with "D" in the middle `findLocation` will continue searching in the left part of the array.
14. The `while` loop finds the right spot to insert `current`; the `for` loop shifts the elements in `a` to make room.
15. `a[1]` and `a[2]` have been inserted into the right places, so the first three elements in `a` must be now in ascending order.

16. ... and information hiding.

17. Constructors do not have a return type.

18. `splat("**")` calls `splat("****")`, then prints `**`.
     `splat("****")` calls `splat("********")`, then prints `****`.
     `splat("********")` prints `********`.

19. By default, an array is initialized to 0 values, so Option 1 does not work.

20. Choice A doesn't work, because `amps` is private in `Sample`.

21. `numbers` holds two elements: two copies of an `Integer` with value 1. Names holds `["Cathy", "Ben", "Anya"]`. Then the element at index 1 is deleted twice from `names`.

22. `Jet` inherits `addFuel` from `Airplane`. `plane` is created with fuel 4, `jet` is created with fuel 8.

23. Naturally.

24. Choice C does not work, because `Mammal` must have a constructor that takes one parameter.

25. The signatures of both `tuneTo` methods in `MyTV` are different from the one in the `TV` interface.

26. `BoxBug` has only one constructor and it takes an `int` parameter.

27. See the documentation for the `Location` class.

28. You cannot override the `turn` method in `Bug` (without also changing `act`) because `turn` is called when a bug cannot move.

29. See `Bug`'s code.

30. `Actor` doesn't have a method `setGrid`.

31. See `Critter`'s code.

32. `Track` does not have a no-args constructor.

33. `duration` is private in `Track`, so Choices B and D are wrong.

34. `tracks` holds 13 copies of the same track of duration 200.

35. Option I fails to create `ArrayList tracks`. Option III attempts to set a non-existing element, which causes `IndexOutOfBoundsException`.

36. If `somethingIsFalse` returns `true`, then the `else` clause is executed, and the code segment also returns `true`.

37. References to objects are passed "by value" (that is, `swap` receives copies of addresses of `a` and `b`), so Option I does not work. Arrays are passed as references to the original arrays, so both Option II and Option III work.

38. What else?

39. `msg[0]` is not initialized (`null`), so you can't call its methods.

40. A standard array has a fixed size.

Answers and Solutions

Exam #3 ~ Free Response

1. (a)
```
public abstract class PhoneCall
{
  private int duration;

  public PhoneCall(int mins) { duration = mins; }

  public int getDuration() { return duration; }
  public abstract double getRate();

  private int getTotal()
  {
    return (int)(getDuration() * getRate() + .5);
  }

  public String toString()
  {
    return "Duration " + getDuration() +
           " Rate " + getRate() + " Total " + getTotal();
  }
}
```

(b)
```
public class LongDistanceCall extends PhoneCall
{
  public LongDistanceCall(int mins) { super(mins); }

  public double getRate() { return 6.0; }

  public String toString()
  {
    return super.toString() + " LD";
  }
}
```

(c)
```
public class ReducedRateCall extends LongDistanceCall
{
  public ReducedRateCall (int mins) { super(mins); }

  public double getRate() { return 0.5 * super.getRate(); }

  public String toString() { return super.toString() + "RR"; }
}
```

2. (a)

```
public void processActors(ArrayList<Actor> actors)
{
  for (Actor a : actors)
  {
    if (a instanceof Clover)
      ((Clover)a).pollinate();
  }
}
```

(b)

```
public Location selectMoveLocation(ArrayList<Location> locs)
{
  Location next = getLocation();
  Location cloverLoc = findNearestClover(next);
  if (cloverLoc == null)
    return next;
  int minDistance = distance(next, cloverLoc);
  for (Location loc : locs)
  {
    int d = distance(loc, findNearestClover(loc));
    if (d < minDistance)
    {
      minDistance = d;
      next = loc;
    }
  }
  return next;
}
```

(c)

```
public void makeMove(Location loc)
{
  setDirection(getLocation().getDirectionToward(loc));
  super.makeMove(loc);
}
```

3. (a)
```
public static int linkStrength(String word1, String word2)
{
  int len1 = word1.length();
  int len2 = word2.length();
  int n = len1;
  if (len2 < n)
    n = len2;

  while (n > 0 && !word1.substring(len1 - n).equals(
                              word2.substring(0, n)))
  {
    n--;
  }
  return n;
}
```

(b)
```
public static void keepFirstChain(List<String> words)
{
  int k = 1;

  while (k < words.size() &&
          linkStrength(words.get(k - 1), words.get(k)) > 0)
  {
    k++;
  }

  while (k < words.size())
    words.remove(k);
}
```

4. (a)

```
public int findLeftCol(int[][] image, int charWidth)
{
  int maxSum = 0, maxCol = 0;

  for (int col = 0;
            col <= image[0].length - charWidth; col++)
  {
    int sum = 0;

    for (int r = 0; r < image.length; r++)
      for (int c = col; c < col + charWidth; c++)
        sum += image[r][c];

    if (sum > maxSum)
    {
      maxSum = sum;
      maxCol = col;
    }
  }

  return maxCol;
}
```

(b)

```
public double calculateFitRatio(int[][] image,
                                Template t, int leftCol)
{
  double fit = 0;
  for (int r = 0; r < t.numRows(); r++)
    for (int c = 0; c < t.numCols(); c++)
      fit += t.getWeight(r, c) * image[r][leftCol + c];

  return fit / (t.numRows() * t.numCols());
}
```

(c)

```java
public String ocr(int[][] image, List<Template> templates)
{
  double bestFit = 0;
  String result = null;

  for (int k = 0; k < templates.size(); k++)
  {
    Template t = templates.get(k);

    int leftCol = findLeftCol(image, t.numCols());
    double fit = calculateFitRatio(image, t, leftCol);
    if (fit > bestFit)
    {
      bestFit = fit;
      result = t.getCharName();
    }
  }

  return result;
}
```

Answers and Solutions

Exam #4 ~ Multiple Choice

1. D	11. B	21. C	31. D
2. B	12. E	22. D	32. A
3. A	13. A	23. C	33. E
4. B	14. C	24. B	34. A
5. A	15. D	25. E	35. A
6. C	16. E	26. D	36. E
7. A	17. E	27. C	37. C
8. B	18. C	28. E	38. D
9. B	19. B	29. A	39. E
10. D	20. E	30. B	40. B

Notes:

1. `arr` is passed as a reference to the original array, `len` is passed by value.
2. Can't convert a `String` into an `Integer` — no "autoboxing" here.
3. `encrypt("SEC")` returns `"CES"`; `encrypt("RET")` returns `"TER"`.
4. `&& z` in Choice B gives it away.
5. `arr[0]` is never changed, and, on the last iteration, `arr[7]` is assigned the value of `arr[5]`, which is 6.
6. `findMax` first counts the number of times each brightness value occurs in `image`, then finds the largest count.
7. `url.indexOf(...)` sets `pos` to 0; `url.substring(0,0)` returns an empty string.
8. `return mid` must remain unchanged for the method to work when the `searchVal` is in `list`. Try a list of size 1 to see where to insert `searchVal`: at the beginning, both `first` and `last` are 0; after the loop `mid` is undefined and `last` becomes –1 when `searchVal < list.get(0)`, so `last` cannot be used as the insert position.
9. At the end of an iteration, `i` is 3, then 4, then 5; `k` changes from 0 to 3 to 7 to 12.
10. `n /= 10` is the correct choice for <statement2> (to eliminate the rightmost digit). This leaves only Choices A and D. If $n = 0$ the return is 1 only when $d = 0$, so Choice A is wrong.
11. `[] => [1] => [1, 2] => [1, 1, 2] => [1, 1, 2, 2] => [1, 1, 2, 3, 2]`
12. For Option II, both `Salsa` IS-A `Dance` and `Swing` IS-A `Dance`; for Option III, both `Salsa` IS-A(n) `Object` and `Swing` IS-A(n) `Object`.
13. Recall that the concept of "privacy" applies to the whole class, not a particular object, so Choice A works.
14. The loops correctly traverse the whole array and fill all its elements in a diagonal pattern, starting with 1 in the upper left corner.
15. Option I has nothing to do with information hiding (it is inheritance).

16. `list` is an array; `getExams` returns an `ArrayList<APTestResult>`, `getExams().get(2)` returns an `APTestResult`.

17. Option I doesn't work because `3/2` is truncated to 1.

18. 4 times for each pair + 2 times for each quadruplet + 1 time at the top level.

19. 40 ms + 40 ms to sort both halves + 0.01 * 2000 = 20 ms to merge them.

20. Simplify using De Morgan's Laws and notice short-circuit evaluation.

21. Option II does not necessarily work: consider {2, 3, 4, 0, 1, 5, 6, 7, 8} and `target` = 3.

22. Since `House` doesn't have a no-args constructor, `super(someInt)` must be the first statement in its subclass's constructor.

23. Superclass's `compareToOther` will be called, which returns the difference in sizes, `2000 - 1800 = 200`.

24. Can't assign a `House` to a `HouseForSale` (because a `House` is not necessarily for sale).

25. `getSize` is inherited from `House`.

26. `if (canMove()) move(); else turn();`

27. When a `SpinningBug` cannot move, `super.act()` calls `turn`, then `act()` calls `turn` for the second time. Both times `SuperBug`'s `turn` is called, due to polymorphism. The two 90-degree turns produce a 180-degree turn.

28. Options II and III work because a `Bug` IS-A(n) `Actor`. In addition, in Option II, `Bug` has a constructor that takes a parameter of the type `Color`.

29. `ChameleonCritter`'s default no-args constructor calls `Critter`'s default no-args constructor, which in turn calls `Actor`'s no-args constructor.

30. Inheritance and polymorphism are not the same thing.

31. The loop is set up correctly in Choices A, C and D; `get(loc)` returns a `Location`, not an `Integer`.

32. The code segments in Options II and III essentially work the same way; in both of them `"*"` is appended to a local variable, not an element of `letters`.

33. You might notice that `guess` implements Euclid's Algorithm for finding GCF.

34. In Option I, you cannot access an instance variable `score` from a static method. You are allowed, of course, to access static variables in constructors and instance methods.

35. For Operations 2 and 3, finding a player in a sorted list (Design B), using a binary search, takes less time than finding a player in Design 1.

36. It is important to test the basic operation but also any special and boundary conditions.

37. This has nothing to do with encapsulation or information hiding.

38. Option I is already guaranteed — no change is necessary for that.

39. `ArrayList<Double>` implements the `List<Double>` interface, so `MyList1`, a subclass of `ArrayList<Double>`, also implements `List<Double>`.

40. After the first outer loop: `counts` holds 0, 2, 3, 4, 5, 1; 1 swap
    After the second outer loop: `counts` holds 0, 1, 3, 4, 5, 2; 1 swap
    After the third outer loop: `counts` holds 0, 1, 2, 4, 5, 3; 1 swap
    etc.

Answers and Solutions

Exam #4 ~ Free Response

1. (a)

```
public int distance(Student other)
{
  if (street.equals(other.getStreet()))
    return Math.abs(getNumber() - other.getNumber());
  else
    return 99999;
}
```

(b)

```
public class SchoolBus
{
  private int numSeats;
  private ArrayList<Student> students;

  public SchoolBus(int capacity)
  {
    numSeats = capacity;
    students = new ArrayList<Student>();
  }

  public int getNumStudents() { return students.size(); }

  public boolean isFull()
  { return getNumStudents() == numSeats; }

  public Student getStudent(int i) { return students.get(i); }

  public boolean add(Student student)
  {
    if (!isFull())
    {
      students.add(student);
      return true;
    }
    return false;
  }

  public void printOut()
  {
    for (Student s : students)
      System.out.println(s);
  }
}
```

(c)

```
boolean enroll(Student student)
{
  int minDistance = 10000;
  SchoolBus bestBus = null;

  for (SchoolBus bus : buses)
  {
    if (!bus.isFull())
    {
      for (int i = 0; i < bus.getNumStudents(); i++)
      {
        int d = student.distance(bus.getStudent(i));
        if (d < minDistance)
        {
          minDistance = d;
          bestBus = bus;
        }
      }
    }
  }

  if (bestBus != null)
  {
    bestBus.add(student);
    return true;
  }

  return false;
}
```

2.   (a)

```
public class FlatRateEnv extends PriorityMail
{
  public FlatRateEnv() { super(1.0, 1); }
}

public class FlatRateBox extends PriorityMail
{
  public FlatRateBox() { super(1.0, 1); }

  public double calculatePostage()
  {
    return 2 * super.calculatePostage();
  }
}
```

(b)

```
public class InsuredMail extends Mail
{
  private Mail piece;
  private int amount;

  public InsuredMail(Mail p, int amt)
  {
    piece = p;
    amount = amt;
  }

  public double calculatePostage()
  {
    double insCost = 0.50 * ((amount + 99) / 100); [1]
    return piece.calculatePostage() + insCost;
  }
}
```

Notes:

1.   Or, a bit longer but perhaps more straightforward,

```
double insCost = 0;
int amt = amount;
while (amt > 0)
{
  insCost += 0.50;
  amt -= 100;
}
```

3.   (a)

```
public boolean isValidGrid()
{
  Grid<Actor> gr = getGrid();
  if (gr == null)
      return false;

  ArrayList<Location> occupiedLocs =
                      gr.getOccupiedLocations();
  for (Location loc : occupiedLocs)
  {
    Actor a = gr.get(loc);
    if (!(a instanceof Rock || a instanceof Flower)
                                      && a != this)
      return false;
  }
  return true;
}
```

(b)

```
public void moveLeft()
{
  setDirection(getDirection() + Location.LEFT); [1]
  move();
}
```

Notes:

1.   Or:

```
setDirection(getDirection() - 90);
```

(c)

```
public boolean canMoveLeft()
{
  Grid<Actor> gr = getGrid();
  if (gr == null)
    return false;
  Location loc = getLocation();
  Location next =
          loc.getAdjacentLocation(getDirection() - 90);
  Location corner =
          loc.getAdjacentLocation(getDirection() - 135); [1]
  return gr.isValid(next) &&
          !(gr.get(next) instanceof Rock) &&
          (!gr.isValid(corner) ||
                  gr.get(corner) instanceof Rock); [2]
}
```

Notes:

1. Or:

```
Location next =
        loc.getAdjacentLocation(getDirection() +
                        Location.LEFT);
Location corner =
        loc.getAdjacentLocation(getDirection() +
                    3 * Location.HALF_LEFT);
```

2. An alternative solution:

```
public boolean canMoveLeft()
{
  Grid<Actor> gr = getGrid();
  if (gr == null)
    return false;
  Location loc = getLocation();
  Location next =
        loc.getAdjacentLocation(getDirection() - 90);
  if (!gr.isValid(next) || gr.get(next) instanceof Rock)
    return false;
  Location corner =
        loc.getAdjacentLocation(getDirection() - 135);
  if (gr.isValid(corner) &&
            !(gr.get(corner) instanceof Rock))
    return false;
  return true;
}
```

(d)

```
public void turn()
{
  super.turn();
  super.turn();
}
```

4. (a)

```
public static int countHits(List<String> text,
                                        String word)
{
  int count = 0;

  for (String s : text)
  {
    if (word.equals(s))
      count++;
  }

  return count;
}
```

(b)

```
public static String mostFrequent(List<String> text)
{
  int maxCount = 0;
  String freqWord = null;

  for (String word : text)
  {
    int count = countHits(text, word);
    if (count > maxCount)
    {
      maxCount = count;
      freqWord = word;
    }
  }
  return freqWord;
}
```

(c)

$$n^2$$

_____

Index

1.	Ⓐ Ⓑ Ⓒ Ⓓ Ⓔ	21.	Ⓐ Ⓑ Ⓒ Ⓓ Ⓔ
2.	Ⓐ Ⓑ Ⓒ Ⓓ Ⓔ	22.	Ⓐ Ⓑ Ⓒ Ⓓ Ⓔ
3.	Ⓐ Ⓑ Ⓒ Ⓓ Ⓔ	23.	Ⓐ Ⓑ Ⓒ Ⓓ Ⓔ
4.	Ⓐ Ⓑ Ⓒ Ⓓ Ⓔ	24.	Ⓐ Ⓑ Ⓒ Ⓓ Ⓔ
5.	Ⓐ Ⓑ Ⓒ Ⓓ Ⓔ	25.	Ⓐ Ⓑ Ⓒ Ⓓ Ⓔ
6.	Ⓐ Ⓑ Ⓒ Ⓓ Ⓔ	26.	Ⓐ Ⓑ Ⓒ Ⓓ Ⓔ
7.	Ⓐ Ⓑ Ⓒ Ⓓ Ⓔ	27.	Ⓐ Ⓑ Ⓒ Ⓓ Ⓔ
8.	Ⓐ Ⓑ Ⓒ Ⓓ Ⓔ	28.	Ⓐ Ⓑ Ⓒ Ⓓ Ⓔ
9.	Ⓐ Ⓑ Ⓒ Ⓓ Ⓔ	29.	Ⓐ Ⓑ Ⓒ Ⓓ Ⓔ
10.	Ⓐ Ⓑ Ⓒ Ⓓ Ⓔ	30.	Ⓐ Ⓑ Ⓒ Ⓓ Ⓔ
11.	Ⓐ Ⓑ Ⓒ Ⓓ Ⓔ	31.	Ⓐ Ⓑ Ⓒ Ⓓ Ⓔ
12.	Ⓐ Ⓑ Ⓒ Ⓓ Ⓔ	32.	Ⓐ Ⓑ Ⓒ Ⓓ Ⓔ
13.	Ⓐ Ⓑ Ⓒ Ⓓ Ⓔ	33.	Ⓐ Ⓑ Ⓒ Ⓓ Ⓔ
14.	Ⓐ Ⓑ Ⓒ Ⓓ Ⓔ	34.	Ⓐ Ⓑ Ⓒ Ⓓ Ⓔ
15.	Ⓐ Ⓑ Ⓒ Ⓓ Ⓔ	35.	Ⓐ Ⓑ Ⓒ Ⓓ Ⓔ
16.	Ⓐ Ⓑ Ⓒ Ⓓ Ⓔ	36.	Ⓐ Ⓑ Ⓒ Ⓓ Ⓔ
17.	Ⓐ Ⓑ Ⓒ Ⓓ Ⓔ	37.	Ⓐ Ⓑ Ⓒ Ⓓ Ⓔ
18.	Ⓐ Ⓑ Ⓒ Ⓓ Ⓔ	38.	Ⓐ Ⓑ Ⓒ Ⓓ Ⓔ
19.	Ⓐ Ⓑ Ⓒ Ⓓ Ⓔ	39.	Ⓐ Ⓑ Ⓒ Ⓓ Ⓔ
20.	Ⓐ Ⓑ Ⓒ Ⓓ Ⓔ	40.	Ⓐ Ⓑ Ⓒ Ⓓ Ⓔ

1.	Ⓐ	Ⓑ	Ⓒ	Ⓓ	Ⓔ	21.	Ⓐ	Ⓑ	Ⓒ	Ⓓ	Ⓔ
2.	Ⓐ	Ⓑ	Ⓒ	Ⓓ	Ⓔ	22.	Ⓐ	Ⓑ	Ⓒ	Ⓓ	Ⓔ
3.	Ⓐ	Ⓑ	Ⓒ	Ⓓ	Ⓔ	23.	Ⓐ	Ⓑ	Ⓒ	Ⓓ	Ⓔ
4.	Ⓐ	Ⓑ	Ⓒ	Ⓓ	Ⓔ	24.	Ⓐ	Ⓑ	Ⓒ	Ⓓ	Ⓔ
5.	Ⓐ	Ⓑ	Ⓒ	Ⓓ	Ⓔ	25.	Ⓐ	Ⓑ	Ⓒ	Ⓓ	Ⓔ
6.	Ⓐ	Ⓑ	Ⓒ	Ⓓ	Ⓔ	26.	Ⓐ	Ⓑ	Ⓒ	Ⓓ	Ⓔ
7.	Ⓐ	Ⓑ	Ⓒ	Ⓓ	Ⓔ	27.	Ⓐ	Ⓑ	Ⓒ	Ⓓ	Ⓔ
8.	Ⓐ	Ⓑ	Ⓒ	Ⓓ	Ⓔ	28.	Ⓐ	Ⓑ	Ⓒ	Ⓓ	Ⓔ
9.	Ⓐ	Ⓑ	Ⓒ	Ⓓ	Ⓔ	29.	Ⓐ	Ⓑ	Ⓒ	Ⓓ	Ⓔ
10.	Ⓐ	Ⓑ	Ⓒ	Ⓓ	Ⓔ	30.	Ⓐ	Ⓑ	Ⓒ	Ⓓ	Ⓔ
11.	Ⓐ	Ⓑ	Ⓒ	Ⓓ	Ⓔ	31.	Ⓐ	Ⓑ	Ⓒ	Ⓓ	Ⓔ
12.	Ⓐ	Ⓑ	Ⓒ	Ⓓ	Ⓔ	32.	Ⓐ	Ⓑ	Ⓒ	Ⓓ	Ⓔ
13.	Ⓐ	Ⓑ	Ⓒ	Ⓓ	Ⓔ	33.	Ⓐ	Ⓑ	Ⓒ	Ⓓ	Ⓔ
14.	Ⓐ	Ⓑ	Ⓒ	Ⓓ	Ⓔ	34.	Ⓐ	Ⓑ	Ⓒ	Ⓓ	Ⓔ
15.	Ⓐ	Ⓑ	Ⓒ	Ⓓ	Ⓔ	35.	Ⓐ	Ⓑ	Ⓒ	Ⓓ	Ⓔ
16.	Ⓐ	Ⓑ	Ⓒ	Ⓓ	Ⓔ	36.	Ⓐ	Ⓑ	Ⓒ	Ⓓ	Ⓔ
17.	Ⓐ	Ⓑ	Ⓒ	Ⓓ	Ⓔ	37.	Ⓐ	Ⓑ	Ⓒ	Ⓓ	Ⓔ
18.	Ⓐ	Ⓑ	Ⓒ	Ⓓ	Ⓔ	38.	Ⓐ	Ⓑ	Ⓒ	Ⓓ	Ⓔ
19.	Ⓐ	Ⓑ	Ⓒ	Ⓓ	Ⓔ	39.	Ⓐ	Ⓑ	Ⓒ	Ⓓ	Ⓔ
20.	Ⓐ	Ⓑ	Ⓒ	Ⓓ	Ⓔ	40.	Ⓐ	Ⓑ	Ⓒ	Ⓓ	Ⓔ

1.	(A)	(B)	(C)	(D)	(E)		21.	(A)	(B)	(C)	(D)	(E)
2.	(A)	(B)	(C)	(D)	(E)		22.	(A)	(B)	(C)	(D)	(E)
3.	(A)	(B)	(C)	(D)	(E)		23.	(A)	(B)	(C)	(D)	(E)
4.	(A)	(B)	(C)	(D)	(E)		24.	(A)	(B)	(C)	(D)	(E)
5.	(A)	(B)	(C)	(D)	(E)		25.	(A)	(B)	(C)	(D)	(E)
6.	(A)	(B)	(C)	(D)	(E)		26.	(A)	(B)	(C)	(D)	(E)
7.	(A)	(B)	(C)	(D)	(E)		27.	(A)	(B)	(C)	(D)	(E)
8.	(A)	(B)	(C)	(D)	(E)		28.	(A)	(B)	(C)	(D)	(E)
9.	(A)	(B)	(C)	(D)	(E)		29.	(A)	(B)	(C)	(D)	(E)
10.	(A)	(B)	(C)	(D)	(E)		30.	(A)	(B)	(C)	(D)	(E)
11.	(A)	(B)	(C)	(D)	(E)		31.	(A)	(B)	(C)	(D)	(E)
12.	(A)	(B)	(C)	(D)	(E)		32.	(A)	(B)	(C)	(D)	(E)
13.	(A)	(B)	(C)	(D)	(E)		33.	(A)	(B)	(C)	(D)	(E)
14.	(A)	(B)	(C)	(D)	(E)		34.	(A)	(B)	(C)	(D)	(E)
15.	(A)	(B)	(C)	(D)	(E)		35.	(A)	(B)	(C)	(D)	(E)
16.	(A)	(B)	(C)	(D)	(E)		36.	(A)	(B)	(C)	(D)	(E)
17.	(A)	(B)	(C)	(D)	(E)		37.	(A)	(B)	(C)	(D)	(E)
18.	(A)	(B)	(C)	(D)	(E)		38.	(A)	(B)	(C)	(D)	(E)
19.	(A)	(B)	(C)	(D)	(E)		39.	(A)	(B)	(C)	(D)	(E)
20.	(A)	(B)	(C)	(D)	(E)		40.	(A)	(B)	(C)	(D)	(E)

1.	Ⓐ Ⓑ Ⓒ Ⓓ Ⓔ	21.	Ⓐ Ⓑ Ⓒ Ⓓ Ⓔ
2.	Ⓐ Ⓑ Ⓒ Ⓓ Ⓔ	22.	Ⓐ Ⓑ Ⓒ Ⓓ Ⓔ
3.	Ⓐ Ⓑ Ⓒ Ⓓ Ⓔ	23.	Ⓐ Ⓑ Ⓒ Ⓓ Ⓔ
4.	Ⓐ Ⓑ Ⓒ Ⓓ Ⓔ	24.	Ⓐ Ⓑ Ⓒ Ⓓ Ⓔ
5.	Ⓐ Ⓑ Ⓒ Ⓓ Ⓔ	25.	Ⓐ Ⓑ Ⓒ Ⓓ Ⓔ
6.	Ⓐ Ⓑ Ⓒ Ⓓ Ⓔ	26.	Ⓐ Ⓑ Ⓒ Ⓓ Ⓔ
7.	Ⓐ Ⓑ Ⓒ Ⓓ Ⓔ	27.	Ⓐ Ⓑ Ⓒ Ⓓ Ⓔ
8.	Ⓐ Ⓑ Ⓒ Ⓓ Ⓔ	28.	Ⓐ Ⓑ Ⓒ Ⓓ Ⓔ
9.	Ⓐ Ⓑ Ⓒ Ⓓ Ⓔ	29.	Ⓐ Ⓑ Ⓒ Ⓓ Ⓔ
10.	Ⓐ Ⓑ Ⓒ Ⓓ Ⓔ	30.	Ⓐ Ⓑ Ⓒ Ⓓ Ⓔ
11.	Ⓐ Ⓑ Ⓒ Ⓓ Ⓔ	31.	Ⓐ Ⓑ Ⓒ Ⓓ Ⓔ
12.	Ⓐ Ⓑ Ⓒ Ⓓ Ⓔ	32.	Ⓐ Ⓑ Ⓒ Ⓓ Ⓔ
13.	Ⓐ Ⓑ Ⓒ Ⓓ Ⓔ	33.	Ⓐ Ⓑ Ⓒ Ⓓ Ⓔ
14.	Ⓐ Ⓑ Ⓒ Ⓓ Ⓔ	34.	Ⓐ Ⓑ Ⓒ Ⓓ Ⓔ
15.	Ⓐ Ⓑ Ⓒ Ⓓ Ⓔ	35.	Ⓐ Ⓑ Ⓒ Ⓓ Ⓔ
16.	Ⓐ Ⓑ Ⓒ Ⓓ Ⓔ	36.	Ⓐ Ⓑ Ⓒ Ⓓ Ⓔ
17.	Ⓐ Ⓑ Ⓒ Ⓓ Ⓔ	37.	Ⓐ Ⓑ Ⓒ Ⓓ Ⓔ
18.	Ⓐ Ⓑ Ⓒ Ⓓ Ⓔ	38.	Ⓐ Ⓑ Ⓒ Ⓓ Ⓔ
19.	Ⓐ Ⓑ Ⓒ Ⓓ Ⓔ	39.	Ⓐ Ⓑ Ⓒ Ⓓ Ⓔ
20.	Ⓐ Ⓑ Ⓒ Ⓓ Ⓔ	40.	Ⓐ Ⓑ Ⓒ Ⓓ Ⓔ

Other Computer Science and Mathematics Titles from Skylight Publishing

Java Methods A&AB: Object-Oriented Programming and Data Structures, AP Edition ISBN 978-0-9727055-7-8

250 Multiple-Choice Computer Science Questions in Java
ISBN 978-0-9727055-9-2

100 Multiple-Choice Questions in C++
ISBN 978-0-9654853-0-2

Mathematics for the Digital Age and Programming in Python
ISBN 978-0-9727055-8-5

Be Prepared for the AP Calculus Exam
ISBN 978-0-9727055-5-4

800 Questions in Calculus
ISBN 978-0-9727055-4-7

Solutions to 800 Questions in Calculus
Part 978-0-9727055-C-D

Calculus Calculator Labs Student Pack
Part 978-0-9727055-S-L

Calculus Calculator Labs Teacher Pack
Part 978-0-9727055-T-L

---

www.skylit.com
sales@skylit.com
Toll free: 888-476-1940
Fax: 978-475-1431

Skylight Publishing, 9 Bartlet Street, Suite 70, Andover, MA 01810